ROPE OPERA

ROPE OPERA
HOW WCW KILLED
VINCE RUSSO

BY VINCE RUSSO

ECW PRESS

Published by ECW Press, 2120 Queen Street East, Suite 200,
Toronto, Ontario, Canada M4E 1E2
416.694.3348 / info@ecwpress.com

LIBRARY AND ARCHIVES CANADA CATALOGUING IN PUBLICATION

Russo, Vince
Rope opera : how WCW killed Vince Russo / Vince Russo.

ISBN 978-1-55022-868-7

1. Russo, Vince. 2. Wrestling promoters--United States--Biography.
3. Total Nonstop Action Wrestling. 4. World Championship Wrestling, Inc. I. Title.

GV1196.R87A3 2010   796.812092   C2009-905928-2

Editor: Michael Holmes
Cover design: David Gee
Front cover photo © Lee South
Text design: Tania Craan
Typesetting: Mary Bowness
Printing: Transcontinental   1   2   3   4   5

PRINTED AND BOUND IN CANADA

ECW PRESS
ecwpress.com

This book is dedicated to the memory of my brother, Jeff Iorio.

Jeff, I love you more than one friend can possibly love another. My life has never been the same since you passed. A day doesn't go by where I don't think about you, and everything you meant to my life.

You were an angel bestowed upon me by God, and I am just so grateful to Him that I was the "Chosen One." There is no one who will ever replace you in my heart.

I miss you so much.

Contents

Foreword

Vince Russo: the first man to actually make men in tights appealing. For years now I have watched my father work day after day in crafting his unique job position. I remember when I was a kid, my peers would come up to me and ask what my father did. Some dads worked at the Coke factory, some were repairmen and some just sat on their butts for a living. Not mine! My response would always be the same: "My father is a writer for wrestling." Then I would always hear the same reply: "They have writers for that?"

Say what you want about Vince's work; love it or hate it. If there is one thing I understand about my father, it's that he is dedicated to anything he puts his hands on. When he had his own business, his dedication was to have that place as clean as a five-star restaurant. His biggest commitment wasn't to his work; it was to his family. My dad spent hours with me and my brother. Shooting hoops, playing catch — he was always happy just to be around us.

Some of the audience reading this might want to hear the war stories that went on at wcw, but I'm not aware of anything involving a fuming Goldberg or a grizzly old Hogan. The moments I know of Vince Russo were when he'd let me stay up late and watch *Saturday Night Live*. This was the man who watched Hanna-Barbera cartoons and quoted Scorsese films. Dad was the only father I knew who wouldn't dress conservative. You could always find him wearing a baseball jersey and basketball shorts (he was ready for any sport). These are the moments and memories I have of Vince Russo, not him getting whaled on by the Nature Boy.

My dad was always the guy ready to do anything for his family. He always encouraged me to do whatever I was interested in and never restricted me to following in his footsteps as a wrestling writer (every boy's fantasy!) Whenever I took an interest in something different, my dad was there to support me and I'll never forget how close he's been to me in my life.

There really isn't anyone else like Vince Russo. He takes pride in what he does and approaches it in a completely different fashion from other people. He's a loud Italian who loves to express his opinion and doesn't care what you're going to think about it. Vince Russo has taught me so much about this world without having to give me any of the bull$%#@ that most fathers provide. Always sincere and always true to his word, this is a man you don't mind spending an evening with.

I am forever grateful to be Vince Russo's son; I couldn't see it being any different. He brought me into this world and for that I am grateful. To some people he's "the man who ruined wrestling." To me, he's just Dad: the guy who wants to hang with me whenever he's got the time.

Sincerely,

VJ

I was munching on a mouthful of Thanksgiving turkey when my dad initially approached me with the notion of writing the foreword to this book. To be honest, the idea struck me as kind of intimidating at first: Just what exactly do I write? How could I possibly capture all my thoughts and feelings about my father in a few neatly structured paragraphs? I'm sure any son could write an entire book about his father.

First off, what aspect of Vince Russo do I talk about? Do I talk about the guy in the San Francisco Giants jersey, with the thick "New Yawk" accent and baseball bat at his side? The "heel" on national television who everybody loved to hate? The unruly writer who single-handedly "destroyed wrestling"? No way. Because I don't know that guy. The only image I have of Vince Russo is as my dad. The guy who took me to my first rock concert — I believe it was the KISS '96–97 reunion tour (my mother was livid!). The guy who would take me to the movies every weekend. The same guy who would let me stay up late and watch *South Park* when I was still in elementary school (probably not the best idea for a fifth-grader). That's the guy I know and the guy I love.

In response to his work, there is one thing I can say about my dad: he is a man who always, always worked his butt off for his family and for that I will forever be grateful. I won't lie; it was tough those years I would spend at home with my mom and brother when my dad was away working. But as an older man now I fully realize and appreciate what he was doing. He was teaching me then what it was like to be a man. What it means to be a hard-working, providing and responsible man who has his priorities straight and refuses to take crap from anyone.

In my teenage years, I was lucky enough to spend time with my father as he was operating his own business when my family lived in Marietta, Georgia. It was called CD Warehouse and it was a small franchise that sold CDs and DVDs. It was the ideal job for a slacker teenager such as myself, but it was there I would spend days with my dad witnessing first-hand what it was like to really take pride in what it is you do. Every single day the guy would get up early and make sure the store was fully stocked and spotless! That's commitment. He treated that store like it was his little baby and I guess in a way it was. I still to this day remember him saying, "The only reason I want to own my own business is because I want to be my own boss." I loved that. And it's that attitude that he's passed on to me.

My dad has passed on many indispensable traits to my brother, my sister and me and I can't thank him enough. It's because of him I developed a love of great films and comedians. It's because of him I learned how to shoot a jump shot. And it's because of him I have come to love (and hate) the act of writing and learned to find the beauty and self-fulfillment that lies in being creative. There is so much I could say, but I'll keep it short and sweet.

Thank you, Dad. I love you and thank you for bringing me into this crazy world.

Your son,

Will

This book was written between the fall of 2006 and the fall of 2008. Vince Russo's life took many turns during that period and subsequently. Even though his views and opinions on individuals and circumstances may have changed, not a word was altered. The reason? It's simple. We are *all* on a never-ending journey.

Searching for Avalon

A couple of years ago I went to see the house on Avalon. It was gone.

Not just the house, but the whole neighborhood. I went to see the ballroom where me and my brothers used to play. The whole place . . . gone.

Not just that – but the grocery store where we used to shop . . . gone . . . all gone. I went to see where Eva lived off Poplar Street . . . it wasn't there.

Not even the street . . . it isn't there . . . not even the street. And then, I went to see the nightclub I used to have. Thank God it was there, because for a minute I thought I never was. If I knew things would no longer be here, I would have tried to remember better.

> – Sam Krichinsky, in Barry Levinson's **Avalon**

I'm back . . .

Saved or unsaved, I still hate the blank page just the same.

For the last few weeks I have been gearing myself up for "Forgiven II," the book now known as *Rope Opera*. As each day passed, the thoughts began to gather until I knew it was time to begin to orchestrate them together on paper. But once more, the fear of that white, empty, agonizing, blank piece of paper made the trip from the sectional to the computer seem like an endless journey. Yes, some things do change — but not the ugliness of the naked page to the writer.

The truth is, I always knew there would be a second book. Since writing *Forgiven*, my thoughts and emotions have incubated, getting to the point of bursting from me much like Bruce Banner bursts from those hideous purple pants as he transforms into the Incredible Hulk.

By the way, have you ever come across anybody that wears, or has ever worn, purple pants? No, I mean anybody . . . *ever*? Okay, maybe Alan Sues on *Laugh-In*, but aside from him, who else? What was Mr. Banner thinking about when he got dressed in the morning? If Bill Bixby had ever donned purple pants as Eddie's father, he would never have been courted. Getting back to my thoughts . . . I could no longer be a prisoner of my own emotions. Feelings of pain, anger, hurt, disappointment, forgiveness and hope consumed me, a never-ending line of bumper-to-bumper traffic more horrifying than that of the Long Island Expressway. Without pausing for even a moment, my deepest thoughts tossed and turned, ping-ponging back and forth between my restless mind and my unsettled stomach. One way or another, they had to be unleashed — set free into the world to shape young minds and have an everlasting impact on the free world.

And well, here you are.

If you're reading these words, there's a good chance that you've already read *Forgiven*. If you have, first and foremost I'd like to thank you. Writing that book was my greatest accomplishment. Not because I was able to receive my medal of "authorship," but because I know that God Himself simply used me as a vessel to get His words across. There was a message from the Creator to each of you who read it. . . . I hope you received it. But if you didn't, that's okay. The good news is that the "Big Man" has more to say.

Even though God created a new creature in me some 27 months ago, the old one still rears his ugly head every now and then — not so much in my actions but sometimes in my thoughts. You see, no human being is going to be 100% perfect, 100% of the time. Only God is capable of that, and that's why . . . well, that's why he's God. But as I began to map out this book, the first street I strolled along the way was "Sensationalism Avenue." How do I start this book to reel you all in? Remember that in the last manuscript, I started with the short but powerful sentence of "I hate Jeff." Well, in plotting this bad boy, I thought what better place to start than at Bash at the Beach 2000? Let's face it; years later, that's still all everybody wants to talk about. Hey, why don't I start it with my infamous *scripted* promo on Hulk Hogan? Yeah . . . that will get them!

But you know what? Something didn't feel right about that. That's not where the *real* author of this book wanted to start. No, that was simply a case of yours truly wanting once again to drive the car — just like old times.

So the writing process was stalled. I sat and I waited for God to speak. That's right . . . I waited. One thing you learn — and learn quickly — after becoming a Christian is that God works on His clock, not ours. God makes decisions when He's ready, not when we want Him to. Like the late, great Jim Croce once said, "You don't tug on Superman's cape, you don't spit into the wind, you don't pull the mask of the ol' Lone Ranger, and you don't mess around with Jim." Well, add to that: you don't force the hand of the Creator! *He*'s the Clock King, not you (chalk up my first Caped Crusader reference). So, while biding my time, I decided to watch a DVD chosen from my personal collection. The movie is called *Avalon* and is no doubt on my all-time top-ten list. The film depicts a family of Polish immigrants, the Krichinskys, who make their way over to America in the first quarter of the twentieth century, and settle in Avalon, a small town near Baltimore. Through the handing off of one generation to the next, we can clearly see the breakdown and deterioration of the traditional family.

I have watched this film many, many times, and after each viewing my river of tears is deeper than the last. I could never understand my emotional connection to *Avalon* until God Himself broke me down at my very core to make me realize why the film had, and still has, such a traumatic impact on me. But that's all part of the process. Once we fall to the base of the cross, God becomes the tour guide of our very lives. In order to show us where we are going, He must first show us where we've been. The process can be painful, but through Him, we must know who we are.

In hindsight, I now understand that God began prepping me years before I ever turned myself over to Him. At the age of 40, I really began to re-evaluate my life — where I was, where I had been and where I was going. I began to examine my very existence under a magnifying glass. Who was I? What made me tick? Writing *Forgiven* was a huge part of that process. I learned so much about myself in those pages that came from my hand — meaning, ultimately, God's hand. My first realization came when for the first time I truly realized how much I miss the family. No, not my immediate one — Amy, Will, VJ and Annie — but the very foundation: the tradition that my grandparents and my great-grandparents before them built their lives on. We were the Krichinskys; nothing mattered back then but the family. That's how I grew up. That's what I knew. And that's what I miss.

But it all goes so much deeper than that. All of us are searching for Avalon in one sense or another. That one place in a certain time in our lives where we felt secure, safe, loved. Years later in our adulthood we would realize that it was our closest taste of heaven, right here on earth. And we spend the rest of our years just trying to get back to that place . . . but we can't. As Sam Krichinsky himself said, "It's gone." What's simply amazing about this is that we can trace it all the way back to Adam and Eve. Through the grace of God, they experienced heaven right there in the Garden of Eden. God showed them His master plan; they witnessed it with their own eyes. "This is the way I meant it to be," He was saying. Then with one sin, they lost it — they lost all of it. They spent the rest of their lives trying to get it back, but they never could — not in this life, anyway. Ironically, we are no different than our fig leaf–clad ancestors.

As I sit here I can only wonder, did God take my grandparents' house at 21 Poplar Street (amazingly enough, Sam Krichinsky's wife, Eva, lived on the same street in Avalon . . . coincidence?) away from me because I, too, sinned and am a sinner? As a child did He show me, through that blessed house, "this is the way I meant it to be"? Did He give me a taste of heaven on earth only to take it away? In my very humble opinion, I believe He did. I believe it because some 35 years later it is still the very thing I chase . . . while chasing Him in the process. And at the end of the day, that's all God wants . . . for us to pick up our nets and follow Him.

"Daniel Elsberg's Psychiatrist" and "Negro Sneakers"

At least at one point in all our lives, we sat at the perfect place. For me, I can remember three times where it was just *right*. Beyond Poplar Street, there were my childhood and teen years at 5 Melvin Court in Farmingville, Long Island. Those summers are so fresh in my mind that I can pull them out any place, at any time, and just replay them in my mind. It's summer. It's eight a.m. I can hear the sound of small stones (they had to be small enough not to break the window) raining upon my window. My crew of neighborhood friends would "quietly" toss the stones from the ground below in an attempt to wake me from my slumber so we could start the day with some baseball at St. Margaret's of Scotland Church. The cast would vary some day to day as the younger kids from the neighborhood would occasionally show up (mainly Doug, Kenny, Jimmy and Bobby), often in a futile attempt to make the "show," or the "big kids'" game. But the core group was always there: Ralph, Duge, Mike and Chykirda, and what a diversified bunch they were.

Starting with the youngest and smallest, Ralph DeStephano was perhaps the best all-around athlete on the block. A rookie southpaw with great promise, Ralph had some nice pop in his bat as he loaded and cocked his Louisville Slugger with visions of impressing yours truly, who at a few years older was his idol. Now, even though Ralph showed tremendous potential as a kid trying to make the cut, there was one small thing that kept him back . . . his mother.

"Raaaal-pheee, Raaaal-pheee!"

Those were the echoes that "bing-bing-bing, ricochet-rabbited" throughout every street in the Barclay Meadows development, courtesy of Flora DeStephano, when it was time to call her youngest son in to eat. And, unfortunately for Ralphie, that would just erase it all. No matter how many hits he got that day, or how many saves he made in street hockey guarding the pipes like his idol Ken Dryden, or how many touchdown passes he caught in the fat part of the court, Ralph would forever be known as a "momma's boy." And that's where Mike never let up — *ever!*

No doubt the smartest of the bunch, Mike DelPiore also had to be the meanest. Man, this guy would just flat out make Ralphie's life miserable. I mean, the guy just never let up. I remember Mike and Ralph literally fist-fighting from Melvin Court all the way up Roberta Avenue. Some of the best brawls I ever saw took place during those summers. But the ironic thing was that the next day they'd be right there, together, throwing blue-gray pebbles at my window attempting to wake the veteran up. But Mike was my boy. Being that I lived in the court, and he right off it, we were always together. Mike and I would play *everything*, and not only your traditional games. We would also invent some of our own.

You see, all Mike and I needed was a ball. It didn't even matter what size; it just needed to be round, and we would be set for the day. The truth is we invented two of the greatest games ever known to man: "Daniel Elsberg's Psychiatrist" (even though we had no idea who he *or* his psychiatrist were — we were just hearing their names on TV every day) and "Negro Sneakers," named after a hideous pair of black, green, red and yellow sneakers my mother bought me that we *thought* were the colors of the African flag. Okay, so they were both versions of boxball, but it really didn't matter: they were *ours*. But that's how it was back then; we played *everything*. From sun-up to sun-down, we were out there playing. Baseball, basketball, hockey, stickball, football, wif-fleball, boxball, kickball, kick the can (remember that one?), "Daniel Elsberg's Psychiatrist," "Negro Sneakers" — it didn't matter! What was a video game? Are you kidding me? We were *kids*. Honest to goodness *kids!*

Then there was Chykirda. One word, like Cher, or Madonna: Chykirda. And, Chykirda was an icon . . . in his own right, of course. One bandmate shy of a group, Chykirda wasn't known for his brains, but the kid had a huge heart. But he was just a screw-up, plain and simple. I mean, we loved the kid, but he just came across like an imbecile. Looking back now, I can't even tell you why, but he just was. Maybe it was that real bad haircut: thick, black, brillo hair over his eyebrows, just above his eyes. I mean I never saw anything like it . . . and I still haven't! Napoleon Dynamite is Heath Ledger compared to this guy! And to boot, he always had acne — even before the age you were supposed to get it. Do the math: this kid had issues. But he was the greatest!

I loved Chykirda — there just wasn't another like him. I loved him despite all the baseballs he hit through the windows of St. Margaret's of Scotland Church. Oh, I haven't told you about that yet? Okay, I'm coming clean again. You see, in the back of St. Margaret's, there was a little league baseball field. No, I mean *little* league. You played there until you were 11, and then you moved up to the majors. I broke out as an all-star on that field, coming into my own as a catcher. But you see, we continued to play on that field well into our teens. I mean, I think the right field porch, where the sanctuary sat just beyond the chain-link fence, was about 150 feet away. We were *way* too big for the field. So what did we do? We hit everything over the *left* field fence. Only one problem with that theory: Chykirda was left-handed — with absolutely *no* bat control. Get the picture? At least once a week Chykirda would sail a baseball high above the right field fence, through the window into the church sanctuary. We would then proceed to hop on our bikes — without castrating ourselves on our banana seats — and peddle for our lives. Now do you see why the kid was one sock away from a pair?

A few months back I visited my old stomping grounds and one of my first stops was St. Margaret's. I had to laugh when the first thing I noticed was that they flipped the entire field around so that home plate was now where the right field porch used to be so you were now hitting *away* from the church. And it took them *how* many years to figure that out?

But I've got to tell you, in his defense, Chykirda was the only one who listened religiously to *"that"* rock music. I mean, he even put it before sports! He was all over it: Queen, Van Halen, Blue Oyster Cult . . . and KISS! Yup, Chykirda and I were generals in the KISS Army. I point that out for a very significant reason. There was an instance in my life when I was about 15 or 16 (the same age as Christine — KISS fans will get the reference) and I was home sick. Keep in mind, after admitting to being a full-fledged hypochondriac in my first book, it probably meant that I was I was on my deathbed. This was it — this time I was really going to join Elizabeth (for all you *Sanford and Son* buffs). Then, all of a sudden, there was a knock on the door. Who could that be? I wasn't expecting anyone. Everybody was in school. It was just me lying here, dying, watching *Sigmund and the Sea Monsters*. So, I answered the door — and keep in mind, this is sometime in the middle of winter — and before me was a sight that I'll never forget. In full Gene Simmons makeup, Chykirda stood, ever so proudly, on my stoop. Shirtless, and with his hair pulled up in the middle, looking somewhat like a Gene ponytail anyway, Chykirda looked at me with those wide-eyed Gene eyes — if you're a KISS fan you know the ones that I'm talking about. Then, with one mighty strum of his guitar that wasn't there, Gene — I mean Chykirda — proceeded to spit ketchup, in lieu of blood, all over himself. Then, standing there smelling like a cold tomato with a hint of B.O., he said nothing; he just turned around and walked back up Roberta Avenue. Now that is a true friend.

Last, but not least, rounding out the crew was Frank Dugnan, or "the Duge" for short. There were two unique things about the Duge; one was that he could hit a ton. I mean he would hit *everything* over the fence at St. Margaret's, and that was important when we played our neighborhood rivals "College Hills." Duge could flat hit, man. I wouldn't admit it then, but I'll admit it now: he was a better hitter than me . . . maybe. But the second thing that stood out about the Duge was his head. The guy had the longest head I ever saw — I mean, it just went on and on and on. You remember back in the old days when your parents would take you to an amusement park and you would look into that mirror that distorted everything? Well, that was Duge's head . . . all the time! And Chykirda was all over this. He never let up on the Duge's melon. So, on the right-hand side of the street you'd have Mike and Ralph whaling on each other, while on the left you had Chykirda and Duge hammering it out. As the great Archie and Edith Bunker would say as they sat at the living room piano, "Those were the days."

I know, I know, I have to get to the rasslin' stuff, and I will — in a minute. Just one more stop.

The last place I experienced Avalon was in college. My days at Indiana State University, Evansville Campus, were the last of my best days for a very long while. The relationships I made in only three short years were some of the best relationships I ever experienced. In a sense I left home and found another home. My early days with my wife, Amy, just can't be repeated. I can remember winning a huge stuffed animal at the Fall Festival and dropping by the Delta Zeta booth where she was working to give it to her. I didn't even know her at the time, but I knew in my heart that I wanted to. Then came our first date, the movie *Arthur*. I remember dropping her off at her house at the end of the date and *not* kissing her goodnight. I didn't want her to think I was like all the other guys, because I wasn't. I remember her cooking for me at her house when I had little or no money for food. I remember the feeling of starting to get jealous over other guys who I thought might be interested in her. I remember the excitement and anticipation when she would come at to see me at Campus Apartments. It was Avalon . . . it was simply Avalon.

We must savor those moments . . . and we must never forget them.

Gone Like a Thief in the Night

"Dad, can we take the video game machine?"

"No Veej, the video game has to stay. It's not mine."

He was only nine at the time, but he was already addicted. Man, my son VJ, now 15, will just sit in his room by himself for hours playing video games while listening to dead rock stars croon. *Tetris*, Morrison, *Tetris*, Hendrix, *Tetris*, Cobain, *Tetris*, Dylan (he counts because he *looks* like a dead rock star). That's it — all day! Maybe an occasional Depp film, or *Simpsons* episode, but that's the extent of it. He never leaves the room . . . never. Unfortunately, I know he gets a lot of that from me, but even I leave the basement from time to time. I mean, you have to eat!

Are there any games going on in the streets of the country today, ANY-WHERE? What happened to that? No wiffleball, stickball, hockey – forget about "Negro Sneakers"! Man, have kids today changed, or what? I remember when I was young and my father would buy two box seats at four dollars a pop to go see the Giants play the Mets at Shea Stadium. Man, the anticipation would build for months. I would literally count down the days. I took my kids to Fenway Park and they wanted to go home after two innings because it was too hot! Do you get that? Fenway – the Green Monster – Nomar – TOO HOT? Man, my kids are nothing like me when I was growing up. Scarily enough, they're more like Chykirda! All they do is listen to music, play music, play video games, eat and sleep. That's it. My kids have never – I mean NEVER – sat down to watch a game with me . . . any game . . . ever! They don't even watch the Super Bowl. What happened?

Getting back to the video game machine:

It was a Friday night, about nine o'clock. My two sons, vj and Will, who was twelve at the time, and I were cleaning out my office at Titan Tower. Having a pass key, I could get into the building 24/7. I guess that was one of the perks for being a "big deal": you could come to work all hours of the night . . . and I do mean to *work*. Man, I had such mixed emotions. I was relieved, yet scared to death. This would be the last time I would ever be in this office, or costume closet — pick your poison.

At that time (and I'm sure it's probably the same way today), it was a huge deal to have a spacious corner office at Titan. To this day I never understood why the corner was such a big deal. Why was corner real estate worth more than something on the street itself? That is a corporate question I've yet to find the answer to. I guess it has something to do with the view. Maybe that made sense at Titan because let's face it: the view was all you were going to have, being you were never allowed to leave the place! Yeah, the first three floors were all about placement and position, but if you went one floor higher, now we're talkin' *prestige* . . . real prestige. If you happened to be a lucky winner and occupied a corner office on the fourth floor — Vince's floor — you were talkin' prime, Donald Trump–type real estate. If you had a corner office on Vince's floor, the workers weren't even allowed to look you in the eye; you were the burning bush.

Ah yes, status symbols for important people. Me? I always hated that. That's why I hand-picked an old costume closet, on the second floor, on the street, with no window in sight. The fact was, there weren't even any lights! I fired up the place with a ten-dollar gooseneck lamp that I bought at Staples. But that was how I preferred to be, quiet and left alone. However, to be honest, I guess I did have room for one perk: standing tall in the corner of my costume closet was an old-school WWF video arcade game. They moved it in on my request when I became a "big deal" in my own right. Where others had windows, and corners, and addresses on the fourth floor, I had Jake "The Snake" Roberts battling it out with the Big Boss Man on a classic, WWF arcade game. And life was good.

Yeah, I froze in time for a moment as I took in the surroundings around me. This is the place where so much had happened for me. All the hopes and all the dreams had become a reality . . . and now I was leaving. I had a ten a.m. flight scheduled for Atlanta the following morning and by the time the next "official" workday rolled along, I would be employed by WCW. There was no turning back. Once I scheduled that meeting with Bill Busch, VP of WCW at the time, I knew it was over. I had already accepted the job, not physically, but mentally and emotionally. I knew that the minute my fingers push-padded his number.

"Dad, why can't we take the video game?"

"I said it's not ours, VJ. It has to stay."

"But, Dad . . ."

I remember thinking, "We're moving to Atlanta." I remember selling Amy and the kids a whole bill of goods on moving down south when I didn't believe a word of it myself. I was a northerner, a *New Yawker*. This was my home — all I had ever known. What would life be like without reading *Newsday* every day, or watching *The Odd Couple* at 11 and *The Honeymooners* at 11:30 on Channel 11? I just couldn't fathom it. But I had to put on a front — especially for my son, Will. He was at that age where he was going to miss his buds. He had lived in Connecticut from the time he was seven — that's when I first started with the WWF. It was going to be tough on Will; I could see it in his eyes and hear it in his voice. But, being everything a dad *shouldn't* be, I couldn't worry about my own son's emotions; I had to worry about mine first. I kept going back to Vince McMahon's words in one of our last conversations: "Get a nanny to raise your kids, Vince." I couldn't get those words out of my mind. They played over and over again like a bad, skipping Milli Vanilli record. Those words *iced* this decision and though Will would never understand that now, I hoped that one day, when he was old enough and had a family of his own, he would. In my heart of hearts, I understood that I had to walk away to stand up for what was right. No nanny was *ever* going to raise my kids and Vince should never have spoken those words to me. They were cold, heartless, insensitive and badly — very badly — thought out.

But, as the boss himself would often say, "That was yesterday." We needed to pack up my office and get out, hopefully with nobody seeing us. So I took all my belongings, left the video game machine, and we were on our way. I'll never forget how on the way out, we bumped into a girl that I had worked with on the second floor. Our hands were filled with brown cardboard boxes, some filled with fond memories, others filled with junk, as my coworker asked, "Hi, Vince — are these your kids?" Yes, I said . . . as we never stopped moving. Luckily, to coin a phrase from the Rock, this girl wasn't the sharpest knife in the drawer, and had no idea that that was the last time Vince Russo was going to be seen at that building for a very long time to come.

You Say It's Your Birthday!

January 24, 2006

I'm a forty-five-year-old man today. Forty-five. I can't believe that. Maybe that's because so many of those years were an absolute blur ... especially those rasslin' years. Writing two shows a week, and one pay-per-view a month on top of that — man, we were just strapped onto the back of a speeding bullet. One day just led into the next and we never had the time to just hit the brakes and enjoy life — *never*. But then again, I didn't stop even in my mid-20s; there was just no time. What with a wife, a mortgage and a kid on the way, who had time to just stop and breathe? You know, I've never done cocaine and I've never experienced riding that drug-induced high of go-go-go, but in all reality, I had a monkey of my own on my back and it was my drive. I was a workaholic and I was an addict.

In hindsight, I realize now that I was just afraid to *stop*. Afraid of what this world might do to me if I did; afraid of losing my "spot"; afraid that somebody might pass me; afraid that somebody else might win; afraid of not living up to the eyes of the world. The world tells you that you must be this, and you must be that, in order to be deemed successful. Successful? In whose eyes? So you spend your whole life trying to be what they're telling you that you need to be, whether you want to be it or not. Then one day, you turn around ... and it's your 45th birthday.

The saddest commentary on this is that without even realizing it, I never had to bear that cross called life ... not for a single day. Why? Because thousands of years ago a Jewish rabbi by the name of Jesus Christ walked up a hill carrying that cross for me. The same cross

13

that He would later die on. Pathetically, less than two and a half years ago all my eyes could see was a man dying on a cross. That's how I looked at it, with about as much impact as that last bland sentence I just wrote. It meant nothing to me . . . nothing. How is it that I was raised a Catholic, received communion and confirmation, went to catechism until I was about 16, but never understood the true ramifications of what Jesus Christ did for *me?* Either I wasn't listening, or somebody wasn't doing their job. Maybe it was a little of both.

I wake up every day thanking Jesus for saving my life at 42 years old. Not a day goes by where I don't thank Him for that. How sad is it that I lived that long without Him — if you want to call that living at all. Man, I just didn't get it. I just didn't understand. Not even the slightest clue. Nobody ever explained it to me. Oh yeah, there were those who came up now and again and said, "Jesus loves you!" But what did that mean? Nobody explained to me the sacrifice of an innocent man until God himself slapped me upside the head.

So this is why I'm explaining it to you — don't wait until you're 42 to get it — and why I'm going to break it down in terms I believe you'll understand:

1. Eve disobeyed God's instructions in the Garden of Eden and listened to Satan's instead when she took a bite out of an apple which hung from the Tree of the Knowledge of Good and Evil. In other words: Eve turned heel.

2. She was now a sinner for disobeying God. Adam then followed Eve's lead, so he too became a heel.

3. Being that Adam and Eve were the first man and woman on earth, we all come from their bloodlines in one way or another. Therefore, because of Adam and Eve, we were *all* born with the sin gene. Thus, we are all heels!

4. Because of humans obeying Satan rather than God, the earth shifted in power from God to Satan. The world now had a new general manager.

5. We were now all slaves of Satan, or jobbers to him, as we lost all our rights and privileges on this earth.

6. At this point the plot starts to thicken. (WWE writers: here is where you should begin to take notes on how to develop a good story.)

7. God needed to free us from Satan, while freeing us from sin. He needed to win our rights back for us. God is a just God (a true babyface), so there was only one way He could do this. He had to sacrifice a life in order to pay our sin debt.

8. But He couldn't just sacrifice any life. Sacrificing a sinner wouldn't have been *just*. You couldn't sacrifice a sinner to free all the other sinners – it don't work that way. But since we were *all* sinners, what was He going to do? (Are you starting to take note of the conflict in this story?)

9. God knew that He had to sacrifice a man, but this man had to be Godly: sin-free, able to live according to the law. Are you with me? So who is it going to be? Is it going to be someone under a mask?

10. No mask – this *isn't* bad, fake rasslin'. This is the Gospel, which translates to *the truth*. Thus, the Virgin Mary gave birth to Jesus Christ . . . the ultimate babyface. Why did the birth have to be immaculate? Because a man and a woman couldn't be involved since they carried the sin gene!

11. So Jesus, the Son of God *and* the Son of Man, was born.

12. Simply put, Jesus lived the rest of his life to die for *us*.

13. Jesus died on a cross in Calvary.

14. His last words: "It is done."

15. Satan would now be driven out, as he had killed an innocent man – someone he had no right to kill. Thus, the death of Jesus Christ covers all our sins, evening the score in a just way. It's a Broadway! With that, we now had the choice of choosing sides: with the "Prince of the World" or the "Prince of Peace."

16. The death of Jesus also once again opened the door for all of us to have communication with his father, God. All the sins committed by His people had been forgiven. Everything is nicey-nice again.

17. Wait, there's more . . .

18. He died on the cross, not only to free us of our sins – if we 'fessed up first and asked for forgiveness – but also to offer the gift of eternal life.

19. Three days later Jesus rose from the dead to show us all that there is eternal life, if we only believe in Him. In other words, he didn't just talk the talk – he walked the walk!

20. Thank you, Jesus.

There you have it: Christianity 101.

By the way . . . belated birthday cards welcomed.

Billy Bones
Sings Dionne Warwick

So, I'm sitting in a hotel room in Atlanta.

Man, you really have to understand how hard this is for me to write. Even though every second I ever spent at wcw was a total nightmare, I now understand that I had to walk down Elm Street in order to reach Paradise.

But man, those three letters — W-C-W — caused such trauma and hardship for me and my entire family. I should have known it from that very first meeting and, to tell you the truth, I did. But at that point I just wanted to be as far away from Vince McMahon as possible. Working for him the past few years as I did, man, he just burned me down to the filter — he took everything I had until I had nothing more to give. But, in all honesty, it wasn't just about *that* Vince; it was also about *this* Vince. Deep down I knew that I had done everything with the wwF that I could. I knew that the ratings had peaked, and even though we could probably sustain them for some time to come, they weren't going to get any higher. Remember, at that point in my life I was always chasing the next challenge, always thinking that accomplishing it would finally make me happy ... complete ... at peace. And that's how I looked at World Championship Wrestling: this would perhaps be the greatest challenge of not only my career, but my entire life. Did I know the baggage that came with it? Yes, I did, but I also remember thinking, "It can't be that bad." No, it wasn't. It was worse.

Back to the meeting.

I'm telling you: God is at my very hand writing this book, and He just doesn't want to get into detail here. It's just so pointless — so negative — but I will feed you what I'm being fed.

The thing that stands out most in my mind about the meeting was the dog and pony show that was put on for me over a two-day period. Let me pause for a second — what the heck is a dog and pony show anyway? Has anybody ever been to one? Do they exist? Are the dogs and the ponies competing for ribbons, trophies or extra oats? Is there money in this for the dog and pony handlers, or do they do it for the love? Where are these shows held? How many people attend? Are they ever televised? Why do donkeys get the snide? And how do they feel about it? Do the donkeys have their own show? If they do, are the promoters the same guys who promote the dog and pony shows? Man, I just love old using old clichés, especially when I have no idea what they mean.

But . . . back to the dog and pony show.

Remember when Dorothy — and her little dog Toto, too — crash-landed in Oz? Remember the royal treatment she got from all the munchkins in Munchkinland? It was a living, breathing rainbow of thousands of small people singing, dancing and jumping about. Oh, the joy! She's here! She's here! Who will ever forget those three height-challenged guys who went on and on about representing the "lollipop kids" or something like that (I can replay the DVD a million times and I still have no idea what they're saying). I can't think of any welcome that's come even close. Not even the brave men and women who come home from the armed forces after serving their country get this kind of fanfare. Man, there were balloons, candy, edible flowers . . . sorry, I'm getting confused with Willy Wonka's intro, but you get my point.

Well, that October day in 1999, the atmosphere was quite similar, except the midgets were replaced by a very tall, very thin man by the name of Billy "Bones." Now, if you were seeing Bill Busch (that was his real name) for the first time, you might have thought you saw him somewhere before — perhaps in Tim Burton's *Nightmare Before Christmas*. Man, the guy was just so thin: eyes sunk in, caved cheekbones, he was every supermodel's dream! But he was also the nicest guy you would ever want to meet.

I've said this a hundred times about the wrestling business: You can't be a good guy and *survive*. You just can't. Unless you're fully prepared, and go into the battle with your armor tightly strapped on, they will chop you down with their weapons of lies, deceit and betrayal so fast that you won't even realize what they've done until you're standing on the outside of their bubble looking in. It happens that fast. But they are gentlemen about it: the nicer you are, the quicker the execution. It's painless and fast . . . real fast. Bill Busch never had a chance. I knew it the moment I met him.

An accountant by trade (I have no ideas why accountants are always appointed my superiors), Bill Busch was put into the role of overseeing wcw after Eric Bischoff was relieved of his duties. Unfortunately, Bill was in the wrong place at the wrong time, and I don't know if he ever even saw it coming. But he was a great guy, a real stand-up guy, and I liked him the moment I met him.

Rounding out the Vince Russo welcome wagon that day was J.J. Dillon, who I believed headed talent relations at the time, and Gary Juster, who was in charge of booking the buildings where wcw would play. At the time, they were Busch's confidants, Duvall's Tom Hagen to Brando's Vito Corleone. Even though the comparison is correct, the motives — in my opinion — may have been much different. You see, Hagen had the Godfather's back: all that he cared about was Corleone's best interests. At the time, I don't know if the same could be said for J.J. and Juster. You see, they were "rasslin' guys," and Bill Busch wasn't. The truth is that "rasslin' guys" just have a natural instinct to look out for themselves before they think about anybody else. No offense to Busch's right-hand men, and nothing personal intended, but that's just the way it is. It's the nature of the beast, the law of the land: nobody has anybody else's back; they are too busy getting their front to the head of the line.

It was no different in the wwf. Vince had guys hanging on his Brooks Brothers suit with the same intentions: "me first"; "I've got to think of myself first"; "I've got to get myself over first." The only difference was that Vince was smart to the business — smarter than anybody else — so you couldn't "work" him. That wasn't true for Busch. He was a rookie in a world filled with cagey veterans who didn't care one iota about him or his family. Again, that's just the way the business makes you. You are constantly guarding your "spot" no matter what the cost . . . or should I say *whose* cost? You are always looking to get on the good side of the brass above your boss, even if it means taking him out in the process. Yes, you tarnish your actions and your words to get ahead, and the boss is no exception — unless his initials were vkm. In the case of Billy Bones, his "under guys" would have bought the shovel and dug the hole themselves. There is always someone above your superior to impress, and impress by any means necessary. At the end of the day it just doesn't matter — that's just the way it is. It's called "The Wrestling Business," or perhaps more appropriately, "The World."

"Sound the trumpets! Russo's here! Russo's here!" Oh, they sang chorus after chorus of Dionne Warwick's "Promises, Promises"! They promised me the world and everything in it, just like Tony Montana said in *Scarface*. The world was my oyster, my clam . . . and everything else that God's great blue ocean had to offer. And the parade just kept coming. The next day, Sunday, two more execs joined the big top: Brad Siegel, who was not only the head of both TBS and TNT, but perhaps more importantly to me, "a Jew from the Island" (that's how the guys from Long Island would have referred to him) and Dr. Harvey Schiller. Now I knew Schiller was a big deal, but to this day I still have no idea what he did. But Siegel — Siegel I liked. He was one of my own. A New Yawker at heart, Brad was brilliant — you know, the type that runs TV networks! And the thing that really stood out about him was that he wore a baseball cap to the meeting. No big-deal suit and tie, but a baseball cap. Now that's my kinda guy!

Did I mention that this turned into a *two*-day meeting? Oh, and also that they had me call my WWF buddy Ed Ferrara in because they were going to give him a job too! Yeah, I could have gotten anybody a job . . . were the "Banana Splits" still around (la, la, la, la-la-la, la)? I mean, I was *huge* in that hotel room!

"Vince, as Creative Director, you will have complete control of all TBS and TNT wrestling-related programming. That includes *Nitro*, *Thunder* and all the WCW pay-per-views. Complete control."

Let me tell you something. These guys were no Howard Weiner (my red-headed, Jewish salesman friend who could sell morals to Hollywood). Not even close. They were selling, but inside, I wasn't buying. Now please don't misunderstand me here: I don't think for one minute any of these guys were blatantly lying to me. I think they honestly believed what they were telling me, but in reality it just wasn't going to work that way. For starters, I've never had complete control of any job in my life unless the person I was working for was *me*. If there are people above you, so to speak, then there is always — *always* — going to be somebody else involved: someone's opinions, ideas, questions and most importantly, two cents. That's just the way business is. Then, there's good ol' standards and practices; TBS and TNT were full-fledged television networks, so there were going to be rules and regulations as to what their programming could — and could not — contain. I knew that going in, so the thought of complete control was never really taken seriously by me from the offset. But did they ever paint one brilliant Picasso.

Man, these guys were in dire straits, and I was their answer. Knowing what they were expecting, I took the time to make it clear to them that ratings didn't happen overnight. I explained that at the WWF, the ratings climb was a slow but steady one. It took a good year to build a ratings point, and everything had to go according to plan in order for it to happen. It was patience and precision and you couldn't have one without the other. Man, I took out my black bat and beat them over the head with that because I knew they were expecting ratings yesterday. But they said they understood . . . even though I knew they didn't.

At this point it was just a matter of signing the contract. I knew that "Billy Bones and Friends" (great name for a CD) weren't going to allow me to get on a plane until that contract was signed. There was a lot of pressure on both Ed and myself, but at this time we were just so burned out on Vince. There was no turning back and we both knew it, but the truth was we weren't even thinking about turning back. Too much damage had already been done. Sure, we had heard all the stories of the overpaid inmates running the asylum at WCW, but it had to be better than Vince. And that's what it came down to: Vince. Not the WWF and not the people in it, but Vince. Yeah, I wanted a new challenge, and yeah, I wanted to be off on my own, but perhaps more importantly, no, I didn't want to go back and work for Vince. Aside from his "infamous" nanny comment, it was never anything personal — never — but at that point in my life, almost 39 years old, I just knew that there was more to life than Titan Tower in Stanford, Connecticut. There was more to life than the World Wrestling Federation twenty-four hours a day, seven days a week.

As I signed the contract, I reflected back on giving the last five years of my life to Vince McMahon, just serving them up on a silver platter. That's the only way you can ever be an employee of his. But let me make one thing clear: that was my choice and nobody forced me into it. I put everything else in my life second, on the back burner: my wife, my three kids, everything. I didn't know why. I had no idea what I was chasing. Thank God, I found it before it was too late.

In closing this chapter, I need to make a small side note of *extreme* importance.

To set it up let me just say that my writing-mate and dear friend, Ed Ferrara, is a genius. The guy is just brilliant. When it comes to the written word, Ed can flat pen rings around me. In 2004, Ed had his own book, *Dark Consequences*, published (you can purchase it at edferrara.com), and after reading it I just wanted to retire my pen forever. If another word was never written again after that masterpiece, the period would have been left in just the right place. His mastery of the English language is a true art. I just kept hearing "Olé! Olé!" imagining every stroke of his keyboard as it danced across the naked page. If Ed's name weren't on the front of his book, you'd swear Stephen King had penned it. Compared to Ed, the "He-Man of Horror," I'm nothing more than a five-year-old scribbling things on a brown paper bag with a crayon. But that's nothing compared to his spoken word. Whereas Ed comes across as a polished and dignified Harvard professor, I come across as a guy wanting to sell you a watch on the corner of 42nd and 7th. I mean, I'm in my mid-40s and Ed still uses words in our conversations that I don't understand. You should have seen me when I was reading his notes on my first book before I sent in the final draft. I literally had to blow the dust from the dictionary and put it to use just to figure out what he was talking about!

That's why he was so valuable to me at the big wcw contract signing. Ed read the fine print when I couldn't even understand what the *big* print said. After literally going through it word for word, Ed made sure that there was a "Play or Pay" clause in the contract which stated that wcw had to pay us in full even if they decided not to use our services at any time during the duration of the two-year contract (actually, wcw wanted me to sign a *three-*year contract, but I knew I was done after two — no matter what!).

Who knew what huge dividends that would pay only three short months later?

Stay-at-Home Mom

Back to the present . . .

I'm 45, and I'm a stay-at-home mom. The only problem is that there are no kids to stay at home with. After leaving TNA (Total Non-Stop Action) and closing my CD Warehouse store in Marietta, Georgia, I knew I was going to be spending a lot of time at home, alone, as I waited on God's word. And don't let Him kid you: He lets you wait on it. It's called obedience and patience, two things that we *all* could use a refresher course in. God uses the Holy Spirit to work through you in order to mold you into the type of person He wants representing His Kingdom. Throughout this period, you will be tested, and tested again. Are you *sure* you want to do this thing? You see, once you are called by God, you then have to be *chosen* by Him; this is all part of the process. So He takes His sweet time — and why shouldn't He? I mean, He's *only* the Creator of the Universe, that's all.

So I bought a dog — if you want to call him that. His name is Yogi, and he's half Shar Pei, half Chow. To put it as nicely as I can, Yogi is about three scoops shy of a full can of Alpo. I mean, can one dog really be dumber than another? After spending time with Yogi, I answer that with a big, resounding *yes!* To give him the benefit of the doubt, I think it may be all that extra fur that Shar Peis have. I mean, he just looks stupid — like that dog on the *Beverly Hillbillies*. But then I watch him harass our two cats, which begins with him chasing them, and ends with them chasing him. No, it's not the skin. He's an imbecile . . . just like Chykirda.

So now, I have a new best friend and we spend a lot of time together — when the cats aren't chasing him around the house.

That's how simple my life is now. That's how simple it can be. But I'll tell you what's incredible: the things I now see in everyday life as I'm hangin' with Yogi, waiting for God's call. Things that were always there, but I never took the time to stop and notice before — the simple things.

I got on my soap box in my last book and wrote about the phenomenon known as Hollywood award shows. But, upon closer examination, I realize that it goes much further than the show itself. And I'm not even talking about the pre-show before the show, or the post-show after the show; I'm talking about something completely different. A Versace gown of a whole different color. Yeah, that's right; there are actually shows about what these people wear to the show!

What is going on with our society? I mean does anybody *really* care about what Eva Longoria wrapped herself in to attend the Golden Globes? All right, bad example — I cared a little, but how about what tux Brad Pitt wore or didn't wear? People, *what are we doing?* Is this where our priorities are today? Whether or not Marcia Cross is wearing a bra with that dress that Paul McCartney's daughter made? Have we gone mad? There *can't* be anybody out there who really cares about this stuff. And this is what I really don't get: Okay, maybe some people do care because they want to be "in style," but wait a minute . . . are they ever going to be able to afford the dresses that the Tinseltown divas are parading around in on the red carpet? Look at what's become important to us. It's all about *material things*. Talk about false idols! I don't know what was worse: that golden calf back in the days of Moses, or Star Jones in that Vera Wang! Man, she must have had to enlist the use of two shoehorns just to get into that thing!

Now I understand how Jerry Seinfeld made a living from this. We learn so much about society and ourselves by just stopping and perceiving the little things in our everyday lives. Okay, okay, I'll get back to rasslin' in just a minute, but there's one more item on my agenda. Every day on television we hear about how out-of-shape America is. From Dr. Phil to Oprah to Maury, they are all jumping on the carb-wagon. And you know what? I think that's great! I think America does need to shape up and become healthier. So, I buy into all this. Next thing I know, I'm in Kroger and I'm browsing the "natural" food aisles. Yup, I have to do the shopping too — it's all part of the stay-at-home mom gimmick. So I'm comparing prices like any good mom would do, and the thing that flips my wig (that saying was stolen from an old, old, Beatles board game I used to have) is that the healthy food is twice as expensive as the junk food! Now is it me, or is that backwards? If we truly want America to get healthy, then shouldn't the healthy food be affordable to everybody? Then we wonder why everybody's eating junk. Why wouldn't they? It's cheaper! If the word "natural" is in front of any food item, it's double the price. What is going on here? Is somebody working from behind the scenes? "All Natural Breakfast Cereal," $5.99 per box; "Captain Sugar," $1.99. How can we shape up America when nobody can afford to?

But there's more . . .

Why did the price of gas go down considerably before Christmas? It was under $2.00 a gallon in Atlanta, and then shot up 30, 35 cents as soon as everybody was done with their shopping? What is that? Were we "allowed" a break to spend our hard-earned money on big business retail before the holidays, only to give it back to the gas companies once the Wise Men, the donkey and the manger were put away?

Trust in Me

I'll never forget the feeling as Ed and I drove from the airport to our first *Nitro* in Biloxi, Mississippi. E.T. must have felt the same way — I could immediately relate to why he wanted to go home so bad. Let's face it: even though we were "in" the business, we were still outsiders to the WCW locker room. Many of the wrestlers had never worked with either of us before. The only things they knew about us were what they read in the "dirt sheets."

You know, the dirt sheets, or wrestling newsletters (and you can also throw the Internet into that mess) as they're "professionally" called, have such a profound effect on the wrestling business. First and foremost, no matter what they tell you, 95% of the boys read them — it's their *National Enquirer*. I mean, wrestlers love gossip, plain and simple. I always had a vision of replacing the yentas on *The View* with professional wrestlers and calling the show *The Pew*, where everybody in the wrestling business could just air dirty laundry — no, not their own, but everybody else's! And I have the perfect Barbara Walters: Glenn "Disco Inferno" Gilberti. Disco loves gossip! To this day, every phone conversation I have with him opens with, "Do ya got any hot news?" But there's a difference between Glenn and many other dirt sheet addicts. You see, Glenn is intelligent enough to do it all in jest. Not only that, but the guy just loves to hear himself talk. In other words, Glenn gossips for laughs. But others . . . others use it as a sword, to simply shape their opinions on others. They'll believe what they want to believe and disregard what they don't want to believe. I can't tell you how many people out there hate me because of something they read about me. They take a statement they read somewhere — which is more often than not, an opinion — and then they process it in their minds and create their own interpretation. So now that *third-hand* information is passed along to someone else, who in turn seasons it with some of their own opinions and by the time the concoction is complete and ready to be served, Vince Russo is the Anti-Christ of Professional Wrestling!

And so goes the world.

So, in speaking for myself, I knew that walking into that locker room wasn't going to be pretty. In fact, it was hard — very hard. I just didn't know what the boys thought of me. I just didn't know what they read and believed, or chose to believe. But maybe I didn't give them enough credit either, because upon our arrival we were first greeted by what many referred to as the wcw "mid-carders." Man, I hate that title — always have. If you'd made it to the level of the wwf or wcw, you had *made it*. You were there because you deserved to be there. You were a *pro*. Now what separates a "mid-carder" from a "main-eventer"? Lack of talent? In some instances, but not all. Now I'm not going to talk about other sports here, because I've never worked behind the scenes where some kind of ball was involved. I lack the knowledge, experience and insight to discuss major league locker rooms and front offices. But when it comes to professional wrestling, I can speak based on having been there. It wasn't just lack of talent that held you back; it went much further than that.

One word: Politics. And I hate that word. I wish that word didn't even exist in the English language. There is nothing good that can be associated with that word . . . nothing. You know one of the ways *Webster's* defines that word? "Factional scheming for power." Could Satan have said that any better? And that's what it is: scheming, from the moment the ring crew starts to assemble the ring to the moment they take it down. Who's going to bury who today? What a tragic, tragic game. But again, that's not just wrestling — that's the world. But in all honesty, when it comes to politics and politicians, I've never come across a business that is more vicious than professional wrestling. And remember, it only takes a few to poison the whole.

But the politics really came later in my career. I have to admit, while with the wwf there really wasn't that much politicking happening behind the scenes, and if there was I wasn't privy to it. It was just a different layout than you had in wcw. Vince was the boss and it started and ended with him. Plus, on top of that, everybody was generally happy. Mostly all the boys — and girls — were involved in a storyline, and with the ratings being what they were, everybody was making money. But the underhandedness is never totally absent. Whether it be the locker room or the office, you still had your elephants and your donkeys, but they just picked their spots.

I remember one occasion, when a senior member of DX didn't want to put over D-Lo Brown (who was a member of The Nation at the time) — which would have surely helped to catapult the "Human Bobble-head" to the next level. I was so hot at Triple H: all I could think about were all those who lay down at his boots before, helping pave the road to his fame and fortune. I also witnessed Sable being single-handedly taken down by one of the boys who had Vince's ear. She was literally in favor one day, and on the outside of the bubble looking in the next. And on yet another occasion, Ed and I had written a script — our last script — where Chris Jericho would defeat the Rock at the conclusion of *Raw*. At the time the Rock was *huge* and Chris had just come over from WCW. That upset would have gotten Jericho over instantly, but once we gave our notice, the script was changed. Now understand, I'm not implicating the Rock *at all*; that simply wasn't his style. But at the time I felt that somebody had it in for Jericho. Either it was a personal thing, or the fact that he was an ex-WCWer thing. Ironically, it took the WWE almost two years to get Jericho over — something that perhaps could have been done with one single job two years earlier. Yes, there were traces of politics in the WWF, but it was nowhere near the infestation of its competitor, WCW.

But in getting back to that first day at WCW, I was both relieved and optimistic as the "under-utilized" talent all made their way over to me, seemingly the minute I walked in the door. I remember being approached by Dean Malenko, Eddie Guerrero, Chris Benoit and Konnan, just to name a few. Man, I just liked Konnan the second I met him. The guy is just so real — been there, done that, and don't make any bones about it. I greatly enjoyed working with him over the years, both in WCW and later in TNA. Meeting these guys — I don't know — it just felt like they had been waiting forever for a guy like me to walk in the door: a guy that would just give them a chance. By the reception it was obvious that they knew what Ed and I had done with the *entire* roster in the WWF. They knew that with us it would be an even playing field. The ball would be handed off to anyone who wanted it, not just the self-proclaimed superstar running backs. No, in our world, all were created equal. They were just men and women looking to make a living and support their families. They all deserved a chance; they all earned it.

Unfortunately, in conjunction with the pyro and ballyhoo reception from those of the boys who were glad to see us, there was a much different reception offered by those who maybe *weren't* so glad. In other words, a high-paid fraction of the locker room failed to greet Ed and me with joy, love and balloon animals.

For some reason, this memory has always remained vivid in my mind. I remember approaching a makeshift office backstage at wcw that they may have named the "War Room" — not sure. Present were many of the agents, guys on the booking committee and various veterans. This is where I first locked eyes with Hulk Hogan. Now before I begin to tell you about that experience, I'm going to write down something *ten times*, because every time I say it, nobody seems to want to listen.

Hulk Hogan is a legend. He paved my way in this field. I am 4ever grateful.
Hulk Hogan is a legend. He paved my way in this field. I am 4ever grateful.
Hulk Hogan is a legend. He paved my way in this field. I am 4ever grateful.
Hulk Hogan is a legend. He paved my way in this field. I am 4ever grateful.
Hulk Hogan is a legend. He paved my way in this field. I am 4ever grateful.
Hulk Hogan is a legend. He paved my way in this field. I am 4ever grateful.
Hulk Hogan is a legend. He paved my way in this field. I am 4ever grateful.
Hulk Hogan is a legend. He paved my way in this field. I am 4ever grateful.
Hulk Hogan is a legend. He paved my way in this field. I am 4ever grateful.
Hulk Hogan is a legend. He paved my way in this field. I am 4ever grateful.

Now, I went through that writing exercise not to be sarcastic, but to simply get my point across. In every interview I've ever done, I always make that *same* statement, yet nobody seems to want to believe me. And I know it has to do with a "worked" promo that I cut on him one night later on that summer . . . but we'll get more into that later.

If you grew up on Long Island in the '80s, you were a Hulk Hogan fan — plain and simple. I mean, I just don't know how else to toot his horn. The guy single-handedly — that means not Vince McMahon, but Hulk Hogan — put sports entertainment on the map. Both Vince and Vince Sr. had been in the wrestling game many years before Hulk came around, and nobody — *nobody* — even came close to having the impact of "Hulkamania." I myself once waited in line for three hours to get an autographed picture of the Hulkster for my son. *Three hours* — do you understand that? I never even waited in line that long to buy kiss tickets! Man, the guy was the Beatles in the sports-entertainment world: George, Paul, Ringo and John — all of them put together. Throw in Yoko and Linda too — he was *huge!*

I actually watched him beat the Iron Sheik for his first wwf title on

Cablevision, live from Madison Square Garden. You just knew that night that the entire business was going to change. Years later, I even remember going to see him wrestle Randy Savage for the first time at MSG. I swear to you, that was the one and only time I ever felt the rafters shake in that place, including the '69–70', '72–73 Knicks, the '93–94 Rangers and the '77 KISS Army. The guy just had *it*. At one point I even remember shelling out eight bucks so my son could proudly wave his Hulkster foam hand to and fro in the air. Was I a fan? No . . . I was a *Hulk Hogan mark!*

I'm just going to lay it all out to you here. After I had signed my WCW contract and it started to sink in, I remember my thoughts went to working with Hulk Hogan and Ric Flair. Why? Because I had such a respect for them that there was a part of me that was nervous . . . yes, even intimidated. I just wanted them to respect me, that's all. Had I achieved what they had in the business? That's like comparing SpongeBob's acting ability to Al Pacino's; of course I hadn't, and never would, but on a different level I did leave my mark on the WWF. I proved I could be successful at what I did. I proved I belonged here, in their world.

But that night, I'll never forget the look in Hogan's eyes. Was it one of unkindness, hostility or even hatred? No, not at all. Perhaps a long, cold stare? Nope. Did a stern look that suggested intimidation rear its ugly head? No; that one stayed home.

Time out.

I need to take a break from the Hulkster's eyes to discuss something that's weighing heavy on my mind.

I just came back from dinner with VJ. I take great joy in spending as much time as I possibly can with my kids, even if that means having to talk about dead rock stars in a smaller-than-it-should-be IHOP booth. I don't know — I just love dragging my kids everywhere with me, all three of them. Sure, 95% of the time they don't want to go, but that doesn't faze me, or even hurt my feelings; I'm used to it. So I'm not cool any more, okay, I get that, but who cares? "Get in the car; we're going to a mall!" Notice I said "a mall." My kids loathe the fact that I'm a mall junkie. I just love going to malls. New malls, old malls, malls I've never been to before, malls I've visited a thousand times; doesn't matter — I'm a MALL ADDICT! If that in itself doesn't irk my kids, what really sends them over the top is that I never buy anything; I just look. Amy hates that part of my mall ritual as well, but after 23 years, what is she really going to do? But, in getting back to IHOP, VJ and I just finished discussing another dead musician, who I'm sure is immortalized on a T-shirt at Hot Topic, when my pancakes were served.

Here's the thing. Can somebody, anybody, please tell me why the pancakes at IHOP are served on a plate THE SAME SIZE AS THE PANCAKES? Is this just me? This question has to go right up there with where is the Ark of the Covenant? Why? Why? Why? I know they have bigger plates in the back — you know, the ones they serve the omelets on. What's the deal here? where is the syrup supposed to go? There is no way to keep the syrup on the plate when the pancakes are the same size as the plate itself. The minute you carve out the first piece, syrup is all over the table. What's with this? What's their angle?

Speaking of angle . . . let's get back to wrestling.

That day, Hulk's eyes housed a look of total distrust. "Who is this guy . . . and how is he going to screw me?" But let me make it clear: this was simply my opinion. During my five-year journey in the WWF, I had spent many hours in locker rooms that were both painted and carpeted in paranoia. The stench just reeked. Nobody trusted anybody and that's the way it was supposed to be. That's the foundation that the founding promoters built it on. We (the promoters) make all the money while pitting all our employees, or "independent contractors" against each other. Independent contractor: that is the biggest joke in the bubble to date. "Wait a minute . . . I've got it! We'll hire them as 'independent contractors' so we don't have to give them any benefits, then we'll write the contract in such a way that even though they are 'independent contractors' and they don't have any benefits, they will also be exclusive to us! Of course they'll sign it . . . they're wrestlers!" And they did . . . and they still do.

I once had a promoter say to me, "Vince, not only would the boys work our TV for free, but they would *pay us* to be on our TV." And that was 2002, not 1952. But that's their MO; that's the way promoters work. They put the fear of God in you, constantly reminding you how lucky you are to be working for them, always telling you that there are 100 wrestlers standing in line to take your spot. I witnessed all this with my own eyes. But, the truth is, as long as the boys allow it, business will continue to go on this way. No union; no fairness. Why do the boys allow it? Again, that disgusting word: paranoia.

The total belief that if they take one step out of line and speak up, the promoter would write their last angle . . . one that puts them out of work and on the unemployment line.

You know what's ironic? Reading back that last line, I don't even believe it. How can business practices be that archaic in 2006? The answer is simple: time has simply passed them by, both inside *and* outside of the ring. And the promoters, owners — call them whatever you want — will continue to get away with it as long as the boys allow them to. I often wondered what would happen on a Monday night, or better yet on a Sunday night — a pay-per-view night — if the boys, all the boys, went up to management say two hours before showtime and said, "You know, there isn't going to be a pay-per-view tonight unless all our families receive full medical coverage — you know, like normal people with normal jobs do."

Would the show be canceled?

The boys: that's how the wrestlers are always referred to behind the curtain. Think about that for a minute. These are grown men: husbands, fathers, *adults*. But yet they are referred to as "the boys." They are referred to as children. Man, if you don't think there's any promoter psychology that goes into that, look at it again. "Boys" aren't capable of taking care of themselves; they always need someone to take care of them. "Boys" aren't capable of thinking for themselves; they need someone to think for them. "Boys" can't make grown-up decisions on their own; they always have to rely on someone else to make their decisions for them. "Boys" will be "boys." Again, this is 2006 we are talking about. When do the "boys" start being treated like men? When do they start getting treated with the respect they deserve? When do they start being treated like husbands and fathers? I'll tell you when: the day they start standing up for themselves; the day they will no longer allow themselves to be used and abused; the day they will no longer be taken advantage of; the day they will no longer be treated like children.

Nuff said.

The paranoia gene is instilled in all the wrestlers — and Hulk Hogan was no exception, especially when it came to me. But again, neither was this his fault, or a character flaw. It was simply based on all those who scarred him years before he ever met me. I never took it personally; I always understood. But it wasn't just Hogan — in large part it was most of the veterans (we're not allowed to say old-timers) who had never met me before. I got the same vibe from Ric Flair. I could just hear him asking, "Who is this guy? Who did he ever beat — and what is he going to do to ruin my career?" There was just no trust — *none!* I felt like Kaa in Walt Disney's *Jungle Book*. Remember him? Who could ever forget that big scene where he emphatically vied for Mowgli's trust? "Trust in me . . . just in me." Man, that python could act!

I believe that both Hogan and Flair construed my developing of the under-card as an attempt to hurt their careers and tarnish what they had already accomplished. What neither stopped to realize was the impossibility of that notion even if it was my objective — which, of course, it was not. They were legends, honest-to-goodness legends. Nobody was going to erase their legacy even if they attempted to. First and foremost, I was a fan of both — a *huge* fan. I stated my admiration of Hogan earlier, and Slick Ric was no different.

To this day, there isn't a guy who cuts a better promo than Ric Flair — not one. Back in the day, when Flair began tearing off his own clothes in mid-sentence during one of his monumental promos, you could hear my *pop* from Long Island to Long Beach! There has never been a more charismatic figure in professional wrestling than Flair, not even the Rock, not even Mick Foley, and I think I'm safe to say there never will be. Secondly, being that the bonus structure of my contract was based on ratings — the higher the rating, the more money I would receive — why in even Vince Russo's wildest dreams would I set out to destroy two of the biggest draws, attractions and ratings-grabbers in the game? Based on my income alone — money that would take care of my family — that idea is simply ludicrous! It just doesn't make any sense. Are you suggesting that this ego trip that some proposed I was on was more important to me than earning as much money as I possibly could for my family? The truth is, if I could have found even a yard ape capable of drawing a rating, I would have told him to clear his schedule on Monday nights because he was going to be on TV! I put myself in the ring — in harm's way — in an attempt to draw a number and I'm not going to use the two biggest icons in the industry?

Even though I am certain that both Hulk and Ric will never understand this, rather than attempting to destroy their careers, I was trying to accomplish the complete opposite. A few weeks prior to signing with WCW, I witnessed Hogan wrestle Flair on *Nitro*. Now strictly from a fan perspective, it was very hard to watch. What I witnessed that night was two legends that were shells of their former selves still trying to do it. And I don't say that in a mean-spirited way at all; it's just what I saw. It brought me back to 1973 when I saw Willie Mays play center field for the New York Mets in the World Series. Seeing Willie that way just broke my heart. He just wasn't the same guy; age caught up with him, as it does to all of us. That's just life; that's just the way it is. I tell many people who ask me if I would ever go back and write for Vince again that quite honestly, I don't know if I could. That was seven years ago and time has passed me by. I don't have my finger on the heartbeat of America like I did ten years ago when I was 35. Watching Flair and Hogan go at it that night at 33 RPM speed — it just wasn't right. In my opinion the bookers were just exploiting them to try to pop a number. It was a desperate situation and that's exactly the way it came across on TV.

Being a fan, I knew that both these individuals deserved better. Was there still a place for them in the business? Of course there was; they built it. Was it as the main event on Monday night? Probably not. Again, these are *all* just my opinions — nothing less, nothing more — but I felt that both Hogan and Flair needed to be elevated to icon status. Being just "one of the boys" was a ridiculous notion. Was Babe Ruth just another baseball player? No, these guys had to go from just being a part of the show to rising above it — and that's exactly what I was going to attempt to do. That's why Ric Flair was left out in the middle of nowhere by the Filthy Animals in the first PPV that Ed and I wrote, and Hogan wasn't even a part of it. Personally, I felt that we had to first undo the damage that had already been done with both superstars, and then start from scratch, putting both icons in a role that better suited them, and better suited the product. Unfortunately, neither one of them understood that. Why? Because the animal known as the professional wrestler is infested with the gene of paranoia. That's their mentality and it will never change. The minute I was no longer booking the show, Hogan and Flair were back on TV in the same roles as they were three months prior. And guess what? Nobody cared . . . and nobody watched. What a sad commentary.

If I'm suppose to take this part of the book to apologize to both Hulk Hogan and Ric Flair, I will. I'm sorry. But, with God as my witness, I really don't know what I'm apologizing for. At this point in my life, is there really any reason for me to be untruthful? Every word I write is directly from my heart, and if my own words are suppose to beat up the author, I have no problem with that, but that's not the case here. To this day I am a fan of both Ric Flair and Hulk Hogan . . . through all the heartache, that never changed. All I tried to do was what I thought was the right thing. I just don't know what else to say about it.

You know, in backing off from those last few paragraphs and re-reading them, I have to ask myself a question: Could I have been the one who was paranoid? Is it possible that Hogan and Flair weren't really thinking what I thought they were thinking? Man, is this world destroying us, or what? Who do we believe? Who don't we believe? Who can we trust? Who can't we trust? Who is speaking the truth? Who is lying? How hard is it for man's intentions to be pure? How hard is that? How hard is it to just have the mindset of doing the right thing? How hard is it to put others before ourselves? How difficult is it for us to serve, rather than be served? Man, in reading the Bible it is just so clear to see how we are doing everything backwards. We are all doing the things that Jesus tells us *not* to do. Then we wonder why the world is in the shape it's in? The wrestling bubble just exemplifies that world, that's all; it's at a much smaller, less complex scale, but it's all the same.

Over the past few years I've used the expression that "the wrestling business is killing the wrestling business," but the truth is, it goes much deeper than that. The world is killing the world, and it's just a matter of time before it catches up with all of us.

Edges First

The jigsaw puzzle was a mess. It was like somebody had dumped out the box and scattered pieces all over the place. Not in one vicinity, mind you, but rather throughout the entire house. Pieces that were supposed to fit, didn't; pieces that weren't supposed to fit, did. There were too many pieces, while at the same time important pieces were missing.

That's what the landscape was like when Ed Ferrara and I took creative control of wcw in October of '99.

Nothing seemed to make sense; nothing was working. At the time the ratings were in the mid-twos, keeping in mind that only a year earlier they had been more than double that. Yeah, wcw was the *Titanic* when Captain Ed and I were given the helm. But all you can do is take one wave at a time, much the same way we did at the wwf. Remember, we had already told the head honchos at wcw that ratings weren't going to happen overnight; they had to be built brick by brick, no different than a house. You had to start from the ground, then build your strong foundation and continue on up. Fortunately, there was much to build on at wcw, including one under-utilized superstar that I knew could be an integral pillar of that foundation. His name? Bret "The Hitman" Hart.

I often wonder if Eric Bischoff and wcw signed Bret Hart because they had plans for him, or simply because they wanted to get him away from the wwf. The reason I ask that question is because once they had him, they had no idea what to do with him. At best, Bret was floundering in a sea of mediocrity, and if anybody knew that Bret had much more to bring to the dance than that, it was me. Having worked with him for the past five years, I knew that Bret was a pure main-eventer, and he got there without any politicking. Bret got to the top of his profession by simply being the best there was, the best there is and the best there ever will be, and I mean that with the purist of sincerity. In order for wcw to be successful, I knew that the Hitman had to be a cornerstone of the company. But remember our history? Well, let's just say there were some personal issues that had to be ironed out between us before that could ever even be a possibility.

The last time I saw Bret Hart prior to me joining wcw was at that 1997 Survivor Series, or the Canadian nightmare, as I like to refer to it. Following that eyesore (no pun intended, vkm), I had spoken to him only once on the phone in the fury of the aftermath. Then, following his departure to wcw, Owen died at a show that I was part of. Not only was I there, but I had written it. Yes, Bret and I had a lot to talk about before we could even think about rebuilding the company that we now both worked for.

Talking with Bret was my number one priority at that first *Nitro*; not stroking Flair, not stroking Hogan, not stroking Goldberg. Bret and I had some issues that needed to be settled and I wanted to do it sooner rather than later. I can remember not being nervous because I simply knew Bret; he was a gentleman, not some testosterone buffoon looking to intimidate you with every sharp word and cold stare. I knew whether Bret agreed with me or not, he would listen, and that's exactly what he did when I found him sitting alone at a cafeteria table.

I have to be honest: Bret made it easy because he was just Bret. His main focus was on what happened the night that Owen died. I explained to Bret every detail that I could remember. After listening to every word I said, and never once interrupting me, Bret went on to tell me that Owen didn't want to portray the Blue Blazer persona. He said that Owen didn't want to be some kind of silly character, that Owen just wanted to do what he did best: wrestle. I explained to Bret that if that was indeed the case, Owen never expressed it to me. I also told Bret that if he had, we would have never done it. Bret listened, and even though he might not have agreed, he was very respectful.

I can't put into words the impact that conversation had on me that night; the truth is that it has stayed with me for all these years. At the time, with what Bret had gone through over the past few years, anybody else would have just lost it and taken every ounce of their inner pain out on me, at least verbally. But not Bret; when he talks about being a hero, or being a role model, he means it — and he lives it. You know, Bret and I were never super tight, but for some reason I miss him more than most. I just think I miss what he represented, in a world that let me down in many, many ways. Bret never let me down. He was always the person that he said he was. That's something that's very rare in the business; it's also something that I'll admire forever.

So now with Bret on board, we were ready to back the ship out of the iceberg. There was no doubt in my mind that this could work — the talent was there. But I also realized that the success of wcw would depend on much more than just the gifts of its crew. The success would depend on the entire landscape of the Ponderosa. Could the chiefs work alongside the Indians? Would the sergeants allow the privates to advance in rank? Could there be one general of this army, or would his own people eventually take him down — and not in gingerly fashion, but rather by beheading? These were the issues that were destroying this company at its very crux. I knew it the second I walked into that building in Biloxi, Mississippi. Nobody was on the same page . . . not even the same book . . . not even the same library. Everybody just had their own agenda. Everybody was looking out for #1. Within the walls of that locker room, nobody trusted anybody. It was a far cry from the atmosphere I had just left at the wwf. But again, there was nobody to blame but myself; this is why I took the job. I knew that I was in for the challenge of a lifetime and call me stupid, hopeful, naïve, ignorant or all of the above, but I really felt I could make a difference if allowed to do what I did best.

I never stopped for a second to think that this one career move could eventually cost me everything I had: my health, my sanity, my family and perhaps even my very life.

Church

If you want to know why this book isn't written in chronological order, it's simple: I want you to read the whole thing. That especially goes for you wrestling fans. I refuse to allow you to seek out and read all the grapplin' parts and then bury this book next to your VHS tape wrestling collection. Not gonna happen!

You know, there was a time in my life — I'd say the good part of five years from 1994 to 1999 — where professional wrestling was my everything. I was obsessed with it, much the same way fantasy baseball managers are obsessed with statistics (oops — did I just give myself away?). That was all I ever thought about, and it wasn't because of my love for it, or because I was a mark; it was because I wanted to succeed in my field. I just wanted to be the best at what I did . . . ever. I thought achieving my goals and being the greatest writer/producer in the history of the wrestling/sports-entertainment business was going to fill the black hole that I was being engulfed in. Man, what a costly mistake. If only I had spent my time and energy concentrating on things that *really* meant something, rather than make-believe wrestling angles — say, *God* for instance — I could have saved myself from years of depression and hopelessness. But no, I didn't know . . . nobody told me, not even The Road Dogg (bless his heart). You won't have that same excuse because this sentence — the one you're reading right now — this sentence *is telling you!*

I often wonder: For those of you reading this who are just fans of wrestling, why does the business consume you? I don't mean *all* of you, but you know who you are. Why is wrestling so important to you that you spend more time on Internet wrestling sites than you do with your own families? If it's not putting money in your pocket (which to me isn't even a good enough excuse), then why does it dictate your life? Where is all this time and money invested going to get you? Do you have this master plan that one day it is going to miraculously put you in the squared circle as the #1 contender facing off against RVD for a fake wrestling belt at Wrestlemania L?

Man, I've got to tell you, with the release of my first book, I had the opportunity to hit the road and do various book signings across the U.S. In all honesty, what I experienced concerned me a great deal. I came across so many men — I'm talking 25 to 35 years old, with families — who were putting the wrestling business far and above everything else. Many of these individuals attended independent wrestling shows every weekend, drove for hours on end to wrestling conventions, and waited in line at the nearest (or furthest) Kmart to get a wrestler to autograph a picture they took 15 years ago. I'm talking grown men here — *fathers* — and they weren't getting the autographs for their kids, either! I've got to tell you, my infatuation with KISS during my teen years was puppy love compared to the love-fest these hardcore mat fanatics have with pro wrestling! Now, don't misunderstand me: there's no judging going on here at all — whatever jams ya slam — but I just don't understand their "passion" (pardon the pun).

But it's not just wrestling; Hollywood is consumed with award shows and plastic surgery. Rappers are consumed with women, explicit lyrics, fake stage names (usually one word) and touching themselves when they perform. TV execs are consumed with ratings. Models are consumed with diets and looks. Businessmen are consumed with money. Football players are consumed with winning the Lombardi Trophy. Joanie is consumed with Chachi. Politicians are consumed with power. Linus is consumed with his blanket. The Crocodile Hunter was consumed with crocs. Teenagers are consumed with *The O.C.* Paris Hilton is consumed with publicity. The paparazzi are consumed with Brangelina and who Jen is dating. Do you get my drift? In the big scheme of things, what does all this really matter? When the time nears for you to leave this earth and you take a look back, do you know what you're going to see? How much time you wasted placing time, importance and emphasis on things that absolutely did not matter. You die; somebody else is getting your toys — even that "Superstar" Billy Graham autograph that you waited in line for two hours to get.

Why is this? Why do we just not know any better? Why do we not know and truly understand what is important in our lives? Now, feathers are going to be ruffled here but I can only go back to my own upbringing to try to make some sense out of this. Could the church possibly have something to do with this?

Relax. Sit down. Have a cream soda. Shake yourself off. Before I go any further, there is one thing that I need to make clear: I'm not condemning the church in any way, shape or form. The raw fact is that the church is governed by man and man is imperfect. Thus, there are going to be some flaws in the church — not all churches, but some. However, those flaws shouldn't be a deterrent for us not to go — that's where I made my mistake. In the Bible God makes it clear that the church is the Body of Christ and we all need to be a part of it. If we experience what we feel are shortcomings within our home churches, then we have two choices: we can either walk away or choose to make a difference. Some 30 years ago I made the decision to walk away from the Catholic Church. Why? Because I had been attending church "religiously" up until the age of 16, and with all due respect I took very little from it, if anything at all.

When I was a small boy, I can remember my parents literally dragging me to church every Sunday. I never wanted to go. It was torture, it was boring — I hated it. My relentless longing to go home to watch a game, or be in a game, combined with having to endure a 60-minute diatribe by a man wearing a gown was a Molotov cocktail just waiting to be lit. Years later I would experience the same feeling in Mr. Bennett's College Algebra class. I know that language is English — but I haven't a clue to what he's trying to say. Are those *letters* he's trying to add? That's how I felt every time the priest spoke. The words were so far over my head that I would have needed a trampoline just to get even close to understanding. The language was just foreign. Say two Hail Marys and call me in the morning; what was that supposed to mean? From the time I wasn't old enough to understand to the time that I should have understood, nothing related to my everyday life — nothing.

When I was in elementary school, there was never any talk about the trials and tribulations that I was experiencing in the fourth grade. I'm sure at some point they told us to "love one another," but that ideology seemed to fall short when the school-bus bully Joe Bennacasa threatened to beat me up every day simply because I had four eyes to his two. The only guidance I ever received concerning that problem was when the "Fruitinator" (my mother) would show up at the bus stop after school, five days a week, with our large dog Brutus, to ensure that there would be no drumming of her beloved son. Okay, maybe that church wasn't geared to the needs of ten-year-olds, but I thought that would surely change as I grew older.

At about fifteen or sixteen, I started experimenting with girls and, man, I had a lot of questions concerning temptation. Unfortunately, that church wasn't geared for teenagers either, because the man in the robe had no words of wisdom for me — nothing! Obviously, I couldn't go to Fruitsy with that one, but luckily I was "guided" through without ever getting myself into a situation that I might have regretted for the rest of my life. Yes, God instilled His very fear in me, and that was plenty to protect me from myself.

I just can't comprehend how I was able to spend well over a decade in the Catholic Church only to take zip away from it. Communion, conformation, catechism — I did it all! Granted, when I was younger I wasn't listening, but as I got older, I was. Could it be that I wasn't being spoken to? Sure, there are those who say that you won't hear the word of God until he readies you. While that does have credence, the truth is that I very much believed in God at the time. I never questioned God's existence for a second. He was working on me; He was in my heart. I knew Him, but I didn't *know* Him. I was never taught how to build a personal relationship with Him. In my opinion — and this is only my opinion — those spreading the Gospel may have failed to meet me where I was.

So I existed in the world for more than 25 years not having a single clue as to what life was all about — I mean, the *real* meaning of life. And you can't say that I didn't search either, because I did. I was Indiana Jones in constant search of that covenant Lost Ark, the one that was going to bring joy and happiness to my life. But think about what blueprint I had to follow, being that the church didn't have the impact on me that perhaps it should have.

I was a boob-tube junkie, more or less raised on the social values I viewed on television. What was important? What was deemed success in the eyes of the world? The answer was simple: money. Everything revolved around money. The more you had, the more successful you were. The more successful you were, the more popular you'd become. It was, and still is, all about the greenback. Even though God clearly states (and I'm paraphrasing here), "You can't serve two masters, meaning me and money; you can only serve one," I chased the Washingtons because nobody told me different. No, not even that guy in the gown on Sunday mornings.

Back during that time, the church I attended was so scripture-heavy. They spoke the written word of the Bible, but never translated it to a language I could understand. In wrestling, you have to know who your audience is. Christianity is no different. You have to know who you're talking to, while always remembering that everybody is different. You need to speak their language; if you don't, they're never going to hear you, just like I didn't. So yeah, I put some fault on those governing the church. You might say, "Vince, get over it; that was a long time ago." Was it? Or are some churches still speaking that same foreign language some 30 years later?

Can you book 1970 rasslin' in 2006? Can the church teach the Gospel the same way today as they did 30 years ago?

The answer to these and many other questions is what follows.

The Glue That Binds: Terry, Bill, Skull & the Harris Boys

Some call it the "Good Ol' Boy Network." I call it filling the chairs of your cabinet with people that you can not only depend on, but who can also perform.

In traditional rasslin' the "Good Ol' Boy Network" has always been a rusty nail in the newly bought tire. The chosen "savior" is brought in to turn the "territory" around, and the first thing he does is hire all his boys to back him. Sure, there is some credence to doing the right thing and returning favors to those who may have lent a hand when you were down and out; the major flaw in this wrestling bubble tradition is that the guys that the "new guy" brings in are usually more incompetent than the poor sap that just found his way out the door. Why is this? It's simple: the new honcho usually surrounds himself with two kinds of people, politicians and yes men.

Look around at the major wrestling promotions operating today. Those at the top (the people I've worked for) have surrounded themselves with individuals who simply tell them what they want to hear. Good, bad or indifferent, those following up — and kissing — the rear will tell them, "It's all good! Everything and everybody is great!" And from where I sit, that's a major problem in wrestling today. There are just too many people employed who are scared to death of telling the boss how it *really* is. I've experienced this at every promotion I've known. From the "Tower in Connecticut" to the "Ugly Blue Building in Smyrna" to that "Dreadful Flea Market in Nashville," politicians and yes men are killing the business. It's like that tick that just gets fatter and fatter as it sucks the blood from an unsuspecting K-9. And that's what they are: ticks. They just suck every drop of blood from you. Sorry if I've lost a bit of my Christian flavor here, but I'm human and this facet of the business is part of the reason why I left. The older I got, the more my tolerance and patience wore. There has to come a point in somebody's life where they just get too old to get their nose caught up in somebody else's briefs, but no — not in professional wrestling. As Vince (the other Vince) would say, "It's a time-honored tradition!"

In all honesty, outside of my right-hand men, one of the few stand-up second bananas I ever worked with in the wrestling circles was Pat Patterson. Pat just told Vince the way it was, whether he liked it, or not. And, ironically, Vince liked it! Vince probably respected Pat more than he did anybody else. And that's the funny thing: Vince knew a hiney-hugger when he saw one. And let me tell you: regardless of what those individuals may think, when Vince knows that you're blatantly puckering up, he is only going to allow you to go so far. He knows your cap; he knows what you bring to the table — or under it — and that's as far as he will allow your leash to extend. If there's one thing Vince McMahon is not, it's stupid.

While at Titan, I also think JR was a pretty stand-up guy. No, he would never stand there and go toe-to-toe with VKM. He wasn't stupid enough for that — he left that to me — but he was always honest. Jim always told the boss what he genuinely felt. Of course, at the end of the day, Vince always got his way; it was his ball, his court and his team, but JR, as the GM, always laid his cards on the table. I think that's just the "Okie way."

And no, I'm not going to name names here — there's no upside to that — but as I write, you have your share of people in key positions with both the WWE and TNA who have no business being there. Having worked with these individuals, trust me, they've earned nothing by their stripes. Why do I suddenly hear Billy Squier screaming out "Stroke Me, Stroke Me" as I search for the next word to put on this paper? Aughhhh! I just hate that part of the business. Man — *earn your spot!* That's all. That's the right way. Don't step on somebody else to get it: just *earn it!*

With that being said, the boys — my boys — that I brought into WCW when I was hired earned every ounce of their spot. I handed nothing out. You have to understand that you're playing with a double-edged sword here: if you put incompetent friends in high places, that could eventually come back to bite you. It usually doesn't because if you're the boss, you're the boss — who's going to say what? But again, it is your rep on the line. And not only that, but have a conscience, for cryin' out loud! Man, I just detest when deserving people get leapfrogged for somebody's friend. As I brought outside people in from my team, I also made sure that I brought people up from within. Believe it or not, there were many capable people at WCW when I was hired, both in the locker room and in the office. But before I touch on that, let me touch on this: Russo's "All-Cronies Team."

[TEN DAYS LATER]

It's been ten days since I last typed a word. I don't know; the inspiration has just been out to lunch . . . dinner . . . and breakfast. As of late, I'm just consumed with feelings of uncertainty, loneliness, depression and fear. It's been almost eight months since I earned a paycheck, and as a man, that's just hard. Being that in this world your success is measured by the thickness of your wallet, when you're unemployed you really begin to take a long, hard look at your self-worth. It's inevitable: after month after month of sitting at home, you just begin to feel like you're useless, that nobody wants you. Man, I can remember when I was "somebody" at WWE, WCW and TNA. My phone never stopped ringing. It was *I Love Vincey*, and everybody was my Ethel Mertz. "Hey, Vince, how is the wife? The kids? Yeah, okay — what am I doing Monday night?" Even though it was all so shallow and just so empty, they were calling. Not only did they want me, but they *needed* me. Today, my name could be the next on the dead wrestlers list and by tomorrow it would be business as usual.

But that's all part of the journey. That's all part of God's testing. Do I go back to hell? Or wait for His instructions to enter heaven? That's what it really comes down to. I'd be lying if I told you I hadn't been tempted of late to once again dive into the mucky, polluted waters of professional wrestling. But I know that's not what God wants. That's not His plan for me. I know that because He assures me every day. However, with assurances come tests, and as a student of the Almighty, I'm just not ready to graduate to that next level. So I sit in quietness, I listen, I obey . . . and I learn. Remember, it's on His watch, not ours.

So today, why am I back? Why am I sitting in this trailer-made, uncomfortable white plastic lawn chair in the depths of my own personal basement, or "Bat Cave" as I fondly refer to it, feverishly banging the keys? What a stupid question. "You meathead, you!" That's right: last night I was inspired by none other than Archie Bunker.

I've always been an *All in the Family* mark. Man, the writing of that show was pure art. And I was reminded of that yesterday when I caught a special on TV Land showcasing the top ten *All in the Family* episodes of all time. Man, I just take writing so seriously, and you know it's great writing when a sitcom can move a grown man to tears. Last night, Amy thought I had lost it as I sobbed and boo-hooed over two exchanges between Michael Stivic and Archie Bunker.

All in the Family was about seven seasons in when the writers thought it was time to share a side of Archie that the audience had never before seen. After getting locked in the basement of his newly acquired bar with his son-in-law, Michael, the world's most beloved bigot and his "Polack" housemate began to hit the bottle out of boredom. As time passed and more liquor went down, Archie gradually dropped his defenses and spoke some truths that he had obviously been repressing for decades. In what was perhaps the strongest moment of dialogue in the history of network television, Archie reveals to Michael that he was an abused child. As the words slurred from his lips, the look on his son-in-law's face was beyond anything I could ever write here. After seven long years of living with Arch, Michael finally understood "why." Man, it was magical. It's moments like that that make me proud to call myself a writer. They had built this character for seven years, holding those cards from us, the audience, until it was time to play them. That is beautiful. All I ever want is the chance to once again have the privilege of attempting to achieve something that grandiose.

In another episode a season or two later, Michael is getting ready to move Gloria and Baby Joey to California to take on a new job. Moments before leaving, he gets Archie alone on the front porch and for the first time softly speaks the unforgettable words, "I love you, Arch." I just cried as I wrote that last sentence because the feelings in those words were just so moving, so meaningful — so strong. That's what good writers do. But, the amazing part of the scene was that Archie never told Michael, "I love you" back. Why? Because he just didn't know how to. Keep in mind it was quite probable that those words were never said to him by his father. That is powerful writing. That is why I'm back today, and that is why this is what I long to do.

Do you now understand the difference between a writer and a booker? A writer would never allow a character he carefully created then crafted to run around a wrestling ring wearing a chicken costume simply to state the obvious: that his opponent was a "chicken." Please . . . somebody help us all!

Okay, now, back to Russo's "All-Cronies Team."

When you're in the professional wrestling business, you are at war at all times! It's incoming all around you. Friends and foes are sometimes one and the same and you really need to be careful when deciding who to share the foxhole with.

When the bombs started to sail, one of the first guys I wanted at my side was Terry Taylor. But, ironically enough, my history with the Rooster didn't start in a very promising way. Quite the contrary. The truth is that upon our introduction I myself would have taken a hand grenade, painted it white, pulled the pin and then placed it in his nest. From there I would have calmly enjoyed the pyro as it exploded a colorful mixture of his guts and feathers to Bismarck, North Dakota. Then, as the debris flew, I would have just sat back, relaxed and enjoyed a cream soda. But in all honesty, I didn't despise Terry at first because of Terry. I despised Terry because of Vince.

I first met T, as I now affectionately refer to him, one bright yellow morning at VKM's compound. The circumstances were somewhat questionable, but at times Vince just enjoyed working that way. Whether he wanted to keep you on your toes, or just flat out make you want to pull every hair out of your head, Vince had a way of sandpapering you even when everything was velvety smooth. However, in the boss's defense, I myself used to be much like that at times. In my "other" life there always had to be a degree of drama going on.

Smooth sailing was just so boring. Give me the perfect storm; throw a tidal wave in there; let's rock this boat! At that's exactly how Vince used Terry against his successful writing team. As Ed and I were riding the high seas Carnival Cruise–style, Vince decided to throw an iceberg our way in the form of an innocent, unsuspecting fold — or fowl — by the name of T. Taylor!

It was just going to be another writing day at Vince's house. You know, the typical grueling ten-hour day. On many occasions Ed and I would wait up for each other before we walked into the fortress. If I got there first I would just hang out in my grape-purple Geo Tracker listening to KISS tunes, while if Ed caught the worm first he would sit outside the complex sucking down cigarettes. I don't know who got there first that day, but it really doesn't matter. All I know is that we walk into Vince's house as usual, very casual, probably unshaven, and sitting at the war table — shirt, tie, model looks, the whole shebang — is Terry Taylor. It didn't take too long for me to get the picture. Only weeks, maybe even days, earlier, Terry Taylor was let go of his duties from World Championship Wrestling. Now, for whatever reason, Vince was bringing him in as the third wheel of the writing team. Only one problem: the team didn't need another wheel. As a matter of fact, not only weren't any of the tires flat, but we were a well-oiled machine ripping up the tracks, while leaving wcw — Terry Taylor's former employer — miles behind in our rear-view mirror, eating our dust! I mean, what was this guy *doing* here? Forget the ol' "why fix something if it isn't broke," but Ed and I had just crushed this guy and his whole company along with him. What was he possibly going to bring to the table other than his Fabio good looks? Again, nothing personal, but did Mo, Larry and Curly really need a Rico Suave?

I think I took a seat at the war room table for about three minutes, giving Terry just enough time to introduce himself. Then, once the formalities were behind us I asked Vince if I could talk to him in private for a second. Once alone with the boss I curiously asked Vince, "What's the deal?" I'll never forget Vince looking me in the eye and giving me the ol' "What — I didn't tell you?" I don't remember for sure, but Vince might have opened his eyes real wide — like he does on TV when the babyface's music would hit and confrontation was right around the corner — while saying it, and then he may have given the big swallow, or the "big gulp" after saying it. Is it just me, or does every person reading this hate Vince's fake big-eye face followed almost immediately by the big gulp? Don't get me wrong, I think Vince's character on TV is entertaining, but when I get the eyes and the gulp he just loses me somewhere in cartoonland.

So as you can see, the Rooster and I didn't get out of the hen house on the best claw, but, ironically enough, I grew to like Terry almost immediately. What others saw as Terry's weakness, I saw as his strength. Terry just always told the truth, no matter what. Now, although honesty is one of the greatest attributes that any man or woman can possess, that theory just doesn't stick in the wrestling bubble. In the bubble, you have to tell those above you what they want to hear, whether it's a truth or not. Man, I can tell you: that's just not in Terry Taylor. No matter who you are, no matter what the circumstances, he will call it as he sees it. And that often got T in trouble, and still does to this day. You can't be an honest man and survive in a liar's world; you just can't. It's just not the norm to tell the truth. No, you have to "work" everybody. Work them to earn points. Work them to get ahead. No matter what my position of power was, Terry Taylor *never* worked me. If he didn't like something, he told me — and I will forever respect him for that.

But, to take it one step further, today I proudly declare that I love Terry. There is no question in my mind that God places people in all our lives. From the bottom of my heart I know T was one of those people. You see, some time before I became a Christian, Terry himself became saved. Now, as a "newborn," there are various . . . let's call them "factions," who try to influence you to join their . . . let's say "group." And, being who I was, with my background and all, I was highly recruited by some of those Godly gangs. Now, being a new creation of God at the time, everything sounded good. It's like a talent first getting signed in the wrestling business. Oh, the picture is painted with broad strokes of bluebirds singing, fawns drinking from a crystal-blue lake, bright yellow tiger lilies growing wild in the Scotch-green field . . . only to find out six months later the bluebirds have transformed into flesh-eating vultures, the fawns are now vicious wildebeests drinking polluted sludge and bacterial fungus is growing wild over the toxic garbage dump! There were many different opinions and viewpoints being thrown my way and I was in desperate need to talk with somebody who spoke my language. That's where Terry came in.

Traveling over an hour just to come to my side of town, Terry would show up at CD Warehouse, the business I owned in Atlanta, at around closing time. Once the lights were shut and the door locked behind us, Terry and I would go to the neighborhood Applebee's and spend the next few hours there. It was in that booth that Terry shared with me the Gospel of Jesus Christ. A flawed individual, coming from a flawed world, Terry invited in a flawed brother and helped him for the first time truly understand the real meaning of life. The words I write here could never express my love and gratitude to T for being such a major part of my life. It's so sad to know that this is what the wrestling business *could* be. To this day, even though I can no longer do anything for him professionally, Terry calls every week just to lift me as a brother. That, my friends, is true, true friendship.

From me to you, I love you, T, and I thank you for being such a great influence in my life.

Other members of the Russo's All-Cronies Team included Ed Ferrara, who I spoke about earlier, Bill Banks, and an individual I first met while at WCW, Jeremy Borash.

At first glance, Jeremy appears to many as the perfect office stooge, but, when you get to know and understand him, you realize that JB wouldn't hurt anybody for his own personal gain. The truth is, I think the guy just loves to gossip, as does everybody inside the bubble. Man, the wrestling world is filled with more yentas than a Barbara Streisand concert. The boys just love to talk about anything, and anybody. True or false, it doesn't matter; if it makes good locker room fodder, they're talking about it! I think that's where many of the rumors get started. So much gets blown out of proportion within the locker room walls that you just accustom yourself to not believing anything.

Jeremy was just all over gossip. The guy just thrived on it. But, personally, I just found it entertaining. It was harmless; I knew Jeremy's nature, I knew his heart and I knew his mind. Even though he may have not looked the part, JB was hip. He knew what was going on — he had his finger on the pulse of our audience. For instance, many years ago Jeremy told me what a huge star Dave Chappelle was going to be when he was just a dime-a-dozen comedian looking to break into the business. He just had that intuition; he knew what was around the corner. And I was always looking for that. The majority of the creative people in the bubble live in the world of been there, done that, one million times. It just gets so old, so tired. JB was a guy who was ahead of the curve, and to this day he remains miles in front of the pack.

Now, there was one more member of Russo's All-Cronies Team, on the creative side, but this guy is going to get a full chapter. I'll give you a hint: his *nose* is too big to share a chapter with anybody else (of course I'm only kidding, but, I had to get that in there). But, before I get to him, let me talk about my boys in the locker room.

If you read *Forgiven* you know all about Vito LoGrasso, a.k.a. Big Vito.

Since I last wrote about Vito, his dreams have come true as he finally reached his destination: WWE. It was quite a journey for him and a testament as to what you can accomplish if you work hard enough and never quit. But again, that's what *you* can accomplish through *your* will. Take nothing away from Vito, but as I sit here today my only dream, hope and aspiration is to fulfill *God's* will for me, whatever that may be. But in not wanting to get too heavy into that right now, let me get back to my AC Team.

In the past, whenever somebody screwed up I would always tell their closest associates in a loving and joking manner, "That's your boy!" You see, in the wrestling circles, nobody likes to adopt anybody else as "their boy." Remember, this is a game built on individuality and when somebody else screws up certainly nobody else wants to take credit for it. Well, right here, right now, that's all going to change. I'm going to hammer the cast and take claim of two guys who I am both honored and privileged to label "my boys": Ron and Don, the Harris Boys.

For those of you reading this who may not be wrestling fans — all two of you — let me tell you a little something about the Harris Twins, being that they may not be household names. Right now I can hear the wrestling critics say, "How can two six-nine, 300-plus-pound, bald-headed, identical twin monsters not be household names?" Well, that's simple, but I'll get into that a bit later on. I've known Ronnie and Donnie for over a decade now and who would have ever thought that an Italian Yankee from suburban Long Island, New York, would fall in love with two red-neck biker thugs as if they were his brothers. That's right; I'm not ashamed to say that it was a love affair. It was a bond between East and South that could just never be understood, or maybe even explained. Man, I just love these guys. They are the gentlest, kindest and most caring and giving individuals you would ever want to know. Every week when I would see them at TV tapings, all I ever wanted to do was somehow, some way put a charge in them just so I could make their faces light up. No matter how bad things got for me at times, when I could make Ronnie and Donnie laugh it made my day feel a lot less stressed.

When I was first hired as the "Creative Director" (chuckle chuckle) at WCW, the Harris Boys sent me a beautiful pair of snakeskin boots as a gift that I still wear every day, to this day. Now, did they like me that much? Heck no — they were looking for jobs! Did that bother me? Heck no — if I was in charge they were going to have jobs. Even though on a personal level I loved both brothers with all my heart — although to this day I can't tell them apart — make no mistakes about it, part of their being hired was for my own protection. As long as Ronnie and Donnie were around, I knew I was safe. These guys always had my back, and what almost brings me to tears is that I know they still have it today. I just had a bond with these guys, a bond that is very difficult to explain. But like with Terry Taylor, I know God places people in our lives for certain reasons. How ironic is it that today Ron and Don are not only my brothers, but they are my brothers in Christ. That says a lot considering where we all came from.

One of my favorite stories concerning Ronnie and Donnie was when the SEX (Sports Entertainment Xtreme) angle was on fire at TNA (Total Non-Stop Action). When push came to knockin' somebody out, I was taking the SEX angle and we were doing it my way, or I just wasn't doing it at all. I knew the minute that those in control of the creative at TNA took it over it would turn into some namby-pamby, good ol' boy, 1975 Memphis, bad fake wrestling angle, an angle that I wasn't going to have anything to do with. So this was my baby, and first and foremost I was going to make it look as real as possible. How real? Well, a few weeks prior to the show at hand I had taken down an unsuspecting Ron "The Truth" Killings in the middle of the ring on a live wrestling show. Luckily, I exited the building through the back door, got in my Jeep and left, because I was told a few days later that The Truth was looking for me in the back carrying a machete with my name on it.

As the weeks passed, I was starting to live this angle — I'll get into the nuts-n-bolts a bit later on, but yes, I had a bit of a divot on my shoulder. In my view the SEX angle could have been the hottest thing since WCW's nWo, but in the pit of my heart I knew it would end sooner rather than later because the creative in charge just wasn't getting it. Again, more on that later, but for now I did my typical entrance coming in through the back door of the Asylum, or ugly barn-looking structure, and hitting the ring with the force of Universal's *Twister*. Heads were rolling and yes, cows were even flying. So in comes the security, Ron and Don Harris.

Now, for some reason I get the idea in my head that if I'm going to make this thing look real, then I have to *go* with Ronnie and Donnie. Keep in mind, however, that they are totally oblivious of my intentions as they try to restrain me bad fake wrestling–style. Well, to be true to art, I decide that I'm going to fight them right then and there. I'm cracking up as I write this because I can remember that the more and more I fought them off, the madder and madder the terrible twins got as they slowly, but surely, were getting it. Finally, in the midst of my fury, I saw a gigantic smile come across one of their faces (remember to this day I couldn't tell you who was who). With that I clearly understood what those pearly whites were saying: "Oh, all right, Yankee. You wanna play, we gonna play." Suddenly that look of endearment turned into a ferocious mask of death. I mean, I swear — his teeth turned mad-foam yellow and his eyes turned Santa-suit red. Suddenly he was the bouncer at the biker bar and I was the guy who just pinched his girl's butt. Within the blink of an eye, Ronnie (or Donnie — again, not sure which was which) grabbed me and put me in some kind of chokehold. No, not a fake wrestling chokehold — a real bar-room brawl chokehold. Within a matter of seconds I could feel the oxygen being cut off to my brain. I was a pace from out cold when he finally released me. To this day I kid them, saying that if it was a fair one-on-one fight, rather than a single warrior against two blood twins, that I would have been the last man standing! All kidding aside, if wrestling were indeed real, the Harris Twins would be the tag-team champs for the rest of their existence on this planet.

I think the case of the Harris Boys is a prime example of the ineptness of booking today. And make no mistakes: I said booking, not writing. Wrestlers book, writers write, and the difference is like comparing *Hee-Haw* to *The Sopranos*. One is based on cartoon fiction; the other is based on reality. You know, people often ask how can professional wrestling ever be reality-based, when in all reality it's fake. While that is indeed true, my question is why can't people act and speak in the wrestling world like normal people would act and speak in the real world if under similar or the same circumstances? In other words, don't have fake wrestlers act like fake wrestlers, have human beings act like human beings. In wrestling it's all so black and white: heels act one way, babyfaces act another. Is that true of people in today's society? The world consists of shades of gray; there are times when a person is good, and times when he or she is not so good. It all depends on the individual and the circumstances.

Booking is a poor attempt at writing by wrestlers who are attempting to be writers. The truth is, to a writer it's an insult. I've been in the wrestling business for 15 years now and I've never worked with or seen a professional wrestler who can actually pass for a writer. Just like I've never seen a writer who could pass as a professional wrestler — and yours truly is at the top of that list. You see, when wcw pushed me in a corner I made the decision against my better judgment to get in the ring and become a part of the show. However, after receiving several head injuries I learned my lesson the hard way. What's the excuse of bookers? How low do ratings have to go before they hand the pencil over to somebody who knows what to do with it?

That's why the Harris Twins were never "over." With wrestlers booking them what they simply looked at was the fact that these guys were unique. You have identical twin monsters here; they'll automatically be over by just going out there and destroying people. Well, if that's the truth, how come the Harris Boys weren't the biggest thing since the Olsen Twins? The answer is simple: nobody cared about them. Nobody cared about them because we knew *nothing* about them. There was nothing pulling on our heartstrings. They had no personality, no shades of gray. That's where writing comes in. A writer uses his craft to make characters multi-dimensional. A writer makes you care about the wrestler, exposing layer after layer of that character's personality. Then, once you know the character, he is put into certain situations and allowed to act as that character would act given those conditions or circumstances.

That's where bookers lose it. Characters act as characters would act in the bubble, not in the real world — that's all they know. A prime example of that came after Ed and I spent years helping develop Stone Cold Steve Austin into the character that he was. Only months after we left, I came across an episode of *Raw* where Austin was wearing a cowboy hat about six sizes too small and making a total idiot out of himself. How did that happen? Unless the guy was dropped on his head and suffered extensive brain damage, how did his personality change so drastically? How did he go from cold-blooded bounty hunter to big-top Bozo? It just didn't make any sense. And that's where they make their biggest mistake: now they are asking the audience to believe something that is unbelievable, now they are insulting their intelligence. I always felt that was the biggest mistake that anyone with a pencil in their hand could make. Once you've insulted the intelligence of the audience you've basically said to them, "You don't have a brain; you're going to believe everything and anything we tell you, whether you like it or not." Now, where that might have worked in the "glory days," it simply doesn't work today because there are far too many other choices out there to flip over to.

Obviously this is a topic that I could go on about forever and will certainly get back into later, but speaking of flipping, flip to the next chapter because it's now time to talk about Toucan Sam (I've got to stop with that — but it's just too good to pass up).

Disco Doesn't Suck

Boo-hoo, boo-hoo: for years I've heard "famous" (I hate that term) actors interviewed on TV say that they wrote their autobiography because it was a form of therapy. I never believed that, not for a second. In my mind their only motivation was money. I mean, let's face it: isn't that everybody's motivation in la-la land? Then a funny thing happened . . .

I sat down to write my own autobiography.

I can never convey to you in words the therapy that getting these feelings out on these pages has served me. Writing about my life has been such a liberating experience. I have discovered so much about myself, a lot of which have been buried inside for years. I never realized the pain that my heart has been burdened with over the years until I began to open up, analyze . . . and type. There were many times when I was writing where I just had to stop mid-sentence because my eyes were welling up with tears. The loss of family has had a tremendous impact on me over the years. Losing my grandmother at an early age left a devastating and lasting scar on my heart, one that remains open to this day.

My own mortality at times can bring me to my knees. I've often said, when you reach a certain age — for me it was 40 — rather than look ahead at your life with the hunger of the Tasmanian Devil, you begin to look back at what could have been and what mistakes you may have made along the way. I don't care who you are, or what you've accomplished; that is enough to humble any man. I can never take back the years I stole from my own family in favor of writing fake wrestling scripts for human beings who could never have the insight to appreciate what I was attempting to do for them and *their* families. Yes, perhaps the wrestling business has hurt me more than any other. I carry that baggage around my waist like a ripped, torn, worn, battered, patched-up, inflatable tube. I just can't get it off. Part of that surely comes from not getting my due. Not only don't I get credit for anything I ever achieved in my career, but I'm constantly getting blamed for I don't even know what. The Bible tells us that we're not put on this earth to impress man, and I understand that. But I'm human — and that's what I want you to understand throughout this book.

I struggle with demons every single day of my existence . . . and most of them are wearing wrestling tights and ring jackets. You can slice it and dice it with the precision of Rachel Ray all you want, but at the end of the day I know I was wronged. Here I sit almost ten years after the fact only to see the television ratings from the "Vince Russo era" still holding up; yet, there is no real place for me in the business I love. Man, that's a sad commentary. I know how Pete Rose feels without ever having bet on a single wrestling match. I work every day to get over this, asking God for His strength, but then I'll hear something or read something and it just starts all over again. My best friend has shut me out of the wrestling business; how is anyone supposed to deal with that? But this chapter isn't about me; it is about somebody who has been wronged perhaps even more than me over the years. It is about a good friend, with a good heart by the name of Glenn "Disco Inferno" Gilberti.

You know, I often tell the younger guys in the wrestling business who haven't quite made it to the level that they deem successful in their minds that perhaps they didn't reach their goal because they *weren't supposed to.* Perhaps they didn't make it to the (side) Show because it was *their* plan for themselves, rather than God's plan for them. Maybe they didn't make it because they had a conscience, or more specifically, a heart. When I preach that, I truly believe and mean it. Let me say it again: you can't be a good guy and exist in the wrestling business. You know what? Maybe this is the case for other professions as well, but I can only speak of the place where I lived for some 15 years. You can't have a heart and become a megastar in the wrestling industry. The minute you care, or show compassion, or put somebody else's feelings before your own, they'll devour your flesh, pause to pick their teeth, then go back to gnaw on the bones. Throughout my years in the business, the only exception I ever saw to this rule was Mick Foley. And maybe that's because you just couldn't screw Mick. If you screwed any side of Foley, it would have been like screwing Santa Claus. But, again, that's the exception. Here's the rule.

Prior to going to wcw, I was a huge mark for Disco Inferno. All you had to do was watch the guy for 30 seconds on television and you knew that he *got it*. Disco was a tremendous character — the truth is that the brain trust at wcw had no inkling of the talent he possessed. I remember when Disco, or Glenn, was having some contractual problems with wcw. I immediately told Bruce Prichard, who was a part of wwf talent relations at the time, that he had to get this guy — we had to have him on our roster. So Bruce called him. Unfortunately, because Bruce didn't like the way that Glenn answered some of his questions, he never called him back. What a surprise; another wrestling guy in a suit cruising down the highway on an all-consuming power trip. But that's exactly what I'm talking about: if you phrase something the wrong way and just one word gets misconstrued, you're "strued." No follow-up questions, no chance to clarify your statement, no "What did you mean by that?" The only response would be no response and your wonderment as to "why?"

So needless to say (but I'll say it anyway), Glenn Gilberti was one of the guys I was quite anxious to meet upon my arrival at wcw. Within maybe a week of being hired, that encounter came when I introduced myself to Glenn while on an airplane, and sat in the seat next to him for the remainder of our flight. Man, was that a refreshing experience. You see, up until that point I had already had so many lips on my butt at wcw that it felt bruised. Everybody was my so-called friend, putting me over as the genius that they perceived I wanted to be identified as, but not my fellow paisan, Glenn. Not for one New York second.

It's funny, but in sitting down with Disco for the first time, I saw a lot of myself. No, not in the looks department, thank you God (again, only kidding, but I just couldn't pass that one up), but in the confidence department. From the moment we met, Glenn never once tried to kiss up to me, or impress me with what he had done in the business. I mean, nobody — and I do mean *nobody* — can put themselves over in a more consuming way than a professional wrestler. To them it's about as matter-of-fact as just saying their name . . .

"Hi, I'm the Crusher. [They always refer to themselves by their gimmick name, never their real name.] I was 29-time World Heavyweight Champion, 42-time World Tag-Team Champion and 17-time Inter-Global Champion. Many say I'm also an all-around swell guy. And your name is?"

"Vince."

"Oh, glad to meet ya, Vic."

Unlike Crusher, Glenn spoke of his knowledge of wrestling — and I'm not talking the science of working a fake wrestling match; I'm talking about the creative side: birthing characters, developing them and then placing them in intriguing storylines.

Glenn just had a mind for television, maybe because he just watched so much of it. But sitting in front of the boob tube is vital if you want to be a success in the creative side of the wrestling business. You have to know what people are watching on prime-time television. Why? Because if you're writing for the WWE, or TNA, chances are that you're probably on during prime time (or hoping to be, as is the case of TNA as I write this). Like it or not, your competition is shows like *24*, *CSI* or *The O.C.*, not Saturday morning cartoons like it was when it was your grandpa's rasslin'! I'm not exaggerating; I know an old promoter who to this day brags about ratings share on local television nearly three decades ago, when the programming they were competing against (in the same time slot) was *Tom and Jerry* reruns. Speaking of Tom and Jerry, do you know why they were always fighting, but when all was said and done by the end of the episode they always appeared to be friends? Because they weren't fighting at all — they were playing. I found out that little tidbit in my mid-30s and was — and still am — fascinated by it.

I know current wrestlers-turned-television-writers who don't even watch television. In my opinion that's equivalent to a baseball manager who doesn't watch baseball. A prime-time TV slot is a prime-time TV slot, regardless if it's an Emmy award–winning drama, or a real bad fake rasslin' show. That's how we treated *Raw* when Ed and I were writing, and that's why it was so successful. We had two hours in prime time, and that's what we focused on. How do we steal eyeballs from *Raymond*, how do we get the Monday night football audience to switch over? Glenn got this. He understood television ratings.

You know, you tend to be an outcast in the wresting business when you're smarter than your peers. Wrestlers have a tendency to feel threatened by those who carry a higher IQ. Once their own insecurity sets in, that's when you'd better watch your back because the knives — they are a-comin'! Warrior and Raven were two guys who seemed to fit into that same category along with Glenn. All three were just intellectually on a different playing field then the rest of the team. They were the outcasts, not because they were different, but because they were smarter. I worked for a promoter who had it out for both Raven and Disco and it was just so blatantly clear to me that it was solely because he felt intellectually inferior to them. It was only a matter of time before both charismatic individuals lost their prized spot. The truth was, if you couldn't get along with Disco, then you couldn't get along with anybody.

I have known Glenn for almost seven years and have never once seen him without that smile tattooed across his chiseled face. In a world where everybody lives in a state of stress, Glenn was always so happy-go-lucky. Everybody liked him — everybody, that is, who was smart enough not to be threatened by his innovative thinking. And unlike many others, Glenn understood friendship. I've been out of wrestling for 18 months, and the guy continues to call when there is nothing in the world that I can do for his career. That's a friend. Not one who loves you when you can help his wallet, and then disregards you like an old Bay City Rollers eight-track when you no longer have any stroke.

It was only a matter of time before I opened the doors and invited Glenn into the creative meetings at wcw. If not for anything else, I was always highly entertained. Man, at times Terry Taylor just wanted to strangle Disco, just to eliminate his interruptions so we could get on with the meeting. But Glenn was harmless and we all knew that . . . and loved him for it. He made the creative meetings enjoyable, a word that isn't often used in the wrestling business. Glenn always had a way of reminding us that this was supposed to be fun, not the living hell that it had turned into for most of us.

I think for as long as I live I will never forget one of Glenn's favorite pitches. I remember one day walking into the creative meeting a few minutes early and seeing Glenn writing feverishly on the boardroom whiteboard. The diagram he was scribbling seemed somewhat involved and intriguing, but I had no idea what it was. For a few seconds I just watched in amazement watching him work — as a fellow creative brother I just knew his mind was working faster than his hand could draw. I had to interrupt the genius at work and ask, "Glenn . . . what's this?"

Without missing a beat he turned around and said, "This is the angle that's going to change the face of the wrestling business forever!" It's hard to describe his child-like excitement, but let me see if I can. Ah, here's a good one: Remember when Ralphie reached around the living-room curtain and revealed that long, slender box that his father had directed to him. Remember that look of total joy, excitement, radiation and adulation that lit up his face when he fully realized that once he tore off the wrapping, he would finally be holding that treasured and adored Red Rider bb gun in his sweaty little paws. That was the exact look on Glenn's face as he got set to lay out his plan to save the wrestling business.

"It's the Martian invasion angle. There's a takeover in wcw by a hostile heel group" — keep in mind that Glenn is using his self-drawn diagrams to help bring light to his vision — "and in time it is revealed that they are Martians and their leader is Lance Storm. But wait — there's a twist. Just when it looks like the Martians are going to be in total control of wcw, we pan over to the announce desk and zoom in on Mike Tenay. Appearing in almost a hypnotic state, Mike slowly rises from his chair. Then the unthinkable happens. Antennas sprout from Mike's head and we find out that he — not Lance — was the mastermind behind this takeover all along. What do you think?"

The truth? I thought it was genius.

You see, unlike wrestlers who claim to be writers but are actually bookers, Glenn resides outside the box. There is no black, no white, no babyfaces, no heels. As "Hey, Hey, We're the Monkees" once crooned, "only shades of gray." Everybody in the wrestling business is going to hate me for saying this because they're never going to hear the end of it, but yes, Glenn Gilberti is a creative genius. How ironic; here we both are on the outside of the bubble looking in. What does that tell you about the wrestling business in general? It tells you don't be creative, don't be outspoken, don't be smart, don't be different, don't be controversial, and never tell a wrestler that wrestling is fake (yes, they're the only ones who believe it's real). Just close your eyes, pucker up and have somebody point you in the direction of the boss.

The bubble needs more people like Glenn Gilberti; however, his kind will forever be blackballed. Man, you just can't dare to rattle their world. The wrestling business will be doing the same thing, the same way, until nobody buys it any more. The close-knit fraternity is killing off their own business without even knowing it. If anybody comes along with new ideas, or a new way, they'll do everything in their power to squash that person like a bug. And it is done so methodically, in such an underhanded way. It's not loud, it's not noisy, it's not blatant; it's just quiet, almost silent, but the scar it leaves is deafening. Man, as much as I pray to God to mend my wounds from the wrestling business, I still have permanent scabs that still bleed every now and them. It's tough for those old wounds to heal . . . especially when it was friends who did the cutting.

Before I end this chapter I have to use Glenn's Martian invasion angle to prove to you just how cutthroat and ridiculous the whole bubble thing is. A few years ago when I almost went back to the WWE, at our first secretive pow-wow, I told Vince about Glenn and proposed to him that once I came back I wanted Disco to be a part of the creative team. Vince had no problem with this, since I had never steered him wrong before when it came to someone else's talents. As a matter of fact Vince's only request was to bring me in first, and then Glenn a few weeks later in order to prevent any suicides on the writing team already in place. You see, the perception would have been that if Russo's bringing in his boys with him, then we'd better be prepared to go back and work on *Friends*.

Let me sidetrack here for a moment. When I left the WWE, Vince filled my spot with a school bus full of 20-somethings who claimed to have worked on the NBC sitcom *Friends*. Now, not to discredit anybody — because I, to this day, have no idea whether it was fact or fiction — but who in their right mind would have traded in their pencil and stopped writing for Jennifer Aniston to borrow their toddler brother's purple Crayola to write for Doink the Clown instead?

Back to the Martians.

After that first secretive pow-wow with Vince, I went back a few weeks later to further talk things out. Prior to wrapping up our covert meeting, I asked Vince when I could tell Glenn that he could start. Vince paused, and I knew there was a problem. With a look of severe seriousness on his face, the Boss looked at me and said:

"Um, I'm not too sure about your friend Glenn, Vince. I heard something about some ridiculous Martian invasion angle that he wanted to do at WCW and ... um ... I just don't know."

Do you have any idea how *great* that is? That, my friends, is the wrestling business in a nutshell — or spaceship. You just have to be in the business to really understand just how *tremendous* that is. Let me break it down for you.

Somehow, some way, somebody within WCW, who wanted to bury Glenn out of pure jealousy, caught wind of Glenn's Martian invasion angle. Wait a minute — what caught wind of it? Glenn told *everybody* because he thought it was so hysterical (which it was). Anyway, that certain someone took the story to the dirt sheets who printed it, not as a goof, but as Glenn being *serious*. Now, on the other side at the WWE, somebody close to Vince (they had to be close because Vince would have had to tell them about hiring Disco) reads the dirt sheet (Vince never reads the sheets himself). In an effort to discredit Glenn, obviously because of their own insecurities, they tell Vince about the strange and questionable creativity of his new, would-be booker. Vince, in turn, buys the Martian invasion angle as serious, so he now tells me he has seconds thoughts about Glenn.

You couldn't make a story like that up!

To this day, Glenn and I eat that story up. Why? Because that's the wrestling business . . . and that's how ridiculous it really is.

Barry Bonds & Tom Glavine's Brother

Barry Bonds hit #713 last night.

Those who know me know that I'm an avid baseball fan, an avid Giants fan and an avid Barry Bonds fan. Any day now one human being, one great baseball player, is about to accomplish a task that is simply legendary: surpassing the Bambino to become second on the all-time home run list.

Going back to 21 Popular Street, I was only 13 years old when I witnessed Hank Aaron break Babe Ruth's all-time home run record at my grandparents' house. It was April 8th, 1974. After 32 years I can still close my eyes and hear the crack of the bat, for the sweet sound that day was quite different from the thousands of home runs I've heard ever since. Later on in life I would learn of all the controversy surrounding that home run, mostly dealing with racism — a black man "taking" the record from a white hero and legend; how dare he? But on that night, a 13-year-old boy was looking at it much differently. As I saw that ball sail high over the left field wall at Fulton County Stadium in Atlanta, I knew I was seeing history. I realized that I was probably seeing an ageless record get broken, one that would never be broken again.

"Nana! He did it! He did it!" screamed the voice of innocence as I called my grandmother in from the next room. It was magical, a moment in time that I treasured and still keep with me to this day. That's what the game was supposed to be: childhood memories that we would carry with us throughout our entire lifetimes. That night Nana and I celebrated, because that's what it was: a celebration. Not only a celebration of baseball history, but more importantly the celebration of a man: "Hammerin'" Hank Aaron.

713.

There was no celebration in Philadelphia last night . . . none. What should have been a frenzied jubilation when Barry's long fly sailed what seemed like miles into the right-field seats, was more like the reception Metallica would have received at a ballet receital. It simply broke my heart.

For a moment I pondered what Nana's reaction would have been. Would she have booed this man if she had witnessed this great feat? Would she have become God, the Almighty Herself, and judged Barry like the 25,000-plus crowd at Citizen's Bank Ballpark last night? Would she have hurled vile and hateful accusations at him, or thrown a syringe his way onto the field for that matter? Man, I hate what we've become. What gives us the right to judge anybody else? That is such a direct assault on our very Creator. God created Barry Bonds, just like He created you and me, just like He gave us life. And God loves Barry, unconditionally, just like He loves us all. But here we are . . . hating a man. Hating a man created by the hands of God.

Man, I'm a far cry from Barry Bonds, but believe me, I know what it feels like to be scrutinized. Everything wrong with wrestling Vince Russo did; everything right with it, he had nothing to do with. Day in, day out, I get judged by others who don't even know me . . . and it stings.

Imagine how Barry must feel.

Man, love him or hate him, the guy is a son; he's a husband; he's a father. I'm always touched when I see Barry on television with his kids. He loves those kids more than anything in the world; I can see that by the soft glow in his eyes. Can you imagine the pain they're enduring through all this? The stuff they're hearing about their father at school? Nobody deserves that. Nobody deserves to have to deal with the pain of his situation — physically, mentally and emotionally. Let's also not forget that through it all he is still mourning the passing of his dad, his hero, Bobby Bonds. My heart cries for Barry — and yours should too.

Am I an advocate of steroids or illegal substances? No, and that has nothing to do with this; I'm simply an advocate of loving your neighbor as if he were your own flesh and blood. As I stated earlier, we are all sinners, every single one of us. But before you point out that splinter in another man's eye, pull that Louisville Slugger from your own first. I just can't imagine Jesus Christ himself sitting in those stands last night and hurling verbal bomb after verbal bomb at Barry along with the rest of the bleacher bums. No, I see Jesus extending his hand and picking Barry up. Why is it so hard for us to do that, not only for Barry, but for each other? Why do our hearts tend to hate?

Why is that the norm? Why is there always something wrong with every-body else? Why are we always right? Why should everybody else be more like us? Man, the me, myself and I theology of the world needs to stop. It is our downfall, yet we don't recognize it. God put us here on this earth to serve others, not to get ourselves over at the expense of others. Can you imagine what this world would be like if everyone in it put others before themselves? If wrestlers *wanted* to do the job for other wrestlers? Why is that concept just so hard for us to understand and embrace? I mean before I was saved why couldn't I just play on the same team as Tom Glavine's brother?

Wow . . . what a segue!

You've got to be asking yourself how the brother of former Atlanta Brave pitcher Tom Glavine fits into this equation. To be honest, I myself, still find the story quite fascinating. Well, you might say that the crafty lefthander's sibling was the start of the beginning of the end for this former trash/crash TV writer. You know, I'm not even sure what his first name was — I think it was Dan — but since that's totally irrelevant, I'll just refer to him as Tom Glavine's brother from here on in.

In accepting the job with wcw, I knew going in that Ed and myself were going to have to deal with a whole other element that we never had to worry about at the wwf: standards and practices. You see, every time we wrote something at the wwf that we thought might be borderline, or might be pushing the envelope, all Vince had to do was call Bonnie Hammer, an exec at USA Network who was responsible for *Raw*, and give her a heads up. Quite frankly, the only reason for that was so if the switchboard at usa was flooded the next morning with calls from horrified moms, Bonnie would both know why and be prepared to handle it. The bottom line: All USA Network cared about was ratings. All *all* television stations care about is ratings. Do the math: The higher the ratings, the more people are watching your show. The more people who are watching your show, the more money advertisers will pay to advertise on your show. The more advertisers pay to advertise on your network, the more money the network makes. Right now in my head the O'Jays are screaming in my ear, "Money, money, money . . . money!"

But that's what it was all about, is still all about, and always will be about when it comes to TV. But not at TBS, and included under that umbrella is of course TNT. I didn't know, and still am not sure: Was it a southern thing, was it a Ted Turner thing, or were they just dumber than Tennessee Tuxedo's sidekick Waldo? ("Duh, I don't know, Tennessee, should we really say the A-word on television?") Which brings me to another point: Why did Tennessee

Tuxedo, who was brilliant, have a walrus of a sidekick with an IQ lower than the dead, raw fish he ate? What was the purpose of Waldo? It seemed like all he ever did was second-guess Tennessee. And Waldo surely didn't help Double-T get the babes. Hey, Waldo, I have two words for you — *gastric bypass.*

But to get back to TBS. Now, being a Christian, I really want to believe that TBS had higher values than the other networks, but in keeping it real, that just wasn't the case. In the middle of the day TBS would run those adolescent movies that were nothing less than what we were doing on *Nitro* and *Thunder* at nine o'clock at night. And they weren't only playing the movie once a day; they were playing it three times a day! You know how TBS thinks. Wait, let me stop there . . . no I don't. What are they thinking when they play the same movie three times a day? If they missed *Can't Hardly Wait* the first time, they have two more chances to watch it? Great, but what happens if they watched it the first time? Then you lose that viewer for four hours when you're replaying the movie, right? I guess they knew something that I didn't, but regardless, how many times can we really watch Jennifer Love Hewitt? Twice, maybe . . . well, probably.

However, it wasn't just the movies. In the middle of the day, Roseanne would be swearin' at Dan right there at the kitchen table at three o'clock in the afternoon! But when asked why Roseanne was allow to curse but not Scott Steiner, I was told, "Because *Nitro* is original programming." Do you get that? Since *Roseanne* wasn't an original TBS show, but *Nitro* was, she was allowed to get away with stuff that we weren't. Yeah, read that last sentence over a few times, and call me when you get it, because I still haven't! Then, to throw yet more kerosene into the open, gaping wound, they add *Sex and the City* to the TBS lineup and play that 16 times a day! Now, you can edit, slice and dice all you want, but the only way you're going to make *Sex an the City* acceptable on network broadcasting is to cut it down to about six minutes. That's why it was on HBO, remember? Maybe it shouldn't have been called standards and practices, but rather *double* standards and practices!

Man, that whole thing was a mess and so unfair to Ed and myself and here's why. We knew we had to play by the rules, and we understood that going in, but the only problem was, there was no rule book! Week in and week out, I would ask for the guidelines, in print, so I knew what we could do and couldn't do, when I sat down to write the show. But they never supplied me with one — never — and you know why? Because if they did, they couldn't change the rules as the game played on. Every week, there were different rules and different regulations. Do you know how hard it is to write a show without knowing what you can — and cannot — put on the show? And understand, this wasn't about censoring things that would have burned the eyes from the sockets of the children, or "victims," who would have seen it; this was about censoring things that at times were just outright comical. Things that not even I, in my wildest imagination, would have ever deemed as possible red flags. Let me name a few for you.

1. The NyQuil Incident

In trying to stay true to their characters, we wanted Scott Hall and Kevin Nash to show up to *Nitro* drunk – again – in the storyline. Now, with those two personalities, we're talking straight comedy here. However, S & P wouldn't have it. If two wrestlers showed up drunk to the show, that wouldn't be a good message for kids. Okay, I can see their point – aside from the fact that I saw Archie Bunker get drunk on *All in the Family* in 1973 when I was 12 and, as unbelievable as this may sound, I wasn't scarred for life. Again, understand that this was a *comedy* bit. So after I was told this, which of course was a few hours before the show, I had to think on my feet just to make the segment work. So I throw out, "Hey, what if Scott Hall has a cold and throughout the show he is drinking NyQuil? He cops a buzz from the NyQuil, not alcholol." I hope you're starting to see how ridiculous this was. The S & P censor who came to every show took a minute to ponder that suggestion. After about 30 seconds he looked at me and said, "Yeah, that'll work." So in other words: kids, forget the Jack Daniels, go out to Walgreens and get some cold medicine. Same results, but cheaper and you won't be carded.

2. The Three Fat Ladies

Upon his arrival to the building, Roddy Piper was going to come across three overweight, middle-aged woman. In HOT ROD fashion, he was going to rapid-fire insults at them, again in a straight comedic skit.

No go – red pencil. According to S & P, "Roddy might offend an overweight, middle-aged woman who might be watching our show." Yes, this really happened.

3. Kimberly Slips Slick Ric a Mickey

Without remembering the exact set-up – there are a lot of things I've wanted to forget and have forgotten about WCW – we wrote a skit (you see, it was a SKIT – wrestling really isn't real) where Kimberly Page would slip a mickey into Ric Flair's cocktail in order to knock him out cold. Now whereas Kimberly was allowed to do that, we just weren't allowed to SHOW her do that. WHAT? Tell me and we'll both know!

4. The Radicalz and the American Flag

In an effort to help get "Hacksaw" Jim Duggan's story over, we wrote a skit where the Radicalz were going to burn the American flag. However, before they completed their dastardly deed, Hacksaw Duggan would save the flag, and the day, Rick Monday style (you have to know baseball to understand that reference). However, even though the proud patriot was successful in foiling their plot, the heels would get heat on him, then cover his body with the American flag in the middle of the ring.

S & P: "That's a no go."
Curious Vince: "Why?"
Matter-of-fact S & P: "Because there might be a veteran watching our show who gets offended by this."

You see, these were all the vile, obscene, dirty things that Vince Russo wanted to do at wcw that S & P wouldn't allow.

Now, as a Christian, there is something that I truly want you to understand. All those horrific things I did at the wwf and wanted to do at wcw, many of which I looked at as strictly comedy (yes, even the Mark Henry incident with the transvestite, but not "The Hand" — I had nothing to do with that beaut), I did to draw ratings, *period*. It wasn't about me, or what I liked; it was about what people would watch. It was our job to feed them what they wanted, plain and simple. You have to remember, at the time I was in my mid- to late 30s. Do you think that at that age, with three children and a wife — the same wife for two decades — that I really got excited over bra-and-panty matches? C'mon. I didn't, but I knew a large percentage of our audience did. So, I shovel-fed them and they ate. Yes, I was guilty of making this place worse than it already is. And I did it for the money.

Today, with God's grace, it's just not in my nature to write those sort of shows. God showed me first-hand: it's not about me, it's not about you, but rather, all about Him. Today, I write every word in praise and glorification of His name.

So, what about Tom Glavine's brother? Well, I'm getting fed up with this whole S & P thing. What happened to that "Complete Control" thing that they sang and danced about? And where's my rule book? You want me to follow the rules, give me the rule book. How can I follow the rules if I don't know them? You can't change the rules from week to week; now that's an unfair practice! Where's this S & P guy? The rep who comes to the shows is just that: a rep. I want to meet *the guy!* Where's the curtain? What is he, the great and powerful Oz? I want to meet this guy!

After two weeks of bellyaching, my dreams come true. I'm arranged a meeting with the high and powerful Standards and Practices guy. Man, at this point I'm expecting somebody like Dog the Bounty Hunter. The power and mystique that surrounds this guy is Yoda-like. So I go to Techwood — that's where the TBS corporate offices were — and I prepare myself to meet this righteous mountain of a man. All I could think about was, "Man, I hope this lives up to all the hype," when from out behind the curtain steps this 150-pound guy with red hair and a clipboard. What a letdown. Here I'm expecting a seven-foot, two-ton, hideous monster with the disposition of my third-grade English teacher, wielding a ruler the size of a two-by-four — with spikes — and I get Jimmy Olsen?

So we have our meeting. Where do you think Elaine got yada-yada-yada from? All I heard was a lot of nothing. I was promised a rule book that I knew I was never going to get and then Screech skipped back to his office. Again, without remembering all the details, I recall looking at Raggedy Andy's card when I left the compound, and his last name was Glavine. Then the person I was with — again I'm drawing a blank — informed me that Opie was Tom Glavine's brother.

I knew it! I knew it! I knew I hated him for a reason. It's 1993. The Giants win 103 games and finish second to the Atlanta Braves in the National League's Western Division. With no playoff system yet in place, we're screwed! 103 wins and *nothing!* That is ludicrous! "Hammerin' Hank, you get a pardon, but from this day forward I hate everybody who ever dons an Atlanta Braves uniform. I even hate anybody who is *related* to an Atlanta Brave!

This means *you*, Tom Glavine's brother!

Oh, the trauma! Only about a month in and I find out that the Standards and Practices guy has Atlanta Braves blood running through his veins. This wasn't a good omen. This wasn't a good sign. I hear that dreaded Tomahawk Chop and it's coming down on me. What's next?

Hey . . . why'd it get so quiet all of a sudden?

The Sounds of Silence

"Hello darkness, my old friend. I've come to talk with you again …"

Man, I love Simon and Garfunkel — *love* them. Paul Simon's lyrics backed by Artie's voice: that is pure magic. Put Paul Simon lyrics up against some of the lyrics of today's so-called standards and see what happens.

My milkshake brings all the boys to the yard
And they're like, it's better than yours
Damn right it's better than yours …

Are you kidding me? Ouch!

To this very day, I love the sound of silence. Anything having to do with being alone in a quiet place, preferably my finished basement where my fantasy baseball team plays, and I'm in. I'm a big fan of peace and quiet. I even loathe when the phone rings; nine out of ten times I don't even answer. As a matter of fact the only time I pick up the phone is after 11 p.m. when it has that "death in the family" ring. I know that sounds morbid, but you know exactly what I'm talking about. And of course, having a mother like mine doesn't help the case.

It's been one whole book since I brought up "Fruitsy," my crazy mother, but how can I go another sentence without her having another ailment of some kind? If you read *Forgiven* you know I have my mother to thank for passing the hypochondriac gene on to her beloved son. Every day she chooses yet another entrée from her medical menu to be stricken with. "Let's see — on Monday I'll have the shin splints, and sauté them if you would. Tuesday … Tuesday I think I'll have that 'my corneas are shot; I can't see three feet in front of me' roast. Wednesday? It's Wednesday already?

Well, on Wednesday I've got to have that deadly fungus that's invading my big toenail. And can I have a salad with that?"

You get the picture. But of late it's gotten a bit more serious, I'm sorry to say. A few months ago my mother discovered that she had . . . hammer toes. Man, what fodder with that one. Every day it's, "Look, Jim" — that's my poor, innocent slob of a father (great guy, though) — "look. Do you see my toes? They're curling up — I can't straighten them out. What do I do?" God bless my father, but when this hypnotic conversation takes place and I'm in the room, he'll look at me in the corner of his eye and explode with laughter just knowing what I'm thinking. Then later on he'll get me alone and whisper in a giddy voice, "Vince, what do I do? I don't know what to do with her. Every day it's something." Calmly I put my hand on his shoulder, look down at him and say, "Don't worry, Dad, I have an idea. The next time she's standing in the driveway and she's not paying attention, back the car out over her toes and it will strengthen them right out." Needless to say, within seconds he can't breathe from the laughter.

You know, it's just one of those small things, but I'll do everything I can just to make my father laugh. When he gets going on a good one — usually at the expense of something my mother just said — the ageless 75-year-old man turns into a ten-year-old boy who just heard his first dirty joke. It's those little things in life that just mean so much. Again . . . Avalon.

But getting back to that silence thing: there's good silence, but there's also bad silence. Bad, deafening silence: the silence that could always be heard backstage at a wrestling show. Engined by the power of paranoia, you just never knew who was talking about you when, or what they were saying; you just knew someone was. Within my first few weeks at WCW I could just feel this. Many people didn't want me in the spot that I was in. It should have been their spot; they put in the time, they paid their dues, they were next in line. Again, that's just the way of the world. You just don't give anybody else any credit; it's always about "It should have been me."

Let me first say that J.J. Dillon was my contact for getting into WCW. I had a third party at the WWE contact him to tell him I might be interested in the *writing* — not booking — job. J.J. brought it to Bill Busch and the rest is history. So J.J. Dillon was very instrumental in getting me into WCW. With that being said, I was into the job for about maybe four weeks when I felt like every time I turned around, J.J. and Kevin Sullivan were having private pow-wows that seemed to break up every time my eyes caught them. This happened on more than one occasion. I knew what this meant. I had not only witnessed it many times before in the wrestling business, but I felt it in the very pit of my stomach. Now, could my own paranoia have started to control my very thoughts? Perhaps — I'm not going to deny that — but when these Dillon–Sullivan summits broke up every time I turned around . . . I just don't know.

What I do know is that it had nothing to do with how I personally felt about either of these two individuals. The truth is that I admired and respected both of them. Remember, I had worked with J.J. at the WWE and I was very grateful for him helping me get into WCW. As far as Kevin Sullivan goes, to this day I think this guy is a genius. Sullivan was just one of those who got it. I was always a fan of his, even when I wasn't in the business. I always marked out on his promos. Why? Because they were different from everybody else's. Many people don't know this, but Kevin Sullivan had a much greater impact in steering me towards the direction of "WWE Attitude" than ECW ever did. In my opinion, the Kevin Sullivan–Brian Pillman feud seemed about as "real" as professional wrestling was ever going to get. Whoever was behind that — Sullivan or Pillman or both — was about a decade ahead of their time.

But the plan was starting to kick in; it was starting to take form. It's just something that I knew. J.J. and Gary Juster were spending a lot of time with Bill Busch on a daily basis as their offices surrounded his at WCW. Once they saw my work I knew that neither were big fans of my style. The fact is, many, many purists weren't big fans of my style and I think I totally understand why. From the beginning, when I was handed the pencil from Vince, my style was always entertainment first and wrestling second. That's what I grew up on. Look at all the greats that I followed in my childhood: Chief Jay Strongbow, Ernie Ladd, the Valiant Brothers, "Superstar" Billy Graham — all were great entertainers first and good wrestlers second. Again, when you're sick with paranoia and you see the wrestling business change more and more towards this new trend of "television first," it's just a matter of time before you start thinking that there may no longer be a spot for you in the business. That maybe time was passing you by, and being that you really didn't understand this style that was much different from the style that you came up on, maybe they would no longer need you. You know what? I fully understand that. But what *they* didn't fully understand was the great respect I had for their old style. There was always going to be a place for them while I was around — always — because to me they were irreplaceable.

But they just didn't see that. Remember their paranoia. They grew up in a business that told them to destroy — by any means possible — anything and anybody who was a threat to them. It was always about protecting your spot. Whether you were 20 years old, 30, 40, 50 or 60, it didn't matter — *protect it*. Can you imagine what professional sports would be like if the legends didn't clear the way for the rookies? If Hammerin' Hank had never stepped aside and paved the way for guys like Barry Bonds? Well, believe it, or not, that's how professional wrestling functions. They don't pass the torch, but rather they take it and use it as a weapon to burn the guy who's on their heels.

I knew this was going on. As I was planting new soil and changing the landscape at WCW with a new way of doing things, the good ol' boy network was re-digging the old soil and using it to bury me ten feet under the ground. And even though I knew this was happening, I wasn't going to be a part of it: I wasn't going to fight it. If they wanted to bury me, so let it be. If Bill Busch was going to allow himself to be worked, then let him be worked. I knew that the end result would be him replacing me with them, but guess what? Then they would have to deliver and I knew in my heart of hearts they couldn't. Times were changing on a daily basis and living in the bubble didn't allow them to know what was going on in the world. I knew that they would digress back to that ol' style of rasslin' that just wasn't going to cut it any-more. I knew in just a matter of time that without even knowing it, they would use that same old dirt they took to bury me, and bury themselves in the process. And that was okay with me. All I was interested in was writing the best show that I was capable of writing on a weekly basis. My job was to write, not to play politics.

It was no surprise to me when a meeting was called by Busch soon there-after. Present at the meeting were all my gravediggers: Dillon, Juster, Sullivan — why they didn't come to the meeting in muddy overalls I'll never under-stand. But to his credit, J.J. was the one who spoke up with me sitting right along next to him. J.J. spoke about everything that he felt was wrong with the product. Good for him. Even though I would have preferred him talking to me in private first, I still applauded him for bringing these things up in my presence. To be honest, I was dumbfounded. You have to understand that at the time all I was looking at was the ratings. The ratings were, and still are, the only barometer. It wasn't about what I liked, or what J.J. liked, or what Kevin preferred — it was about the public. Were *they* watching?

Please keep in mind, when I joined WCW the last rating they did before Ed and I took over was a 2.6. Now, only 12 weeks in, the rating of the last show was a 3.5. That's a fact, and you can look it up. Again, all we were looking at was the numbers. According to the numbers, there was no doubt that we were going in the right direction. So after sitting there in silence, just listening to them attack my writing, when they were done I simply said, "Shouldn't we be looking at the ratings? Three months ago they were at a 2.6. This week's show did a 3.5. That's a jump of almost a rating in a little under three months. We have to be doing something right — you think?" The room was silent; nobody said a word. Man, it's great to fight with numbers — as the old saying goes, they never lie!

Unfortunately, it didn't matter. The writing was all over every wall in the building. I knew then I was done. I was just too tired to fight the fight. At the beginning of my tenure at the WWE, when I took over as the head writer of *Raw*, I had to fight the same war, and here I was over four years later and they were asking me to fight it again. No way. I had already proven at the WWE what needed to be done to save a business that just insisted on being bad reruns of *That '70s Show*. What's funny is if I went back to the WWE tomorrow — ten years later — I'd be fighting the same fight again. They are determined to do things *their* way. It doesn't matter if anybody buys it or not, it's going to be bad wrestling, with bad characters, with bad storylines, and that's just the way it's going to be.

How Tank Abbott Cost
Me My Job

They say that when it rains it pours. Well, I wasn't caught in a rainstorm; I was being hit by Typhoon Mary — from all sides! As if now the added pressure from the office wasn't enough, creatively we were thrown not just a monkey wrench, but the whole Craftsman 150-piece tool and ratchet set — that same week!

For three months the creative team had slowly rebuilt the nWo storyline, but this time the players had changed. Kevin Nash and Scott Hall were still part of the group. But gone was Hulk Hogan who was going to be the lone wolf on the other side, so to speak, now with his former friends being his bitter rivals. In were Scott Steiner, Jeff Jarrett and the last piece: Bret Hart. The idea was playing off the intricacy of these personalities trying to play for the same team. It was going to be a war of egos, and that's where great writing was going to come in. Who was going to screw who first, when were they going to do it, and how were they going to do it? Again, a story that we could just sink our teeth into and play with for months. However, just as soon as the last piece was in place — Bret Hart — the Hitman suffered a bad concussion courtesy of Bill Goldberg's boot to his head, and was going to be out indefinitely.

As if that wasn't enough, Jeff Jarrett suffered a concussion the Monday before the upcoming pay-per-view when "Superfly" Jimmy Snuka splashed him for the top of a steel cage — rattling Jeff's cage in the process. Within a two-week span, the main angle which we had built for some three months was now home sick in bed and the thermometer was stuck up my . . . you know what. So what do you do? Cry? Bellyache? In the wrestling business there is no time for that. The shows come fast and furious and you have to be trained to think on your feet. You have to digest what happened, take it, then make sense out of it. That's all you can do.

But you know what? That was part of the beauty of the job. I thrived on having my creativity challenged. There was always more than one way to do things; you just had to expand your mind so that you could see the alternatives. So without missing a beat I pulled my crack staff together for an emergency late-night meeting to figure out where we were going with this thing. Present were Terry Taylor and reliable Bill Banks. I'm not sure if Ed was there or not — I'd think he would have had to be, but for some reason I don't remember. But regardless, we had to get on with the show.

When your back was against a wall, there was only one way to think: think logically. What would happen if this was real? What would we do if *really* faced with this situation? Well, the fact was that Bret was our champion and he was going to be out for who knew how long, so first and foremost the belt had to come off Bret. Before we just move past that, think about that for a second. I had built the last three months around Bret. He was going to be the WCW Champion, and everything was going to revolve around him. One kick to the head and done. It's that simple — it's that fast. But notice, it was Bret. I felt secure with Bret as the champion; I just felt so safe. I knew that I could trust him; I knew that he would never screw me behind my back regardless of what happened in Montreal a few years earlier. Wow, that's saying a lot about Bret. I couldn't — and still can't — even say that about some in the business who I actually considered friends. Bret was just a stand-up guy. I think that's why he felt so betrayed at the Survivor Series. He felt betrayed because he would have never done anything like that to anyone else. I understand that now — I'm not sure if I did then.

So now the entire landscape of wcw had to change, and change within the next three days. I believe it was a Thursday night when we met, because we had to write the show on Friday. With that kind of deadline working against you, there is no way to know where you're going the next three months. We had to fix Sunday's pay-per-view and then take it from there. That is really where you relied on your writing ability. But tonight wasn't the night to do that. Tonight was basically the night to put a Band-Aid over our newly acquired gaping wound. So as we started everything, I opened up with *what if?*

What if . . . a battle royale of sorts was booked to crown a new WCW World Champion? I love that "World" Champion nonsense. It's hysterical when you think about it. A *fake* wrestling belt that covered the entire world — what were we thinking? Anyway, *what if* there was a battle royale? What if Sid was one of the first three guys in? What if Sid outlasted 26 other opponents in a 30–45 minute span? What if Sid was in the ring alone — battered, beaten, hurt, bloodied, worn out, tired and dead on his feet — when the last competitor made his way out to the ring. What if that last competitor was a fresh, hungry lion, looking to make a name for himself in the wrestling business? What if that competitor was a shoot fighter by the name of Tank Abbott? Well again, let's get back to *what if* this were real? If this were real, Tank Abbott would have hit the shocked Sid one time and sent him sailing over the top rope. Then, much to his surprise — and everybody else's — Tank Abbott would have been standing in the center of the ring WCW "World" Heavyweight Champion. That's what would happen if this were real.

Terry, Bill and whoever else was there digested it, tweaked it, and then said, "Let's do it." Could they have had reservations and been afraid to speak up? Maybe, and that's cool — to this day I take full responsibility for that decision and would do it again tomorrow. Where did we go from there? Who knew? We weren't going to figure that out tonight. But, I had enough confidence in my writing ability to know that we would have taken it where it needed to go. All you have to do is listen to the fans. If it works, you go with it; if it doesn't, then on to the next thing. There is no doubt that I would have just let the fans create our direction for us. They are the ones buying it. That's why I wasn't afraid to try it. Within the next few weeks they were going to tell us what to do. Unfortunately, that type of philosophy just doesn't work today. Here's an example.

Recently *Raw*'s numbers were down — way down. So they pull a surprise at a recent pay-per-view and Edge, shockingly, walks away the WWE "World" (they have one too) Champion. The next two weeks the ratings *spike*. The people never saw this coming and they're with it. Wrestlings fans love to get fooled because the majority of them think they have it all figured out. When they get sincerely surprised, you have 'em. With Edge as champion, the WWE had 'em. So what do they do? Three weeks later at the next pay-per-view, the title comes off Edge and the rating plummet again. Now, why did this happen?

This happened because bookers had written the storylines three months in advance and had no idea how to change their booking on the spot. That's how that happens — that's how it always happens. Wrestlers write according to what their audience is telling them, bookers book according to the way of the bubble for the past 50 years.

Nuff said.

So, the meeting broke and we agreed that this was our new direction.

Where we went from there . . . we'd worry about that later when we had more time. Right then, I had to go home, and get some sleep — with my eyes wide open. I never slept in those days . . . never. This wcw thing was headed for disaster. It was just a matter of time. In the background I could hear James Hetfield, lead singer of Metallica: "Sleep with one eye open." Don't worry, James — in the wrestling business you always do.

The Meeting That Never Was

Somewhere in this mess a meeting was set up by Bill Busch (who would also be attending), between myself, Hulk Hogan and Ric Flair, to discuss where we planned to go with their characters. Remember, at the time Hogan and Flair were off TV, as we were strategizing a way to build for a monumental return that would position them in the appropriate way at that point in their careers. And that plan was already in gear. Slowly but surely, we were eliminating the major players from WCW. I know at the time Sting was on hiatus, Piper hadn't been around in a while, Savage had been off TV for some time, Page was MIA — so while it looked like the young talent was taking over, the "Legends" (remember, we could never call them old) were plotting their sneak attack in some secret bunker some 100 feet underground — you know, like that Fox show *Unanimous.*

Talk about a *work!* Are you kidding me or what? If that show isn't scripted, then there really is a talking bear in the woods who steals picnic baskets! If the show *were* a shoot, wouldn't the contestants just award somebody the one million dollars the first week and then just split the money between them? Then everybody gets to go home as winners! Or is it much like the wrestling business and the players haven't figured that out yet? Do a job and get the other guy over . . . by getting the other guy over we eventually get everybody over . . . when everybody gets over we're *all* over! When we're *all* over we *all* make more money! Yeah — more money for everybody! Nope . . . they still haven't figured that one out.

So, the morning of this big pow-wow, which was the day after we came up with the Tank game plan, I get a call from Bill Busch.

Bill starts the conversation by saying, "Vince, is it true that you're going to put the wcw World Title on Tank Abbott? Vince . . . you can't do that." Okay, so it's not bad enough that the wrestlers are bookers, but now we have our first *accountant* turned booker? No — I was smarter than that. Bill Busch didn't know Tank Abbott from Bud Abbott. Obviously sometime between Thursday night and his Friday morning phone call, somebody had gotten to him. You see how this stuff works? Now, if I'm Tony Soprano, there's a rat in the ranks and Silvio and Paulie are doin' a strip search looking for wires. But in my heart of hearts, I didn't believe that. I believed that somebody in that meeting told somebody in passing what we planned on doing at that Sunday's ppv. That somebody then probably told one of Bill Busch's minions, who in turn couldn't wait to tell Billy Bones. Then Busch, who really didn't have a clue about wrestling — and really didn't care for that matter — gets worked into a frenzy by the said minion, until he's convinced that this one angle is going to bring down not only wcw, but tbs, tnt, cnn, the Atlanta Braves, Ted Turner, Jane Fonda, Jane's co-stars in *9 to 5* Lily Tomlin and Dolly Parton, and last but not least the entire chain of Ted's Montana Grills. Thus the frantic phone call to yours truly. At that point I didn't even try to explain the angle to Busch. Maybe I should have, but at the time the whole notion was ridiculous. So I told Bill that I'd see him later and we'd talk about it. At that point I hung up the phone, picked it up again . . . and called my attorney. I told him that no matter what it took, no matter how much money I would have to forfeit, that he just had to get me out of my wcw contract. In three short months, I was done. They won; I lost. Another innocent victim devoured by the vicious, un-pop-able bubble.

Later that day, I got in my car and headed to the office. For some reason I felt something was up. I was now infested with that same wrestling paranoia that I swore I would never allow myself to be infiltrated by. It had seeped into my skin. It was pumping through my veins. Man, at the time all I could think about was *Invasion of the Body Snatchers*, a movie I had seen many, many years ago. I was now a different person, both on the outside and in. I was now just like them — every single one of them. Upon entering the building, there was no sign of Hogan, no sign of Flair, just a milky-white Bill Busch.

Time to digress.

It's 11 a.m. Footsteps from above my head wake me from my slumber as my oldest son Will (who just finished his first year at college last week) returns home after having slept the night at a friend's house. Barely awake, I pull myself off the couch in my dungeon and within seconds fold the sleeping-bag-turned-blanket and throw it into a nearby closet along with an old pillow that lost its feathered plump years ago. I had to hide the evidence; I didn't want him to know that I wasn't up yet. Man, it gets harder and harder. Another sleepless night disrupted by one bad dream after the next. During the night, as I lay still on the sofa bed that I'm always too lazy to pull out, my adrenals race to a beat that only Secretariat would know. And that's exactly what it feels like at 2 a.m.: the hoofbeats of a thoroughbred racing within my heart. That's why I sleep in the basement in the first place . . . or at least attempt to. Even after all the late west coast baseball games are over — usually about 2 a.m. — I just lie there staring up into the darkness. I haven't slept with Amy in my own bed for years. There is no normalcy to this madness.

Many nights I'll lie with Amy until about 11 p.m. Usually when she begins to snore delicately. I look at her and wish that could be me. Why can't I snore on the contact of my head hitting the pillow? The insomnia has been going on since the moment college ended and real life began. It got worse during my WWF days, and became almost unbearable during my WCW nightmare. Looking back now, that's actually when I discovered current TNA announcer Don West. Once the sheep got tired of being counted and left me for somebody else's dream, I turned on the TV; I think it was 4 a.m. I don't know how else to say it, but there was this lunatic on the screen, screaming at me at the top of his lungs, telling me why I had to pick up the phone and order this 1,000-card lot of Matt Williams's rookie card. And even though I had never met him, I knew nothing about him and he knew nothing about me, he was making it perfectly clear that it was a matter of my own life or death: that I needed to order these cards. Man, I was in a trance. I had never seen or felt such energy in my life. This guy was Robin Williams ? 2, working on ten cups of coffee and a good hit of speed. All I could think of was, "I've got to get to the phone and order these cards — now!" I knew right there that if this guy could sell a piece of cardboard with a picture on it with this kind of conviction, then he could sell professional wrestling. I immediately brought this idea to Brad Siegel at WCW. No offense to Brad, but even though he was with it, the corporate machine dragged, till it stalled . . . till it eventually died. That's why when I went to TNA I made the call to Don West myself.

I know that I'm rambling a bit here, but it's because there's something that I want you to understand clearly. There is no magic switch you turn on or off when God is at the center of your life. No matter what you may or may not hear in church, life doesn't just become Wonderland. God or no God, you are still living in *this* world — day in and day out. No matter how strong your convictions, you are still an element of your own environment. It's not that easy to constantly have pleasant thoughts when society is continuously reminding you of how screwed up we are and how screwed up our world is. Watch the evening news any day of the week — pick one: Monday, Tuesday, it doesn't matter. We're painted to be failures, losers, inadequate, liars, cheaters, killers. For every 100 dark news stories, there's maybe one with that single ray of light shining through. It's not that easy to grab onto that bright beam and ride it when everybody else is desperately trying to pull you down.

Through the eyes of the world: look at my life right now. At my age, it's not "supposed" to be like this. At this point in time, my life is in a place that it has never known. I'm 45 years old and I haven't worked on the clock for nearly ten months now. Every day my savings — the money that I now support my family on — decreases in size and I feel it with every dollar I spend. Every time I leave the house it's ten dollars in the gas tank just to get to where I'm going. And even though I'm not working, the day-to-day needs of supporting a family don't go away. The car needs to be fixed, the lawn mower is broken, we have no milk . . . and on and on and on.

These are things you don't look at when you're making a six-figure salary. But six figures feels like a lifetime ago. Did I save my money? Of course I did, but remember: my run wasn't that long. My high-salary days were between 1997 and 2001 — a four-year period. During that time I also listened to a friend of a friend, who advised me to invest in blue-chip stocks — you know, the "safe" ones. So, when the Twin Towers came crashing to the ground, so did my nest egg — to the tune of over $200,000. How do I live with that? That isn't normal in anyone's life. That wasn't supposed to happen. It was the American Dream, remember? Or at least, that's what they told me. Depression or suicide — which is it going to be? To be honest, I don't know which is more painful.

Losing that money, three years ago . . . I didn't know what to do. I was just sick to my stomach. How many times can you say, "If only . . . "? But here, right here, this is where having God in the center of your life changes everything. With everything we go through in life there are lessons: lessons that, if we examine and learn from them, will make us better people in the long run. That's all God wants to do: make us better, bring us closer to Him. Today, when things don't go according to my plan, rather than put on my swim trunks and belly-flop into that sea of depression that we all know so well, I simply ask God: What are you trying to show me in this? What are you trying to teach me? That puts everything in perspective. Now everything makes sense. Even your disappointments have meaning . . . valuable meaning.

That money? I was never meant to have that money. Look at how I earned it. It was nothing more than dirty wrestling money. Sweaty, filthy, meaningless paper made by throwing every shred of moral value that I had — or didn't have — straight into the garbage. There was no ethical judgement, no scruples and no feelings of responsibility to anyone. I just plain spit in God's face. Nothing I did back then glorified Him . . . nothing. It was all about me. That's why the money was taken away. There was nothing in anything I earned that advanced God's Kingdom. There was nothing that showed my gratitude to Him. There was nothing that showed my love to Him. In the Bible God makes it perfectly clear to those who read it: Me or money. Only one will be your God; you choose. I did . . . and I lost.

I can't talk the "holy talk"; I can only work with what God gave me. Being a Christian, handing your life over to Him, that means that you begin to view the world through His eyes, and no longer through the eyes of the world. That perspective changes everything. That perspective now gives everything meaning. God shows you and explains to you "Why?"; all you have to do is ask, look, listen. Learn and obey. I know that's "why" I'm writing this book. It's not about me, it's not about Bash at the Beach, it's not about Hulk Hogan. It's about speaking in a language you can understand. That's what I never got. Nobody ever spoke to me about Christ in a language I could understand. I remember a lot of people coming up to me and saying, "God loves you." Man, that meant nothing to me . . . nothing. I just couldn't understand what it meant. Now, I know you, I know where you are. Please, just open up your heart and mind. I promise you, God will do the rest.

Back to the meeting with Billy Bones.

So, with Flair and Hogan nowhere in sight, Bill asked me to come into his office and sit down. Man, he looked sick — I mean downright ill. To this day I don't know if I've ever seen anybody so nervous. He was visibly rattled, almost physically shaking. At that point anyone else in my Harris Brother–bought boots would have been overcome with a feeling of "This isn't good," but to be honest with you, I wasn't. As a matter of fact, I was looking forward to what he had to say. Anything had to be better than what I had experienced there over the past three months.

"Vince," he started. Man, he was nervous. I don't even think I was this nervous when I got to meet Gene Simmons after being a fan for almost 30 years.

"Vince . . . we've decided to take a change in direction. From this point forward, we are going to have a 'creative team' that you will be a part of, but not head of."

He then went on to rattle off some names of those who would be on the committee, one being a friend of his who was the lead singer for a band I'd never heard of called Hüsker Dü. How a musician now became a writer I had no idea, but I could say the same for wrestlers turned writers as well. As he continued his list of names, without meaning to sound arrogant, I knew that these guys weren't on my playing field. It would have been like Joe Torre reading off the lineup card and saying, "Okay, Alex, you're at third, Derek you've got short, Robinson you play second, and Vince you're at first." Yes, in my mind it was that far out of kilter.

With the pigment of his skin now absolutely absent, Bill's voice grew weaker with every word. It was obvious to me that this wasn't his brainchild; there was not one shred of confidence in his voice. He had been worked . . . worked by the best in the business. This is exactly what I saw coming, and exactly what I expected. Any hopes of Bill being smarter than those who were pulling his strings were now gone. He was a lifeless marionette, just mouthing words that he was told to say.

Inside I was jubilant. This is just what I had hoped for. As the words continued to stumble from Bill's lips, all I could think of was: They've breached my contract. I can't believe that this is going to be my out. They signed me to be "Creative Director" and now they're telling me that I'm no more than just another member of the band — pardon the pun. I'll be out of this and they'll still have to pay me. At this point I didn't even hear what Bill was saying anymore; I was just too giddy inside to pay attention.

Respectfully, I waited for Bill to finish. There is no question that he was anticipating an angry diatribe as my response since he himself knew this was wrong. But he wasn't going to get an argument; quite the contrary. You have to go back and watch *Kramer vs. Kramer* to really understand how skillfully I played this. In *Kramer*, Dustin Hoffman's character Ted Kramer is in quite the bind as he battles his wife for custody of his son Billy. Just prior to the court hearing, all hope comes crashing down when he loses his job. How would he be awarded custody of his son without a job? So a few days before Christmas he goes on a job interview. The interview even takes place around the office Christmas party. After answering all the questions of his potential employers, who no doubt would rather have been at the party, the head honchos matter-of-factly tell Mr. Kramer, "We'll get back to you after the holidays." Without missing a beat, Ted says, "Gentlemen, you saw my work and you know I can do the job. I'm even willing to take a pay cut but I need to know today — not tomorrow, not after the holidays, but today."

Ted Kramer got the job.

All right, the circumstances were a bit different — I was being fired, not hired — but it reminded me of that scene nonetheless. Without missing a beat, I looked Bill Busch in the eye and said:

"Bill, thanks, but no thanks. That wasn't the position I accepted when I took the job. If you've changed your mind about me being the Creative Director, that's fine, but I'm not accepting your offer to be part of a committee. So, I'm going home now; you need to talk to Brad [Siegel], to figure out what to do about my contract. Call me."

Then I got up and calmly walked out of his office.

You should have seen the look on Bill's face. Let me go through my memory bank of movies and television shows in order to make the appropriate comparison.

Okay, I'm looking for the perfect picture of surprise — no, not surprise, but more like total shock. Let me think. Okay, here's one.

"Luke . . . I am your father."

Okay, maybe that's being a bit over-dramatic, but it was something like that. Bill never expected that response from me. He never expected the outcome to be my going home. No, in his mind I was just going to accept being an equal bandmate, banging the tambourine on my palm as I stood side-by-side on stage with his Hüsker Dü buddy. No offense — you stick to writing song lyrics, I'll stick to scripting fake wrestling shows. Again, how it's so easy for anyone to be a sports entertainment writer I have no idea.

So I took my ball and I went home. Tell me, what would you have done? Played along and been miserable as you sat around a table and listened to singer/songwriters and retired wrestlers who just didn't know what wrestling fans in the year 2000 wanted? Remember, back then Disco wasn't yet a part of the creative process and I wouldn't have had him to entertain me during those meetings; that at least would have made it bearable. No, I was going to go home and watch this thing play out because I already knew what the final outcome would be. When you're brought down by politics, sooner or later, those who brought you down — and have now replaced you — are going to have to perform. Once they're in that spot there's nowhere to hide. At that point they're the main event and they have to deliver. But what they forget is that this isn't a rasslin' ring — this is television writing. There's a lot more to this than just laying out a match. There are characters, storylines, plots, arcs, dilemmas, emotions, twists, turns, conflicts, comedy, drama, tragedy; if they don't know how to write, the ratings would reflect that.

There are times, man, when you just have to bite the proverbial bullet. There would have been no point in me going off on a tirade with Bill. This decision was made weeks ago and right now he was looking through his "Vince is the Anti-Christ" glasses. They had poured him the poison and he drank it. Poor sap . . . it wasn't his fault. So I went home. Thanks to Little Lou Gianfriddo's words from about five years ago, there was nothing to take from my office. "It could be over any day," he said.

And it was.

So, what do I tell Amy and the kids? They had no clue any of this was going on. I held the drama closer to my vest than Bruce Wayne does his secret identity. I had uprooted them only three months ago for a life that I promised would be better. Man, what will Will think . . . what will he say? Will he hate his father for the rest of his life? Will he find himself in Dr. Melfi's office at the age of 18? Back then, there was nothing in the world worse than failing your family. As a husband, a father, a man, that's just something you don't do. In my life today the only greater failure would be the failure to serve my Father, my God . . . the failure to stop pursuing His will for my life.

Life was just so much easier before wrestling. I never intended to get in this deep. I don't know what happened, how it happened. I can tell you this: It had *nothing* to do with a love for the business. This was a job — a job that I could walk away from like any other job. But it was the people — those I worked with, those who just couldn't wait for the "Great" Vince Russo to fall — SPLAT — on his face; the people who never looked behind Vince Russo to see Amy, Will, vj and Annie; the people who had no idea who I was or what was truly in my heart. I was on a mission to never let those people win; never let them beat me regardless of the consequences. Man, I just don't know why. I don't know how I became like this. Yeah, I do know why. It was my Italian pride. The pride that my late great-grandfather, John J. Savarino, instilled in me when I was just a child too young to understand how everlasting his influence would be on me. Nobody — *nobody* — would ever beat my grandfather. And, to take one step back . . . you wouldn't even try.

Pride is a very dangerous thing. Pride can be the downfall of any man, regardless of his position or status. My pride was my worst enemy, not Bill Busch, not J.J. Dillon, not Kevin Sullivan. I could have controlled the situation; I could have controlled my career in the wrestling business; I could have controlled the heartache and the pain, the disappointment; I could have controlled everything . . . if only I had handed it over to God.

I know that now, but back then all I knew was that I had to go home and tell my family that their dad was now unemployed. . . .

I think.

15 CHAPTER

Heaven

May 25, 2006

Soul Patrol!

There is still hope in America. When the masses are choosing a prematurely gray, average white guy over a beautiful, young, body-blessed vixen, you know we still have a chance. Yes, Katharine McPhee was the cat's meow on *American Idol*, but no matter how corrupt our society is we couldn't vote against Taylor Hicks. That really does tell you about the heart of America. It's there; it really does exist. We just need to wipe it free of the filth which stains it: the sewage which corrodes the entire world that we live in.

Living in Marietta, Georgia, some famous Civil War battlefields literally line my own backyard. Whenever I get the chance, or at least get the energy up, I take great pleasure in walking the trails that roll through the historical landmarks. Closing my eyes and a taking a deep breath, I'm exalted by what I believe is God's country. On the surface, the view is velvet to the skin. The full greenness of the forest, the babbling brooks of living water, the baby deer that run in herds — is this the closest I'll ever get to Avalon on this earth?

In my innermost moment of peace, my mind is suddenly interrupted as I'm jolted by a sense of reality upon closer examination of my surroundings. The dead trees, the weeds growing wildly, the litter that pollutes the brooks, the runners who spit on the ground as they pass, the pile of horse manure covered by a family of yellow-blue butterflies.

Horse manure covered by a family of beautiful, yellow-blue butterflies. How perfect is that?

Is it possible that *we* are the beautiful, yellow-blue butterflies: God's unique creations put on this earth — His earth — not only to nurture it but to also live from it? And if so, then why aren't we living off the honey of the land? Why are we instead feeding off a pile of stale, black horse manure? The answer is simple: This earth isn't God's Avalon, but rather the Devil's swamplands. Sure, he'll con you with some of the scenery from time to time — I've been to Boulder, Colorado, but that scenery is only paper-thin. It's a façade, an illusion.

Back After 21 Months

February 24, 2008

It's been a year and nine months since I typed the last word of the previous chapter. During that time, there is no doubt that a healing process was in full bloom. There was no point to writing anything, not another word. It was time to find out what every human being yearns for: Who am I? What am I doing here? What is my purpose?

For a writer, it is a gift to be able to go back and read your own words from an earlier time. Even though God was a part of my life when I stopped writing 21 months ago, look at that last paragraph, in that last chapter. Reread it if you have to. Do you feel the negativity? Do you have a strong sense that the glass was not only half-empty, but bone-dry? Even with the understanding that Jesus Christ Himself was my Lord and Savior, look at the place I was living in. There was still an overwhelming feeling of sadness. Being a writer, that is easy to mask with words, but when you get on a roll, it all seems to find its way out.

I was seven years removed from my WCW experience when I wrote about the world being an illusion. Seven years removed, but yet at the very core of my soul I still had no resolution. Even though God Himself had profoundly changed my life, at my very base I was still desperately seeking resolve to unanswered questions. So much had happened during that time. I had even used God's grace to turn wrestling into a positive, used wrestling as a gift to His Kingdom, to glorify His name, but at the very root of my manhood it is obvious by reading my own words that I still wasn't experiencing the peace that I knew He meant for me. That proves one thing: I'm a human being. We all are human beings. We can be found by God, and yet still not truly understand the blessing. Still be in a place that we don't want to be in. That we know He didn't intend for us to be in.

During the past 21 months, while I was still wrestling with my wrestling past, I kept asking God over and over again: What was the purpose for You placing me in this business? Even the Ring of Glory shows which I wrote and produced in Your honor haven't given me the overall peace that I'm looking for — that I know You meant for me. Why, God? What is it? What are You trying to show me? What are You trying to tell me? I believe in You, and I know there's an answer . . . what is it?

The wait was long . . . but well worth it.

How WCW Killed Me

Writing my first book was never about money. First and foremost, I wanted to share with the world how Jesus Christ had profoundly changed my life. Secondly, growing up it was always my dream. No, I didn't want to be a wrestler; no, I didn't want to be a wrestling manager; no, *I didn't want to be a wrestling writer*; I simply wanted to be a published author. Luckily, a senior editor at ECW Press by the name of Michael Holmes clearly understood my dream, my vision and my intentions, and agreed to let me write *Forgiven* my way — meaning it wasn't going to be aimed and marketed directly to the wrestling audience. There wasn't going to be a wrestling cover, there weren't going to be any wrestling drive-bys aimed at those who couldn't defend themselves, there weren't going to be rumors and hearsay, and most noticeably, there wasn't going to be heaps of dirt left on anybody — perhaps with the exception of myself. I completely understood that Michael, and ECW Press, made a sacrifice in an effort to help me get my word across, in lieu of dollars and cents, and I am forever grateful to them. However, with this book, I feel obliged to return the favor.

So, with that being said, I'm right here, right now, going to name this second book. Here it is:

Rope Opera: How WCW Killed Vince Russo

How ironic is it that ECW Press, my publisher, also published a book entitled *The Death of WCW*, with a picture of yours truly on the cover. This epic manuscript goes on in detail — not factually based, but detail nonetheless — fingering the culprits who killed wcw. Now mind you, being one of the "usual suspects" named, I was a bit taken aback that I was never interviewed and that none of the authors involved in the book ever had any legitimate ties to wcw whatsoever, but regardless — the book's a masterpiece. It's right up there with *The Toilet Zone: A Hilarious Collection of Bathroom Humor* by Reynolds and Gross.

I get tickled, absolutely tickled, when I hear the critics say that Vince Russo killed wcw. Man — that's a lot of hard work and dedication for just one man in just under a three-month span, because that's exactly how long I had any kind of control at wcw. I mean, to take a 13-year-old company and utterly destroy it in a matter of three months — I'm Cloverfield! That alien took Manhattan down in a day, so I guess anything's possible. It must have been that Tank Abbott thing. It couldn't have been that David Arquette thing, could it? No, it was definitely the Tank thing. Damn Tank Abbott! Damn him!

Wait a minute.

Hold the phone . . .

I just had a thought.

If wcw went out of business because of the Tank Abbott thing, then technically, didn't *Tank Abbott* kill wcw and not Vince Russo? But wait! There's a hole in that: the Tank Abbott thing never happened. But what if the higher-ups at Turner Broadcasting caught wind of what we were about to do, and they determined that just the chatter of Tank Abbott winning the WCW "World" Title was enough for them to sell the company? Because if in fact Tank had become the WCW "World" Champion, the company as a whole would have gone out of business anyway! I mean a fake wrestling match does carry that kind of weight whether we want to admit it or not!

Obviously this topic hits a nerve. Why? Because I was *working* at wcw and to this day, I can't tell you why it went out of business. Can I speculate? All day long. But at the end of the day none of us will ever know the whole story. I can, however, tell you this. When I worked at the wwf, everybody embraced the product. You had to, or else Vince would have you out on the last train to Clarksville. At wcw, the product was only embraced by the wrestling division. Everybody else at Turner looked down at professional wrestling. It was beneath them. They were a television station for cryin' out loud, not a carnival! How do I know that? It's simple: none of the higher-ups were ever around — *ever*. They separated themselves much like Britney separates herself from good decisions. They were embarrassed to be in bed with wrestling, plain and simple. Going back to 1988, remember that wcw was Ted Turner's brainchild. He was behind it and gave it his full support. Well, when I showed up on the scene, Ted was well on his way out. The AOL/Time-Warner merger had just taken place, and a whole new sea of bigwigs were now looking down their snouts at grown men grappling around in their underwear. Regardless of the ratings, they didn't want it. To them they were a legitimate television station, and wrestling was a joke. The nameless and faceless suits killed wcw. Not Vince Russo, not Eric Bischoff, not Hulk Hogan's salary — and certainly not Tank Abbott.

You definitely have more of a case if you want to argue that wcw almost killed Vince Russo. Never in my entire life have I had to deal with such depression. It was crippling; it was taking my very life from me. As a man, a husband and a father, I uprooted my entire family to move to Atlanta, Georgia, to work for wcw. I stripped them of all the security they knew, only for Bill Busch to tell me 90 days later that "they" (wcw) were going in a new direction. I took Will, vj and Annie from family and friends. I took them from their schools and familiar surroundings. I took everything from my wife, Amy, that she had built in her life to work for a company that was never worthy of her sacrifices. *Never.* Those who were responsible for ousting me should have been ashamed of themselves. In order for them to jump a spot, they buried an innocent family in the process. I was both ashamed and embarrassed . . . and depressed. Very depressed.

I spent days and nights in the basement of my house, too defeated to even rear my ugly head. I felt I had let my family down, and as the provider, there was nothing worse in the world. I had no game plan whatsoever — none. What was I going to do in Atlanta? I had no contacts; I knew nobody outside of wcw. As far as income went, keep in mind I walked away from the job. I told Bill Busch that I wasn't going to be a part of any committee. Could I have breached my contract? I didn't know; I just knew that I wanted to be as far away from wcw as possible. The nights became sleepless; the days, torturing. At 38 years old, I was absolutely lost.

I spent hours at the computer, following wrestling news sites just to see if there were any updates on my situation. I didn't hear a word from anyone at wcw — nothing but the "Sound of Silence." I had read that there was a small uproar at the tv tapings when some of the boys found out what had happened. Even though I was thankful for their support, it didn't change my situation at all. My only saving grace was that I knew that the product would fall flat on its face without me. There wasn't a doubt in my mind. I was certain that I was on the right track my first three months at wcw, just as certain as I was that those who undermined me had no clue what they were doing. They were now in a Monday night war with the WWF, and a badly booked rasslin' show wasn't going to cut it. I knew that, but how long would it take for the suits at WCW to figure that out?

Within the next three months, the 3.6 rating that we had built over three months was back to the 2.6 where we had started. It didn't take long for my executioners to turn into suicide bombers. Not only were they killing the product, but they were killing themselves in the process. As I stated earlier, politics can be a great knife when you want to cut those in your way out, but sooner or later you're going to have to put up or your superiors will turn that blade on you. That's exactly what was now happening at WCW.

It was sometime in late January 2000 that I received a phone call from Brad Siegel, the executive in charge of TBS and TNT — remember, the New Yawker who wore a Yankee cap to our first encounter.

"Vince, there's somebody I want you to talk to. He'll be calling you."

That's all that Brad said. However, that's all he had to say. I knew immediately who Brad was speaking of. I knew that the next call was going to come from Eric Bischoff. It was no secret that Brad was a huge Eric fan, and rightfully so. During Eric's run at WCW he had been extremely successful for the network. With Eric at the helm, WCW saw heights that nobody in the business thought were possible — Vince McMahon included. There are a million theories out there about why WCW was successful before its decline just months before I arrived. The fact is, many look to give Eric as little credit as possible. The truth? That's a joke. Eric was the mastermind behind it; regardless that it was Ted's money, it was Eric's vision. You can't take that away from him.

From the start I just had a bad feeling about this. Keep in mind that it wasn't until I took over the booking for Vince that the WWF made their dramatic comeback. From 1996 to 1999, we caught, surpassed, then crushed WCW in the ratings, with the end result being Eric losing his job at WCW. He couldn't have been happy about that. Plus the fact that years earlier I gave him the opportunity to hire me before I started booking with Vince, and he never called me back as he stated he would. It was only days after that that Vince gave me my chance and as they say, the rest is history. The only real opinion I had of Eric Bischoff at that time was from my one and only phone conversation with him. It was probably back in late '96 or early '97, during which time he was the cock of the walk, and he knew it. Almost needless to say, his manner reflected this. During that conversation he just came across as arrogant, as if he were doing me a favor by just talking to me. In his defense, he probably was doing me a favor. At that time I was just a nobody looking for a chance, an opportunity. One that Eric Bischoff never gave me.

I think it was only a matter of hours following Brad's phone call that Eric called. He didn't want to talk much on the phone, so he suggested we meet up for lunch. I have to be honest here: I hated this whole thing from the start. Aside from being leery of Eric, I was hired for the job as Creative Director of wcw and now it seemed apparent that I was never going to get the opportunity to do what I was hired to do. Three months isn't a chance — three months is nothing. Unfortunately, I knew I had no say in the matter. At this point all I wanted to do was secure my check for the next year and nine months — that was it.

A Recipe for Disaster

I met Eric at a restaurant in Kennesaw, Georgia, called Hopps. Ironically, that restaurant is also now out of business. The meeting was clandestine, to say the least. After talking to Eric, Brad Siegel had called me back stating that nobody associated with WCW could know anything about this. I knew that Brad was doing all this without even Bill Busch's knowledge. Remember, Brad liked Eric, and I don't think Brad ever wanted to see Eric go in the first place.

Man — I just hated everything about this meeting. From the start, Eric and I never liked each other and never trusted each other. We were cordial to each other because neither one of us had a choice in the matter. I was never asked if I wanted to work with Eric Bischoff, and I'm almost certain he was never asked if he wanted to work with me. If we were, I'm certain that both of us would have said thanks but no thanks. Add to that that I had no idea what the pecking order was. Was I now reporting to Eric? Was he a consultant? Brad never laid any of that out, to me anyway.

Again, it's nothing personal against Eric at all. We were just two totally different animals with two completely different styles and approaches. I've always considered myself a blue-collar guy in the business. I just enjoy working with the boys no matter where they are on the card. I don't enjoy being the boss, and I never play the boss card — *never*. I don't think I'm better then anybody else, and I don't expect people to shudder in fear when I enter a room. That's just not my make-up. I always felt that the most important thing was to respect the boys. Respect their talent, respect their craft, respect their families and respect them as human beings.

I never found joy in being the "big deal." That never impressed me. I wear baseball jerseys, not sport jackets. I talk with people, not at them. I don't get off on being smarter than anybody else. The truth is I have way more street smarts than I do book smarts. To this day my son vj, who's now 17, cannot believe that I'm a writer who hates to read. He always recommends books for me to read and I tell him he's nuts — the extent of my reading is fantasy baseball magazines. I don't want to be smart; I just want to be real. That's why I hate meetings, I hate dog and pony shows and I hate tooting my own horn. I'd just rather work with the boys where the most important thing we share is respect.

It's apparent to those who know Eric that's he's the complete opposite. And hey — whatever makes him happy. He is who he is. I never had a problem with that, but I just knew that because of the differences in personalities, that it was only a matter of time before this experiment blew up in all our faces. But again, I had to go along with it because I had no choice. As long as I was still getting paid, I could handle it . . . or so I thought.

Over the period of a few weeks, Eric and I met in seclusion and laid out the road map that would serve as our springboard back into wcw. The idea was to wipe the slate clean, and start with a huge angle that would bring Eric and me back to wcw together, with an ax to grind with the overpaid veterans. We would ignite an uprising within the younger talent, or "New Blood," who were being blocked from opportunity by the "Millionaire's Club." The idea was the brainchild of both Eric and me, but it was he who suggested that I appear on tv for the first time.

Putting Myself Over

Even though I fully realized that I was about to cross the line from "office" to "talent," I didn't have an issue with Eric's suggestion and here's why. At the time, there was so much pressure on me to deliver ratings that my thought was, if I have to do it, I'll go out there and do it myself. Believe me, it had nothing to do with ego but everything to do with survival. My back, front and every other part of my body were up against a wall. And not just any wall, but one with protruding, sharp spikes that were threatening to slash my skin with every decision made. There was no wiggle room. I had to prove my critics wrong by showing them that not only would my way work, but that it would be just as successful as it had been in the WWF. I was so hell-bent on not losing to the enemy, that I never — not even for one second — considered my physical well-being. At the end of the day, I just wanted to win.

The premiere of the Russo/Bischoff — or Bischoff/Russo — *Monday Nitro* took off without a hitch. I wasn't sure whose name should have come first because Brad Siegel still hadn't discussed the pecking order with either Eric or me. Or perhaps he had told Eric, but he never said anything to me. Nonetheless, even though I didn't know who the boss was, I was working with Eric Bischoff. The New Blood vs. The Millionaire's Club storyline hit the airwaves running, and we were on our way. I remember cutting a shoot promo that night on the politics that cost me my job. I didn't mention names because those responsible knew who they were. My promo was spotty at times, but the truth is that my mouth was drier than Whoopi's cornrows. I was nervous, not so much about my own ability, but rather what others were going to think about me.

Man, that is all our fear, isn't it? It is so important for us to please other people. To make sure that others both think and say good things about us. We make it our #1 priority to be liked by all. It wasn't until I became saved years later that I realized how ridiculous that notion was. Through God I now understand that it's all about pleasing Him — and Him only. Not Vince McMahon, not Eric Bischoff, not dirt sheet critics, not even the fans, but just the One who created us all. What that means is simply going out and being the best that you can be every day that you live on this earth, honoring Him with everything you do. At the end of the day, that's all that any of us can do. Always remember, you are working for God, not an appointed boss, and you should strive to please Him.

Getting back into creative at wcw, I immediately assembled a booking committee, because I was just so sick and tired of hearing those above me saying that's what I needed. The truth is, I didn't need a committee, I didn't want a committee, and — most importantly — in wrestling, committees *never* work. The reason is simple: you only have so many hours in a day to write the show. The more people involved, the more opinions you have to hear; the more opinions you have to hear, the more time you spend; the more time you spend, the more time you waste. On a committee everybody wants to throw in their two cents — good or bad — and with the pressures of a weekly television show you just don't have the luxury of time. So what happens is you run out of clock, and then you're simply writing to get it done. That's why guys at the bottom of the card usually have nothing to work with. Ninety percent of the time, the committee never even gets to them.

That's why what Ed and I had at the wwf was so unique, special and successful. Two guys bouncing ideas off of each other. No big room filled with numerous egos: just the two of us. It's no coincidence that while we were booking, *everybody* on the wwf roster had a role. Everybody was doing something because we had ample time to cover everyone on the roster. But again, those in charge at wcw didn't understand any of this, so I was just going to do things their way.

Oddly enough, Eric never met with the committee from the start, and I think that's what started our ultimate downfall. You have to understand that within the confines of a committee, hours are spent writing the show: not the 10–4 that Ed and I were used to, but rather those 9–7 days that I dreaded so much. When the booking sessions were over, I just wanted to go home and sink my head in a boiling pot of water. So, with that being said, think about how irritating it would be when we would send Eric the shows when we were done writing, and then he would tell us what was wrong with them after they aired. Not before the show aired, but *after* it. I started to get the feeling that Eric didn't know a good show from a bad show until the Internet told him Tuesday morning. Again, not only in defense of me, but in defense of the entire creative team, I started having a huge problem with this. We were spending hours on the show, and you're going to negatively critique it only after it's aired? What about before? Isn't that the way it's supposed to work? Again, it was really hard for me to figure the entire structure out because Brad Siegel had still never told me what Eric's role was.

Aside from that, there were other issues between Eric and me. Our philosophies were just different. Eric was always a main event guy; I was always a mid-card and below guy. Why? Because on many occasions you couldn't tell the veterans anything — *especially* at wcw. In their minds, since they were making a ton of money, they knew everything. In their minds when it came to writing, they were Shakespeare and I was Dr. Seuss. The only problem with that was that they didn't have a clue about writing. You see, wrestlers want to act like wrestlers, and "real people" — our audience — were not wrestlers. Wrestlers want to talk like wrestlers, walk like wrestlers and carry themselves like wrestlers. That's not how everyday people go about their lives. The audience has to be able to relate to these characters, and the only way they're going to be able to do that is if the wrestlers are human beings. That's where storytelling and actions come in. Emotion is everything in the wrestling business. As a performer you have to be able to strike that chord. You have to be able to make the audience care about you. It's not all about spots, but rather all about personalities. Maybe you're asking yourself, when you talk about wrestlers acting like wrestlers, what does that mean? Well, here's a prime example.

How many times have you ever seen a World Champion boxer walk around *everywhere* with the title belt draped over his shoulder? How many times did you see Ali or Foreman or Tyson carrying that thing around? Do you even know what it looks like? Now, how many times in wrestling do we see the Champion with the belt draped over his shoulder? The answer: *every time*! He always has that belt on his shoulder, while he's eating, while he's having sex, on the toilet, at the airport — everywhere! How ridiculous is that? The belt never leaves his shoulder! That's what I mean about wrestlers acting like wrestlers.

So, since they knew more than I did and rarely listened — even when it was for their own good — they just weren't enjoyable to work with. They made the job as taxing as it possibly could be, as opposed to the younger guys who always wanted to learn. The less experienced talent would hang on every word you said because they wanted to get better. It's those guys I'm in the business for, to this day. It is an honor and a pleasure to share with them every ounce of knowledge I have in my 17 years in this business. And that's where Eric and I had massive, unfixable differences. Eric wanted to kowtow to the big stars, and give in to them at every turn, and I wanted to give the younger talent an opportunity. So it's easy to see that we were going to quickly get into a situation where sides were going to be chosen. Hulk goes with Eric, Jarrett goes with Russo, DDP goes with Eric, Kidman goes with Russo, and so on, and so on, and so on. To anybody with half a brain, it was only a matter of time before this thing was going to erupt. And, the explosion would probably come between Eric's top "boy" and yours truly.

Brainwashing the Nature Boy's Son

I'd be lying if I didn't admit to being concerned with how the top guys at wcw were going to view me. The two who weighed heaviest on my mind were Hulk Hogan and Ric Flair. Looking back now, it's easy to understand why I felt this way. First and foremost, I was a mark for the both of them, with a huge respect for everything they had every done in the business. Without guys like Hogan and Flair, guys like me wouldn't exist. Therefore, it was vital to me that I make a good impression on them. Unfortunately, that probably was unrealistic from the start. Remember, I came in to wcw with the reputation of being an advocate for the younger talent and when you piggyback that with the fact that I knew Hogan and Flair's roles needed to change for their own longevity, you're going to have a problem on your hands.

And remember too, I was watching wcw prior to jumping, and at times it was painful — as a fan — to see my heroes from decades ago, trying to legitimately compete when they were mere shells of themselves. Again, I don't put any of the blame on them, but rather on those who were booking them. Just this past week, Disco was telling me a story about wcw that took place a while before I arrived. He told me that Eric booked a match between Hogan and "Macho Man" Randy Savage because — and I quote — "I want Hulk and Randy to recreate some of that old magic."

Now I ask you — can Pete Rose go out there tomorrow and go three for four, with three runs scored and a stolen base? Time doesn't stand still, no matter how badly we want it to. Glenn then goes on to finish his story by telling me that on the same night the wcw booked Hogan/Savage, the wwf booked the Mean Street Posse vs.

Pat Patterson and Gerry Brisco directly opposite them — at the *same time*. Now, even though Patterson and Brisco were much older than Hulk and Savage, the fans weren't supposed to take them seriously. They were buffoons — and great ones, I might add. The end result? McMahon's goons doubled the rating of the "magical" match between Hogan and Savage.

Again, let me make this *perfectly* clear: not the fault of the talent — the fault of the bookers. In conjunction with that, week after week, I would witness Ric Flair come to the ring with his shirt off and let's just say, it wasn't his most appealing look. Again, at his age at the time, who's going to look like Batista? It's the law of gravity. Heck, I'm 47 years old, I diet and work out, and I got a jelly roll around my waist the size of a Michelin snow tire! Even though to this day neither individual buys it, as a fan I wanted to protect them from themselves. Again, what else could my motive have been? Write them off of TV — why? Because I didn't like them? I didn't even know either one long enough to establish an opinion! Man, as a baseball fan that's the equivalent of not liking Joe DiMaggio, or even Babe Ruth for that matter! The entire notion is ludicrous.

Starting with Flair, in my opinion he needed to be "fixed," and the only way that was going to happen was to put him on the shelf for a period of time. That was the objective of the Filthy Animal beatdown in the desert. Ironically, I was crafting his return when Billy Bones decided on the company's "change in direction." That change must have been to bring back Flair with no fanfare in my absence, because that's exactly what they did. That's why on the night I returned, I was right back where I started. Hogan and Flair's characters still needed to be refreshed for 2000. And if Flair wasn't a priority, then why did I take aim on him the moment a microphone was put in my hand?

I remember that first promo clearly. I remember saying that Ric Flair was the !@#$ on the bottom of my shoe. How do I remember it? Because I knew all those "smart" fans out there would believe every word I was saying. I knew that they would buy into the fantasy that I was shooting on Ric Flair and that I had legitimate heat with him. Man, just writing that last line cracks me up. Sometimes you can make the "smartest" fans believe anything. It's called good acting combined with better execution — it's as simple as that. Anyway, from that moment the stage was set: the arrogant, brash New Yawker who single-handedly killed the wrestling business was going to take down the beloved, honored and treasured legend.

The key cog to the Russo/Flair story was going to be Ric's son, David. If one of my weaknesses in the wrestling business is kowtowing to the younger talent, an even bigger Achilles heel is rolling over for second generation wrestlers. Three individuals who I greatly enjoyed working with over the years have been David Flair, Eric Watts and Dustin Rhodes — all second generation wrestlers. Man, I just gravitated to these guys; I think it was simply because I truly understood their plight. How difficult it was for all of them to fill the shoes of their fathers who laid down such a trail-blazing path in this business. Ric Flair, "Cowboy" Bill Watts and Dusty Rhodes were simply legends in the game. Their sons were forever going to be battling their shadows — both inside and outside of the ring. And they all had issues — all of them — but there's also something else they had: hearts of gold. I don't believe for a second that any of the three — David, Eric or Dustin — ever dreamed of living up to the expectations of their fathers. At the end of the day they just wanted a chance to be themselves. It was never them who expected greatness, but rather others in the business who put their fathers on such high pedestals.

To this day it boggles my mind when I'm told of the negative tone that Ric Flair had towards me in his autobiography. Now don't get me wrong, I'm not looking for a standing ovation here, but the truth is I coddled his son like no other. I took care of David, and put David center stage when others — even some on my own committee — saw nothing in him. I would think that Ric would have seen that, and maybe even appreciated it, but I don't know if he ever did. And, to be blatantly honest here, I will never understand that. However, in wanting to make something crystal clear here, I never did any of that for Ric — I did it all for David. In my eyes he was deserving. He had a terrific attitude, and was extremely respectful; that's all that anyone could ask.

In his role as the kid who was brainwashed by the evil New Yawker, only to then turn on his legendary father, I felt David was outstanding. Perhaps the best work he ever did in the wrestling business. In fact, whether he ever wants to admit it or not, there is no question Ric was into the angle, since soon his former wife Beth and younger son Reed also found themselves involved — at his suggestion. It was a family affair, one that I was hoping would bring Ric and David closer together, but again, in reading some of Ric's own words, I don't believe it ever amounted to that.

Throughout the entire angle with Ric, I worked closely with him on everything. I always asked him what he wanted to do first. The fact of the matter is, I could care less what he says and thinks about me today; I know that I treated him with the utmost dignity and respect every day I had the honor and privilege of working with him. To me, it was like pitching batting practice to Willie Mays. I don't think Ric ever realized what the entire angle meant to me. Again, through it all you could just feel that lack of trust. The feeling that the only thought going through his mind was: Somehow, some way, Russo is going to try to get over on me.

I can tell you now — while swearing on my kids in the process — that was never the case. My motive, more than anything else, was to learn from perhaps *the* greatest player in the game.

And since this is a book based 100% on honesty, let me also set the record straight on something. Sometime during my angle with Flair, the Nature Boy approached me with an idea.

"Vince, what if you shave my head?"

Now, even in the wildest imagination of Vince Russo, that thought would have never even have crossed my mind. I mean, we were talking about *Ric Flair* for cryin' out loud, and out of respect alone, I would have never even thought of such a dastardly deed. I remember adamantly trying to talk Ric out of it — *adamantly* — but the truth is, he insisted.

You can only imagine how shocked and surprised I was when in his own book, in his own words, while taking yet another shot at me, Ric suggested that the head-shaving idea was my brainchild from the start.

You know what? I have to believe that people just forget. I can't believe for one second that the truth is twisted just in order to make a good story. If one single person in this book is buried unfairly by me, I will give you your money back. At the end of the day people have differences — we have to, because we are all different. At the end of the day no two people are going to agree. But the truth is, none of us are right and none of us are wrong; it's just the way we see things. That's why I'm not going to hammer an Eric Bischoff, or a Hulk Hogan, or a Ric Flair. I have nothing against them, and never did. If we didn't see eye to eye on certain things, so be it. They all have their opinions and I have mine. But to sit down at my keyboard and just blast them when they can't defend themselves? What's the point in that? I have been attacked in many, many books by many, many people — many who don't even know me, who have never even met me in the case of the *Who Killed WCW* book — and I can only wonder if they feel good after they did it. Any hostile feelings I had left my body a long time ago, just about the same time that God took over. How coincidental is that? Look, I'm never going to change the world, or even the wrestling business for that matter, but man, can't we all try to be a bit kinder? Don't you think that if that approach was taken the world, as a whole, would just be a better place?

There Is No Sick in Wrestling

After a two-week hiatus, I'm back.

I don't know what bird it was — or what country it flew in from — but for the past two weeks I was down with the flu. I spent five days flat on my back in bed, only having to get up to fly to Nashville to write TV with Jeff Jarrett and Dutch Mantel. In my 17 years in this business I have never called in sick — haven't even taken a day's vacation. The relevance of all this: I just wanted to let you know the recent feeling of euphoria that consumed me knowing that I *could* call in sick to a wrestling company if I really needed to.

But that's just *one* very small difference between Jeff Jarrett and Vince McMahon.

As my story progresses, I will go much further into my relationship with Jeff Jarrett over the years; however, having just gotten over this experience the past couple of weeks, there are a few things I'd like to toss around while they're fresh in my mind.

I had my bi-monthly Monday night flight scheduled from my home in Denver to my work in Nashville, Tennessee. I would get in sometime around midnight, get a night's sleep and then go to Jeff's house, where we would work on television for the next two days. This journey is my ritual every two weeks, and something I am very accustomed to by now. Well, sometime around Wednesday night it hit me. I knew it the second it was in my body. You see, I don't often get sick — but when I do I usually take it much the same way an unsuspecting Wile E. Coyote takes an oncoming Acme anvil. Knowing that in only a few short days I had to be ready to fly to Nashville to do my job, I immediately dashed for the covers in an effort to nurse myself back to good health.

After a five-day diet of flu medications, egg-drop soup and *Everybody Loves Raymond* episodes (seasons one through nine of which I own on DVD), I wasn't feeling the least bit better. Monday night was approaching quickly and no matter what my mind was telling me, my body couldn't get out of bed to ready itself for the flight.

On Monday afternoon, my wife Amy kept insisting that I just didn't go, knowing that right after our writing sessions I'd immediately have to fly out again to a PPV in Norfolk, Virginia, followed by two days of TV in Orlando, Florida, which would give me no time for rest. Ignoring her plea, I barked the line at her that Vince McMahon ingrained in my head through my five-year slavery term to him: "There is no sick!"

You know what? When you sit back and read that, I don't really think you're getting the significance. We're talking a sick day here. We work approximately 250 days a year, and some people much more than that. The Vegas odds are that one, two, maybe three days out of the 250, we're going to get sick. So what does the normal employee do? You pick up the phone, call your boss, tell him you're not coming in because you're sick — no big whoop. Well, with Vince it didn't work that way. You see, he didn't "believe in" being sick. To him, there was no sick, and it was as simple as that. Vince even had this bizarre ritual of getting pissed off at himself every time he *sneezed*. I'm not kidding — I guess it was some kind of control thing. And when *he* got sick, he would never even admit it. I guess in hindsight it just wasn't the "manly" thing to do. And vacations? Forget it; there were none. No matter how young your kids were, no matter how badly they wanted to see Mickey Mouse — nuh-uh. No vacations. Even though this wasn't a written policy, and vacations were offered when you got the job, your address would have to be a padded cell if you told Vince you were taking a vacay with the family.

Every second of every day, all Vince McMahon knows — and wants to know — is the WWE. And not only is that his perogative, that's also the reason he makes all that money. And don't get me wrong, I signed up for it — I agreed to it — but after five years of every day being about wrestling, and only wrestling, I was just about to drop through the floor with a noose around my throat at high noon.

That's why I was trained to get out of bed and head to work no matter how bad I felt. But this time, I just physically couldn't do it. So I picked up the phone, called Jeff and told him that I was too sick to make the late Monday night flight, but I would come in first thing Tuesday morning. Jeff's response?

"No problem, Vince, just get yourself better."

You know what? There's nothing to making all the money that one man can possibly make — *nothing*. You could have billions neatly tucked away in safety deposit boxes for all I care, but that doesn't make you a man. What makes you a man is putting other people before yourself. What makes you a man is treating people like people. What makes you a man is treating people the way that you want to be treated; that's the difference between someone who's driven by loving others and someone who's driven by loving themself.

22 CHAPTER

Why Does Bill Goldberg Want to Kill Me?

As I said, upon my arrival at WCW I knew there'd be problems. I wasn't concerned about creative difficulties, because I knew I had the talent to resolve them. But political issues? I knew from the start I'd take a shellacking. You see, politics is the last thing I'm interested in. Even when the Hillary/Obama debates were going on, I could care less. In my opinion, it doesn't matter who the President of the United States is; nothing is ever going to change. It is what it is, and it will always be that way no matter who's in charge.

So if I hate watching, reading and talking about politics, you can imagine how much I loathe playing them. And guess what? That's not a healthy mindset, especially in the professional wrestling business. The world behind that curtain is infested with politics and politicians. That was another great difference between Eric and me — whereas he had the savvy of a young Al Gore, I had the naïveté of that innocent little girl who asked, "How much is that gorilla in the window?" That's why I knew from the start that guys like Hogan and Flair would eat me alive as ravenously as Jared eats his lunchtime Subway. Even though I was aware of it, the fact was that there wasn't much I could do.

The same could be said for Bill Goldberg, but his power came in a much different way. His power came by way of *fear*.

In my years in this business, I don't think I've ever seen any one individual take the profession by the storm like Bill Goldberg. Nobody — not Hogan, not The Rock, Austin or the Warrior — had such a dramatic impact in such a short time. If anyone in professional wrestling was ever a phenom, it was Bill Goldberg. And while his critics would tell you to this day that he couldn't work a lick, I tell you, *who cares?* He didn't have to. Goldberg just had "it" — plain and simple. While the nWo was no doubt responsible for the demise of the WWF in the mid-'90s, to this day I feel it was Bill Goldberg who may have had the most dramatic impact in taking us down. And while he was at the right place at the right time, he still had to go out there and do it. To this day I take nothing away from Goldberg — *nothing*. Sure, there are those who will tell you that it was scripted that he went out there and beat *everybody in the world* in seconds, but remember, with each and every spear he had to make you believe it . . . and Goldberg did.

Backstage, from the moment I met him, I always perceived Goldberg as a regular guy. He was always no-nonsense and told you how he felt. He wasn't afraid to disagree, and I respected him for that, but that also has its limits. Goldberg was in no way, shape or form a politician. The truth? Maybe he wasn't smart enough to be. When you're dealing with guys like Hogan, Flair, Nash, Luger and Page, you'd better be able to play or else you're going to be out of the race before it even starts. However, even though he was no slick, flashy, smooth-talking democratic donkey, Goldberg could get you in other ways.

Again, everything you read here is strictly my opinion, and my opinion only. I have no intention of throwing anyone under the bus: all I can tell you is the way I perceived people, and why. I'm sure if you spoke to them they would have a much different spin, but with all of us being different, we are all going to have a different perspective.

As I've said, when I joined WCW, I felt that Hulk and Flair immediately needed to be fixed — right or wrong, that was my professional opinion. At the same time, I also felt that Bill Goldberg needed his share of some tweaking. Let's face it: he had beaten everybody so quickly for so long — where was it going to go? I'm sure that those who built him before me never stopped to realize that sooner or later, Goldberg was literally going to hit a brick wall that even he wouldn't have been able to bust through. After a while the fans just get tired of the same old, same old. It had happened with the nWo by the time I hit the scene. They were adding guys, splitting factions, doing some very non-creative things just to keep it alive. The truth was, it wasn't working anymore, and from listening to the crowd, I felt that Bill Goldberg was on that same path.

By some means, we needed to humanize this animal. We needed the fans to see a different side of Goldberg — that he was human, flesh and bone just like everyone else. The only way that was going to be accomplished was by him losing. In order for us to take the character to the next level, we had to see how he would deal with adversity. And I'm not talking about Goldberg losing to some slouch, or being upset — my choice of the man to defeat Goldberg was "Big Poppa Pump" Scott Steiner.

Goldberg hated it from the get-go. And not only that, he resented me for even coming up with the idea. I explained to him, face-to-face, man-to-man, that I thought it was the best thing for the company. Bill vehemently disagreed. When I then flat out asked him what the problem was, Goldberg looked at me and said, "If this were real, Scottie would never beat me."

How do you respond to that? Not only wasn't wrestling real, but I also had to question whether or not Bill could legitimately beat Steiner. The truth is, on his best day I don't even think he would have come close. Whereas Bill was a stand-out football player at University of Georgia, Scott was a legitimate wrestling machine at Michigan. He *was* the real deal. Taking nothing away from Goldberg, I think Steiner would have killed him in a shoot.

At that point I realized I wasn't going to get anywhere with Bill. He flat out wasn't going to lose to Steiner — period. At this point I had no choice but to go to the Yankee ball cap–wearing head of TBS and TNT, Brad Siegel, for advice. During our phone conversation, Brad couldn't believe what I was telling him. He kept saying over and over again, "But it's not real — it's wrestling!" Finally, Brad had no choice but to fly Goldberg to his office in Atlanta — with Bill's *agent* — so the head of TNT and TBS could tell him that he had to lose a *fake* wrestling match. Being at that meeting was almost surreal. The head of Turner Broadcasting was taking time out of his schedule to tell a grown man — and his agent — that he had to lose a scripted match. Right there I knew that one day I would be writing about this — and no one would believe me.

After much deliberation, and much coaxing from his agent, Siegel finally won the debate. But let's face it: he won because not even the great Bill Goldberg had more power then he did. Leaving Brad's office that day I knew that the issue wasn't over — Bill made that clear when he left the office red-faced. Unfortunately, I, and I alone, was going to have to make sure that this thing was executed — the day of the pay-per-view.

Even though it was very different from the way guys like Hogan and Flair operated, this was how Bill Goldberg wielded power. When Goldberg didn't get his way, he would just put the fear of God in you, no matter who you were. Through his stare, his snarl, his glare, the redness in his face, the veins popping out of his neck, he would attempt to intimidate you like no other person I have ever worked with. The office was scared to death of him; what

Bill Goldberg wanted, Bill Goldberg got — or else somebody was going to get hurt. On this day that someone was almost certain to be me.

I don't remember dates, I don't remember pay-per-views and I don't remember venues — I only remember incidents. Throughout my entire life I have never cluttered my mind with details — I hate the details. Details are never important to me, nor will they ever be. I'm a big picture guy. That's why Vince and I worked so well together — I laid out the big picture, and he added his nuances. At the end of the day you might not get a Picasso, but maybe you create a Warhol. So despite the details, I'll never forget the day that Bill Goldberg was being forced to do something he didn't want to do: lose a match.

It was hours before the ppv and I was doing what I usually do: making sure that the talent was as prepared as they possibly could be. With my production tunnel vision in full effect, I was interrupted by head agent Johnny "Ace" Laurenaitis, who not only looked like he had seen a ghost — he *was* a freakin' ghost. I mean he was albino white! For some reason his blood had vacated his body — and he was looking for me.

"Vince, Vince," he said, "you've got to go in there" — pointing to Bill Goldberg's locker room. "It's Goldberg . . . he doesn't want to do the job."

You know what? At that point I wasn't scared, I wasn't intimidated, I wasn't panicked — I was just flat fed up. Even after the meeting with Brad Siegel, Goldberg's position had not changed. The fact is, after he left Siegel's office all he did was fire himself up more during the week. At this point he was an inferno, looking to take yours truly down in a blaze of glory.

Genuinely pissed off at this point, I went into Goldberg's locker room without hesitation. I immediately saw Bill sitting in a chair backwards, staring into space, and breathing heavy — real heavy. To this day, I don't think I've ever seen anyone that mad. Suddenly he started this rocking motion, coming across like a coiled cobra just moments before he was about to strike. I remember looking at him, and not being scared at all. Why? Because I just couldn't believe how ridiculous this all was. We're talking about a grown man losing a fake match. At that point I grabbed another chair that was in the room, turn it around just like Bill's was, and sat face-to face with the breathing, snorting, coiled dragon. I remember asking Bill what the problem was and his answer was deafening silence. He just began to snort louder and rock faster. Where these next words came from I have no idea — I'm not that brave, or that stupid. Without hesitation I blurted out, "You're not intimidating me, so if you're gonna hit me, hit me — and let's get this thing over with."

Man, typing that last sentence, I still can't believe those words came from my mouth.

I guess it was the shock of the sentence that caught Bill off-guard and almost immediately changed his demeanor.

"I'm not going to hit you."

And at that point, the conversation was over. I got up and left the room, and later that night Goldberg lost to Scott Steiner. Looking back, I guess I kind of backed Bill into a corner, calling his bluff. I mean, if he wasn't going to hit me, then what was he going to do? Brad Siegel's word was final and he knew that. So no matter what frustrations he was going to take out on me, the end result wasn't going to change — and it didn't.

Throughout my experiences with Goldberg, well, I guess I was just more disappointed then anything else. When Bill wasn't so mad at something, I actually enjoyed the conversations I had with him. On many occasions I sat next to him on private planes and I genuinely enjoyed his company. Beneath it all, he was actually a good guy. When you were able to get that guard down, he was a respectful, kind, human being. But the hard part was getting that guard down. It would seem that right after we had those good talks, back at work the next day Goldberg would be burying me behind my back to who-ever would listen — that's the part that hurt the most.

In hindsight, wcw created a monster in Goldberg before I even got there. They allowed him the power to believe his own hype — to believe he was something that, in retrospect, he really wasn't. I blame the machine for this one; I truly do. Bill Goldberg has too big a heart — as I witnessed when I saw him many times around kids — to be a bad guy. I confirmed this to myself a few months later when Eric Bischoff and I asked Bill Goldberg to turn heel — and he just couldn't do it. His response was, "What will the kids think?" Whereas many laughed at him, I truly believed him. I truly believed that those kids meant everything to the guy.

To this day I wish things could have been different between the two of us.

Another wcw star with a temper was the same guy I scripted to beat Bill Goldberg: "Big Poppa Pump" Scott Steiner. I literally — *literally* — witnessed Scott Steiner foaming at the mouth as he went off on a female producer who gave him the wrong answer. But here's the big difference between Scott Steiner and Bill Goldberg. Every single time Scott Steiner would get into one of his tirades, I would stop and look at him, and he would stop . . . and look at me . . . and then Scott Steiner's face would light up like Christmas morning and he would burst out in laughter. With Scott I totally understood that he was well aware of having to maintain a certain persona behind the scenes. He knew that people perceived Big Poppa Pump a certain way, so — not wanting to let anybody down — Scott Steiner would become Big Poppa Pump in the locker room. However, once you were on to him, and once you understood his mindset and what was actually going on, Scott Steiner would let you in on the joke.

With Bill Goldberg, it wasn't a joke. Goldberg bought into the phenomenon that was created for him. Goldberg never let you in on it . . . because there was nothing to ever let you in on. It was real. And it was created by those who created him.

Not the Same Guy

I just came off a four-day road trip this past week. And so I wanted to make sure that I spent some time with my 17-year-old son, vj. At this point, vj is a massive ball of confusion. With high school graduation less than three months away, he is at the point of trying to decide what to do with the rest of his life. Like any other 20-year-old, that mountainous decision is taking its toll on him. It also doesn't help that he spends a lot of time at his brother Will's apartment, getting schooled philosophically by four 20-year-olds who haven't got the slightest clue.

My older son, Will, and his three roommates — his cousin Greg and two others he grew up with in Atlanta — are in that post-teen, anti-establishment mode. At times, I really don't know if that truly is their mindset, or if the fact of the matter is that they just hate to work. They'll find every excuse out there to not have to join the rat race and make a living. On the surface, their arguments sound good at times, but having been there and done that, they're just so unrealistic. They'll argue with the passion of the Christ how they don't need money, they loathe money, and they protest the "ways of the world." One of their favorite movies is *Into the Wild*, about a 20-something who after graduating college burned all the money he had, ditched his car and lived in the wild of Alaska. This film is their Bible — as I'm sure it is for many kids that age who are too lazy to work. The hysterical thing about the movie is at the finish — since the guy has no dough and the only thing around him is moose — he is forced to eat shrubbery. Unfortunately, one of the plants was poisonous and the dude was dead before his 25th birthday.

But in getting back to vj, there is nothing like the fear of the unknown, especially at that age. As his father, all I can do is listen and tell him that everything will be all right. My instinct is to tell him that there's no need to worry because God is in charge and he just needs to have faith, pray and follow his heart, which will lead to the road that has been paved for him. But, as many parents know, at his age that isn't what a kid wants to hear. Even though he doesn't see it now, he will eventually walk right into it.

So in getting back to the time we spent together, VJ was talking to me about his outlook on life, the latest book he's reading, his cerebral take on *No Country for Old Men* and what makes good music. I'd never tell my own son this, but his conversation is *way* over his old man's head. I mean, how did this kid turn out to be so smart when his father is a moron? The reality of my life is I just came off a road trip where the topics of conversation were Adam West's *Batman*; who's better out of the Three Stooges, Abbott and Costello, or the Marx Brothers; and "Just how ignorant *is* Glenn Gilberti?" That's what we — grown men — talked about for four days. So when VJ hits me with knowledge and wisdom my instinct is to just give him a Moe Howard finger poke, right between the eyes. However, somewhere between his diatribes about legendary black jazz musicians and what makes Woody Allen as great as he is, VJ mentioned to me that he recently saw some old clips of me on YouTube. He described how I was in rare form, berating Mike Tenay while wielding a black Louisville Slugger. He then turned to me and said, "Man, Dad — that was another guy."

And today, I am another guy. I can sit here and type to you all day long about how God changed me inside out, but wrestling fans being the skeptics they are will never believe me. Since I made the transition almost five years ago, wrestling critics are still trying to figure out my angle. How is Vince capitalizing on this, financially? Now don't misunderstand me: every day that I walk this earth, I'm as much a sinner as the next guy — we can't help it; that's our nature — but I try to let God shine through me every second of every day by the way I carry myself. VJ making that statement to me fills my heart with joy, knowing that my own son sees a difference. A difference that was impossible for me to make myself no matter how committed I was, or how hard I tried.

You know I get e-mails on a weekly basis, mainly from fans who want the writing style of the "old" Vince to return. What they don't understand is that since the "old" Vince doesn't exist any more, neither does his writing style. Boys and girls, I'm not the same guy, and I can't write the same way I did ten years ago — it's just not in me. Back in the heyday of the mid- to late

'90s, I was overflowing with you-know-what and vinegar. (See? I couldn't even say it.) My body was filled with such a venomous hatred that it's even hard for me to explain, or fathom. That overwhelming feeling of negativity came out in everything I wrote . . . *everything*. You should have seen my first draft of my first book, all I can say is Lenny Bruce would have been proud.

But my professional attitude didn't just change on paper — it changed on television as well. I can remember an incident when SEX (Sports Entertainment Xtreme) was running rampant in TNA. At the height and fury of one of my in-ring promos, I winged a full water bottle as hard as I could at Don West, literally as hard as I could. Thankfully, Don got out of the way. But looking back now, I can't even comprehend that I did that. I mean, I could have seriously hurt someone who I honestly cared about. It's no secret why Mike Tenay hated me back then. At the time, out of character I considered myself a good guy, with a good heart, but when that camera came on, it was my true feelings and true emotions that came out — how I really felt inside: the hatred, the violence . . . the pain. That's why so many people bought into the character. It never came across as acting because, in retrospect, it wasn't. Being that character gave me the license to turn myself inside-out and really show you the mess I had become. It also gave me the liberty to say, Hey, I'm not that guy — it's just a part I play.

I'll never forget an incident that happened after I became saved that clearly told me that something out of this world had occurred. I was doing a small independent show for a friend of mine, Derek Gordon, in New York. To this day I generally refuse to do indies, but when I get the chance to go home, I pounce. So, in laying out the script to me that night, Derek was all jacked up because it was going to be the return of Vince Russo, the heel. At that time I was featured on TNA television — but as a babyface. Derek really believed that this would be great, especially to the hometown crowd in NYC. But when I got in the ring and did what he wanted to me to, I soon realized that I just couldn't do it anymore. There wasn't one ounce of hatred left in my body for me to pull from. For the first time, I felt like I was acting and I knew that was exactly the way it was coming across. After that performance, I had to pull myself off future shows, turning down good money in the process, because I knew that the old Vince wasn't coming back.

So in the future, save the e-mails; the blood, the violence, the vulgarity isn't coming back any time soon. At least not from my pen. There's a much bigger empty white page out there. One that I choose to fill with stories that may enlighten you or, God forbid, make you laugh.

Vertigo

You probably figured out that it wasn't too difficult for me to make the transition from behind the scenes to in front of the camera. Having just been blatantly tackled by the political machine within WCW, I was fueled with venom. That was the great thing about performing at the time. Being a character on TV gave me a platform to release all the poison that was stored up in my body. You see, as Vince Russo the human being, I am very passive and have always been that way, but as Vince Russo the *character*, I said what was on my mind, regardless of how vicious it was.

The first promo I cut to kick off the New Blood vs. Millionaire's Club era more or less set the stage for the entire company's mind-set at the time. Since there was in-fighting going on at every turn, we might as well make money with it. I always felt that in wrestling — that's what made a great performer. When you legitimately had issues with someone, but you were professional enough to play things out in front of the camera *with* them in order to make money. To me, those types of scenarios were magic, mainly because there was no acting involved. If you shoot on somebody, that usually is coming from the heart. If there is even a shred of reality in your words, those watching at home are going to believe you. That's why I feel that performers always need to draw from something real.

What's ridiculous, however, is when two performers have an issue behind the scenes, but they aren't professional enough to take the story to the screen. And I've seen that many times in the business: where the hatred was so real that one performer would just refuse to work with another. Can you imagine how great the Bret Hart/Shawn Michaels real-life soap opera would have played out in *front* of the camera, rather than them pulling each other's hair out in a locker room shower scene that very few saw? Man, Jeff Jarrett and I have played out some great stories together on TV when we had some legitimate heat. Why? Because we knew it was the best thing for business. There is no issue in this world that can't be resolved — none — and you might as well make some money with it before you get there.

That's why following Bash at the Beach, I would have begged to work with Hulk Hogan. Not because I had any issues with him — because I had *zero* — but because I knew he had notebooks full of grievances with me. Unfortunately, Hogan was one of those guys who let his personal issues affect his professional life, so the Hogan/Russo feud never played out on TV.

Preparing myself to rant and rave in front of a television camera was one thing, but preparing to get into that ring against guys who made a living of doing this was another. You know, if you're going to step between the ropes you immediately think, "Oh, my God — I have to learn how to work!" Although that is the way the mind is trained, the notion is absolutely ridiculous. First off, I was 39 at the time; secondly, *I wasn't a wrestler!* But again, that's a case of the dirt sheet writers finding a way to get into your head. I could see their words before I even started: "Russo's a terrible worker!" Of course I was, because I wasn't one! So that's the theory I went with. As a figure in management, I wasn't supposed to know a lick about how to work a match; however in my arrogance and innocence, I was actually going to talk myself into believing that I could take this guy.

My first match was booked inside a steel cage at the Phillips Arena in Atlanta against Ric Flair on a live *Nitro*. Going in, Ric was great. Granted, he probably hated the whole idea — at the beginning — but he was a pro nonetheless. A few days before the event, Ric met me at WCW's training facility, the Power Plant, and laid out the entire match. I hung on his every word because to me this was no different than Will Clark telling me how to hit a curve ball. Flair was great with me; he was patient and never, ever condescending, even though he was one of the greatest to ever play the game and I didn't have a clue. He was a gentlemen and as respectful to me as I was to him.

The night of the show there was a huge house; no doubt they were paying to see the legendary Nature Boy kick the attitude out of the arrogant New Yawker. Was I nervous? Not as much as I thought I would be. I was focused on not screwing up, and not making Ric look bad — that's the only thing I feared. My words here can't express the respect I had for him, and still do. Now, with hindsight being 20/20, I fully understand that nobody could have made Ric Flair look bad in a wrestling ring — including me.

Things went according to plan as I did everything the exact same way Flair had shown me at the Power Plant. A few minutes in, Flair took me down with a Russian Leg Sweep, and, while I remember trampolining my head off the canvas, I felt absolutely no pain because my adrenaline was racing at a fever pitch. I remember being so locked in that night that I didn't even acknowledge the crowd — the thousands who were in attendance, including members of my own family. I was so intent on not screwing up and embarrassing Ric that I tuned everything else out. At one point I can remember climbing out of the cage with Ric in tow, soon finding myself perched over 15 feet in the air on the steel structure. Keeping in mind that this was my first attempt at a match I was hell-bent on proving to Ric, the boys and the fans that I could play on their canvas.

Standing high atop the cage, I never stopped to realize either the danger or how ignorant I was. I had no business being there — I wasn't a wrestler. But again, with all my critics watching — and each one desperate to see me fail — I was more determined than at any other point in my life. As Ric and I fought back into the cage, the finish was near. The plan was that he was supposed to get me in the figure-four in the middle of the ring, but before I tapped out, blood was supposed to be dropped on him from high atop the arena ceiling — the calling card of the New Blood. Again, going off without a hitch, Ric got me in the middle of the ring and wrapped me up in his signature move. I slapped the canvas with everything I had — for what felt like days — but for some reason the blood never came. I remember screaming in agony, for what felt like hours — but still no blood. Laying in the middle of the ring, I started to feel dizzy and confused — discombobulated. At the time I just thought it was my blood pressure, being that I was pumping everything I had into the theatrics. I remember almost passing out, just not being able to sell for a moment longer when finally the blood was dropped, forcing Ric to release the hold. To tell you the truth, I really don't remember the finish from there. I think I covered Ric for the win, but I'm not sure: look it up on YouTube.

Following the match, I went to the back and the rest is just a blur — I don't remember who patted me on the back and who didn't. The truth is, I didn't care. What mattered is that I didn't embarrass myself — or more importantly, Ric. I remember someone telling that it took so long for them to shower the blood from the arena ceiling because Ric wasn't on his mark. Ric Flair not on his mark? That's the equivalent of Pavarotti just being off a few notes. To this day, I still question that. Was it a last-minute sabotage?

Knowing the makings of the wrestling bubble . . . perhaps. But regardless, I had achieved everything I set out to do that night. But in the process I also learned a very important lesson: I wasn't a wrestler. That night, after being a fan for well over 25 years, I realized first-hand that these guys were pros and the best in world at what they did. I was out of my league — and that was cool with me. Again, I was driven to that spot by those who were rooting quietly on the sidelines to see me fail. Never at any point had I disrespected their craft, or felt that "anybody could do it" because the truth is, only a very few can. Working in the business now since 1991, I can tell you that a good percentage of the boys who make their profession as profession wrestlers *still* can't do it. It's not just about spots, or suicide moves that just don't make sense. It's not the flash, the moonsaults, or the diving over the top rope. It's the science — the science that begins once that bell rings. That's what so many hopefuls today just don't understand, both inside and out of the business.

On that night in the Phillips Arena I was in there with the best. I had both the honor and the privilege of having a front row seat to witness how this thing was supposed to be done. It was art and the ring was Ric Flair's canvas. There are very few things I appreciate more than that night. That's why I will forever be grateful for Ric Flair, not only on a professional level, but on a personal one as well.

Knowing that we had a *Thunder* taping the following day in a nearby town, I left the Phillips Arena the moment the show ended to get home and get some much-needed rest. It was going to be a treat to be able to sleep in the comfort of my own basement. Yes, you heard that right, and my wife is going to kill me for this part — but in a tell-all, you tell *all!* Looking back, I think it was the trauma of my first three months at wcw that sent me to sleep in the finished basement of my house for almost the next eight years. That's right: for nearly eight years Amy and I didn't sleep in the same bed. No, it had absolutely nothing to do with marital problems whatsoever; the truth is in our almost 25-year marriage we've had very few problems. No, what drove me to eight years in the "dungeon," as Amy affectionately refers to it, was simply depression and stress.

It seems that the first day I started working at wcw was also the first night I stopped sleeping. Slowly, over a very short period of time, I would find myself wide awake at two, three, sometimes four o'clock in the morning. In the past, in fact throughout my entire life, the boob tube had always acted as my Nytol. As long as something was playing in the background, I would visit dreamland without any hitches. This ritual started probably somewhere at around age ten. I always slept with a television at my bedside; to this day there's no hope of me getting to sleep without one. However, once I moved to Atlanta, I could have been sleeping in a Circuit City showroom and it wouldn't have mattered. I couldn't catch a single Z no matter how long or how hard I chased them. Every night I would find myself watching Tony Little infomercials with the sun rising just outside the window. As I stated earlier, this is how and where I met Don West: hawking baseball cards at around the same time that children across the country were getting up for school. And night after night after night, I would get more and more pissed off at myself. All I wanted to do was sleep! Knowing that I would be keeping Amy up all night with the TV on, I soon started nesting in the basement. What started as my "temporary" living condition soon became my permanent bed. The minute Amy would turn in upstairs, I would head downstairs. After a few months it just turned into the norm. Even though I knew this wasn't healthy for our relationship I felt I had no other option. I wasn't going to keep my wife up all night because of my insomnia.

Surprisingly, that particular night following my match with Flair, I slept better than usual. Whether it was the euphoria of getting it all behind me or just the impact of the adrenaline crash, it seemed like I was out the moment my head hit the couch. I remember sleeping through the night, something I hadn't done since the confines of the basement became home. I awoke early the next morning knowing that I had to get to the next town, when something quite bizarre happened. Upon opening my eyes, I looked at the TV that had been playing all night, and for some reason I couldn't put the picture within the frame of the set. In other words, the television picture was off to the left of where it should have been. I remember blinking a few times, trying to realign the picture, but no matter how many times I did, the picture still wasn't in the box. Feeling both concerned and confused, I then lifted my head off the coach only to experience the room spinning around like I had just experienced a tornado in Oz. Everything was everywhere and it was swirling and swirling fast. I fell to the floor, not understanding what was happening. I tried to pull myself back up, but my head just felt like a carousel, spinning round and round. The feeling was sickening; a surge of nausea soon came over me as I slumped to the floor again. Finally, I had to call for Amy as the slightest movement of my head sent me off in the cyclone again. I had no idea what was happening to me; I just knew that I had never experienced anything like this in my life.

Amy soon came downstairs and helped me up. I told her that everything was okay because I didn't want to alarm her. I asked her to give me a second as I would get back up on my feet shortly. Using the couch as a crutch, I attempted to push myself again, only to crumble back down to the floor. Now in a slight panic, I crawled over to the stairs and pulled myself up one-by-one until I made it to the cold kitchen floor. At this point Amy was real concerned, as was I. I just didn't know what was going on. Amy helped me over to a chair where I sat down, collected my thoughts and tried to make sense of this thing. I kept wondering how on earth I was able to drive home the night before feeling like this now. Did I hit my head? I don't remember doing so. However, keeping that train of thought I went back to that match with Flair the night before. Then it became clear to me. That simple Russian Leg Sweep early in the match — I forgot to tuck my head. Something so simple that wrestlers learn the first day on the job, I had failed to do. Now, the feeling of dizziness I suffered throughout the course of the match all made sense to me. At the time the adrenaline was masking it, but this morning the rush had subsided and I was feeling the full effect.

Bill Banks was supposed to pick me up in an hour and drive me to *Thunder* as I pondered how I was going to just make it through the day, let alone go to work and perform. Remember, in my line of work not only was there no sick, but I was now quickly coming to the realization that there were no concussions either. Again, how would my peers perceive me? One match, one little concussion and he can't come to work? They would be laughing at me and I wouldn't allow it. So despite Amy's pleading, I gathered myself, got dressed and headed out to the building.

The car ride was torture from every turn to every stop and go. I remember asking myself over and over, How are you going to do this? I knew that aside from Bill, I couldn't let anyone else know. I couldn't "sell it"; that was just part of the wrestler's code. If you got hurt, you didn't sell it. Or show it. Where this tradition derived from, I have no idea. I guess it came from the idea that if a wrestler was injured and he let it on to the promoter, then the promoter wouldn't book him, costing the wrestler a pay day. I knew it had something to do with that — but I also knew it had something to do with ego. Remember, Vince McMahon taught me that there was no sick, and if there was no sick, there certainly was no getting hurt. So, I did what I always do in a situation like that: I sucked it up. I reached down with everything I had, took a deep breath, and packed it all down to the base of my gut. "Suck it up" — something I have been preaching to my kids since they were first able to walk without holding on.

Upon entering the building I can remember attempting to take baby steps while trying not to let on that something was wrong. Everything was spinning around and the vertigo was making me sick to my stomach. I knew in wrestling that the show had to go on no matter what, but I also knew that the longest day of my life was ahead of me. Soon some of the boys began asking what was wrong being that no matter how much I tried to downplay it, they knew I wasn't being myself. I shrugged it off, just telling them that I bumped my head in the match the night before. Man, even though I already had all the respect in the world for the boys, this experience brought it to a whole new galaxy. The guys wrestle with concussions *daily*; to them it's no more than having a splinter. I can't talk for other sports, but these guys are warriors — working through every known injury and never, never letting you know just how serious it may be. Walking the halls that day while bracing myself against the walls, I realized that not only *wasn't* I a warrior, I had no interest in being one. I also understood that I had no business playing in their world, or attempting to paint on their canvas.

That's why from the start this thing wasn't about ego, or wanting to be on TV. The reason was simply because this wasn't any fun for me. My job was to write and produce the show and that's what I did best. I didn't sign up to get my coconut bounced off a mat, or to experience what it would be like to rode Coney Island's Cyclone for 24 straight hours. I wasn't an athlete, nor did I think I was one. I had nothing to prove to the boys on that level — *nothing*. They were the pros and I was the Joe and I had no problem with that. But again, I was so driven not to fail that at this point in the game I would have probably gotten in a boxing ring with Mike Tyson in his prime.

You know, there's one rule that up until this point I had always lived up to: when you attempt to be something you're not, that's when you get yourself in trouble.

Ladies and gentlemen, boys and girls, cats and dogs, that is the golden rule. There is no question in my mind that that life lesson comes directly from God Himself. I truly believe that God created every single one of us with a purpose. He created all of us differently, giving us different gifts that we are to use to fulfill our calling. Those gifts live in our hearts, and if we follow them, we have found our purpose in life. However, if we go down another road — one that we know we weren't meant to tread — that's when we get ourselves in all kinds of trouble.

I knew at that time I wasn't supposed to tread anywhere near a wrestling ring; however, you couldn't tell that to my drive and my passion. I was going to achieve success no matter what the price was to pay — whether it be spiritually, mentally or physically.

Somehow, some way, I got through that day. I remember the show was based around busing in senior citizens from an "old folks' home," and they were going to throw one of their own — Ric Flair — a surprise party. At the end of the skit I was to get myself in a compromising position, only to wind up face first through the cake the old fogies had made for the Nature Boy. The show went off without a hitch, but to this day I don't know how.

Going home that night and waking up the next morning, there is no doubt I had a severe concussion; that was later confirmed at the emergency ward. Whereas that is no biggie to a wrestler, believe me, it is to a writer. In getting back behind the pencil, the first thing I realized was that no matter how hard I tried, no matter how hard I dug in, I just couldn't concentrate on my craft. To me, writing is all about getting in a zone. You put your blinders on, close out the rest of the world, and it's you and that screen. From the first freelance story I ever wrote for the *WWF Magazine* in 1993, up until this point, that is my ritual. When I'm writing I don't hear the TV, I don't hear the kids and I certainly don't hear the wife. As Amy likes to put it, I go off in my own little world, never to be heard from again until that final bell rings at the end of the last match. Not being able to concentrate clearly put a damper on my writing. I mean, I had the attention span of a seventh grader sitting through an algebra class. Everything would distract me: every movement, every sound. What would once take me an hour to write now took three. But again, it didn't matter — nothing was going to stop me and nobody was going to stand in my way.

As we began to build the New Blood vs. the Millionaire's Club angle, the script called for me to further put myself in harm's way week after week. My role as a cocky and brash New Yawker was working because I wasn't hard to hate. Everybody hates a Northerner who thinks he's better then everybody else; just ask Jim Cornette. At the time it was unbelievable to me to see how the fans were actually buying into it. I mean, I was hated at arenas — cursed both inside and outside the building. I was hated on the Internet — hated — with a great deal of it having to do with people thinking that Vince Russo really was that guy he portrayed on TV. For me, the role was easy to play; it was just my New Yawk personality magnified 1,000-fold to become a larger-than-life character. What also didn't hurt was the fuel in my belly at the time. Having a huge target on my head in real life made it real simple for me to portray a screw-you attitude through my character. Unfortunately, whereas talking was my strong point, getting physically involved was another matter. Again, label me paranoid, but every time I stepped into that ring, with the boys knowing my condition at the time, it was only a matter of seconds before they landed one on my aching melon. Coincidence? Maybe. Sending a message? More than likely. One week it was Ernest Miller, the next week it was Scott Steiner; every week it would be somebody else. And you know what? They had every right in the world to do it. In their minds, I was an outsider who crossed the line into their world. Although they really had no idea what my motivations were — they didn't care — I was in a place I shouldn't have been in: their world. Again, it all goes back to trying to be something you're not.

While I constantly tried to no-sell, my physical state wasn't getting better; in fact it was getting worse . . . much worse. I could feel myself just falling deeper and deeper into depression. Everything just seemed so dark, like a Salvador Dali painting. I knew something was seriously wrong, but I also knew that no matter what it was, I wasn't letting up. With each passing day the symptoms seemed to get worse and worse. Every time I cut a promo in the ring I felt like I was just going to collapse. I would become real dizzy, real fast, and I could actually feel my blood pressure rising in my body, sometimes to the point that I thought it would explode straight through my head. The feeling was almost indescribable. I can't even fathom Troy Aikman playing with one concussion — let alone 20.

At the time, the only escape I had was my "man-cave." When I was home, every night after experiencing yet another day of hell I would escape down to my safe haven. There wasn't even any point of turning on a light; no matter how many watts would burn, my world at the time was blacker than the desk I'm currently writing on. It was on those nights, in that basement, that my next symptom would rear its ugly head. No matter what was on TV or what channel it was on, I would find myself sobbing over the show. Whether it was a talk show, *Judge Judy*, a sappy movie or *Lifetime*, I would sit downstairs on my couch in the dark and sob. Not cry, but sob; big difference. Yeah — I guess this is how "Vince Russo killed WCW." A grown man, sobbing in his basement, single-handedly killed a multi-million-dollar company. No, critics, WCW was clearly killing Vince Russo. The circumstances had made me a shell of who I used to be while helping guide the WWF to the greatest heights it had ever seen. I wasn't even a man anymore; men don't act this way. Knowing that this wasn't of the norm, I went back to the head doctor. Upon finishing his examination he said, "Vince, the good news is that you're past the concussion. The bad news is that you now have *post*-concussion syndrome. That's why you're crying over *Scooby-Doo*."

Man, it was just a bad time. What should have been perhaps the most enjoyable time of my life was simply becoming the worst. Aside from my physical issues, Eric and I just didn't trust each other and you just can't work with an individual under those circumstances. And, let me say that Eric gave me no reason not to trust him — I want to make that clear — but knowing him, and knowing his drive, there is no question that he wanted to be the one calling the shots. He wanted to be back in the saddle again, having only been thrown off the horse three months earlier. With the landscape the way it was at the top, the locker room was clearly starting to divide. Money players were going to one side, while the mid-carders who wanted to be main-eventers were going to the other. A volcano was going to erupt, and no question, it was coming sooner rather than later. The only questions were who would be involved and where would it take place.

Not Only Is He Killing WCW — Now He's a Racist!

March 20, 2008

It's been about seven years since the horrifying nightmare of wcw, yet to this day there are remnants, memories, that surface.

I'm not going to get specific, but recently someone has once again brought up that, while at wcw, Vince Russo was a racist. I don't know — maybe it's another case of a wrestler dragging everybody he holds a grudge against through the mud, hurting innocent victims along the way, in order to claim a big pay day that he didn't have to work for. Again, I'm not sure — just guessing — but to that individual, who I won't mention by name, shame on you.

You can say whatever you want about me professionally — I suck, I don't have a clue about booking, I killed wcw, I'm an ego-maniac, I ripped off Paul Heyman, I'm a Vince McMahon wannabe, whatever you want — and I'm fine with that. Last I checked, this is America, and we're all entitled to our opinion. But when you attack my character, that's something that I won't stand for. Being called a racist by those looking to make a quick, easy, *unearned* buck cuts me deeply. The truth is that it hurts now more than ever being that I just lost my best friend, the godfather of my son and the best man at my wedding, to a sudden heart attack at the age of 46. His name was Jeff Iorio, and I will talk about him more later, but what hurts the most about being called a racist, is that the one human being who I loved more than any other outside my family was of Puerto Rican descent.

Now I can go on a tirade hear about what I feel I've actually *done* for minorities in the business since I've been a part of it, but there's no need to. I know the truth and if you look at my history you'll know it too. What's fascinating to me is that a certain someone labeled me a racist at wcw, when the facts will tell you that on my very first day on the job there, Rey Mysterio Jr. and Konnan won the WCW Tag Team Titles. That fact alone makes those accusations absolutely ludicrous.

But since this is my book, and I swear to God above that I will tell you the truth, it's time for me to set the record straight once and for all.

The "racist" label came into play shortly after I first met Ernest Miller at wcw. While still with the wwf, I had become a huge Ernest Miller mark watching him on *Nitro*. To me, the guy had more charisma then anybody else on the entire wcw roster. In my opinion he was drastically under-utilized, and upon my hiring at wcw, I wanted to get Ernest more in the mix. So obviously I was eager to meet him and pick his brain. Sometime during our first conversation, Ernest asked me about his manager, who happened to be of Japanese descent. I told Ernest that I honestly felt that he didn't need a mouthpiece, or anybody talking for him for that matter, because he just dripped charisma.

So based on those last few paragraphs we've narrowed a few things down. I can't be racist towards those of Mexican or Puerto Rican descent, being that I put the tag straps on Rey Mysterio and Konnan on my first night on the job, and I can't be racist towards African-Americans because I just admitted to being an Ernest Miller mark, so at this point I guess I'm racist towards Japanese people because I felt that Ernest Miller didn't need a manager.

But wait . . . the story gets better.

Sometime later I'm interviewed by someone writing either for a wrestling dirt sheet or a wrestling website — can't remember; they're one and the same. Anyway, the question is asked: what are my thoughts on foreign wrestlers? My answer was simple, and it's the same answer I would give today. When it comes to foreign wrestlers competing in the United States, there are two huge obstacles to overcome. Problem #1: Many of them wear masks. In my opinion, it is very hard for the fan at home to relate to someone who's hiding behind a mask. Wearing a mask, you take away one of your strongest weapons in getting over with the fans: your emotions. When they can't read your face, they can't get a true read on what you're feeling. Are you sincere? Are you lying? Are you concerned, or not really worried about it? Facial expressions just tell so much; that's why I always tell the guys to take off their sunglasses during interviews — that plus the fact that the sun isn't glaring down on them on the interview set. Problem #2: Language barrier. If the wrestler speaks a different language, and the American fan at home doesn't understand that language, then Houston, we've got a problem. Sure, you can give him an American mouthpiece, but then the spotlight goes on the mouthpiece and not the wrestler. How are you supposed to get over a wrestler when the fans don't understand what he's saying? Very difficult to do — I'm not saying it can't be done, but very difficult to do. The proof? Go through those notecards in your brain and come up with a list of *five* foreign language–speaking wrestlers who wore masks and who got over with some success in this country.

My statement was based on both opinion and fact. It had absolutely nothing to do with the color of anybody's skin. If you can get over, I'm going to help you get over — I could care less if you're a mountain goat! And as far as being racist towards the Japanese, the truth is that I just haven't worked with many of them in my career. Why? Because most of them are working in Japan! But I will tell you this: I was a huge mark of Mr. Fuji and Professor Taru Tanaka and I draft Ichiro on my fantasy baseball team every year.

Anyway, getting back to that interview, of course dirt sheet writers do what dirt sheet writers do, and I should have known better; they take everything out of context. So of course my words were completely twisted around to make it look like I had it out for all the Mexican and Japanese wrestlers in the world. Take that along with a bitter, unemployed Japanese manager, and Vince Russo is a racist.

Man, now more than ever the old Vince is begging to come out here. He's screaming right inside my left ear saying, Name names! Tell them how you really feel about them! But no matter how much I want to, I just can't. No matter how badly people hurt you, at the end of the day, no matter how difficult it may be, you need to forgive and love.

Out of this fabricated racist thing, the one thing that hurt me the most didn't actually involve me, but rather an innocent individual who I'll always have a soft spot for: Booker T.

Man, not to get all warm and gooey here, but I love Booker T. When all the chaos was swirling around wcw with the impact of Typhoon Mary, Booker T was the calm, soothing ocean. No matter how hectic things got, he was always the same guy: respectful, agreeable, professional and always smiling form ear to ear. It was guys like Book who allowed hope to stay alive inside of me. At the base of my very core I always knew that I was in the business for guys like him.

One day at a booking meeting, I went around the entire table and asked everyone, "If you were to switch the title right now, who would you put it on?" The answer was unanimous — not 5 to 2, or even 6 to 1 — but unanimous. Almost in harmony, the room sang: "Booker T." My next question was why? Again, unanimously: "Because he's a company guy." So at that point, it was simply a no-brainer. When I then asked the group, "Well then, why don't we put the belt on him?" there was no answer . . . silence. So at that point I made my decision: Booker T was going to become the new WCW World Champion, for the first time, at Bash at the Beach.

Man, this should have been storybook. Here was a guy who paid his dues, came up through the ranks, never played a single political game, had been passed over time and time again while never speaking up, who was finally getting his due. This story should have been celebrated in the circles of professional wrestling — but of course it wasn't. Why? Because at the time, that certain Japanese gentleman I mentioned earlier riled up a disgruntled employee or two in the wcw ranks and rallied them to file a racism lawsuit against wcw. In the face of this, well, there was good old Vince Russo, putting the title on Booker . . . to prove that neither he nor wcw as a company was racist.

To this day that story makes me want to vomit. I'm sorry, I can't put it in a nicer way. What was going on at the time with the lawsuit had nothing to do with our decision — *nothing* — and you can ask anybody who was in that room. At the end of the day, it wasn't me who was being discredited — I had already been labeled a racist — it was Booker T. The guy who earned everything single thing he had ever gotten.

What a damn shame.

Prelude to Bash at the Beach

When I hit my 20s, while going to school in Evansville, Indiana, I became obsessively goal-orientated. I guess that had to do with so much being on my plate all the time. By the time I reached sophomore status I was editor of the student newspaper and vice president of my fraternity, Sigma Tau Gamma, while holding down not one job but two. It was during this time that I really became driven. However, as I looked ahead to my future, my main goal was quite reachable and fairly innocent.

You see, I never dreamed about making millions of dollars; the truth is that never in my life had I — or have I — been driven by money. But back in my college days the plan was simple: I just wanted to get up every day and go to a job I enjoyed. To me, the most depressing thing for anybody, man or woman, is when they have to drag themselves up every morning and force themselves to go to a job that they absolutely despise. At that point in my life in college I had been there, done that — and wasn't going back. You see, I was never a big fan of high school, and as a matter of fact wanted to get out so badly that I doubled up on some credits and graduated after my junior year. From there I went to a community college, only to drop out because I wasn't ready. How could I have been ready when all my friends were still in high school? So from there, I had to find a job — a full-time job. At the time my father was working for a company called Hazeltine that dealt in defense government contracting. In doing his son a favor, like all good parents do, my father was able to pull a string on two, and get me a position in his company. Having no idea what I was going to be doing wasn't a concern at all. At least now I was no longer going to carry the moniker "college drop-out," but rather the proud flag of "full-time employee."

Man, a paycheck for 40 hours a week — I was rich! This was a far cry from washing dishes for a few bucks a month at Howard Johnson's while going through high school. You see? I didn't have to go through four years of college to be a major success — I was already there! I knew it would be this easy! The guidance counselor at school, my parents — they didn't know anything!

That was until I became fourth man on an assembly line.

Since a big part of Hazeltine's business was making PC boards for defensive military equipment, I immediately found myself on a six-man assembly line putting the same chip in the same board for the same eight hours a day. The process would start with the first guy, who put in his part and hand it to the second guy, who put in his part, to the third guy, and on and on and on. With all the potential that I knew I had, I was being used as a brainless, emotionless zombie, and I was barely 18 years old.

I'll never forget going home after my first day on the job and just crying like a child who had just been slapped for the first time. Ironically, that was exactly what had happened, but the backhand didn't come from a well-intentioned parent; it came from the cold, harsh world that didn't care a lick about me. Was this the American Dream? Was this what it was supposed to be all about? After getting a dose of reality for about a week, I soon realized that there was no getting around an education. I had to get myself back in school if I wanted any kind of a career. Unfortunately, the new semester had already begun, so I was going to have to wait for the fall to come around again. Even though I knew what I had to do, my dilemma was now how was I ever going to stay alive in this godforsaken place putting little parts in littler boards for the next eight months?

Jim Russo didn't have a lot of stroke, but he had some. The problem my father has always been faced with throughout his entire life was that at no point could he ever throw his weight around because he was only 140 pounds . . . soaking wet! And at five-eight, he wasn't scaring anybody! My dad was one of the good guys — and still is to this day. You wanted something done, you went to Jim. While this may have never catapulted him to the top of the food chain, it worked for him because he was so well liked and respected. And my dad, he didn't care — he was never about the money either. He just wanted to earn his paycheck so he could support his family . . . and then go play softball. That was his passion; I swear to you, the game after work was more important to him then work itself. He played during the week for

Hazeltine, and on weekends with the neighborhood team. And Fruity — that's my crazy, Italian mother — she *hated* it.

If you're Italian and grew up during the '60s and '70s, you understand that every Sunday you went to your grandparents' house — mother's side — religiously. No matter what. It was no different then going to school during the week; it was simply a matter of fact. So there we were every Sunday morning, all dressed up . . . with no place to go until my father's game was over! Every Sunday you could count on Fruitsy waiting for my father just inside the door. Then, the moment his red Chevy Vega pulled up, she flung that door open and had at Jim. She would cut promos on him that not even the Nature Boy was capable of. My mother would blame everything on Jim's playing ball — from the reason why we were late going to my grandparents all the way up to the Kennedy assassination. And Jim? He did the same thing then that he does to this very day, some 40 years later (yes, he still play softball at 77): he somehow, some way tuned her out. How he did this, and continues to do this, I have no idea. I mean she would be all over him like a child on their weekly allowance. Ranting and raving about the heinous crime he just committed. But Jim? He nonchalantly walked into the house, got out of his Pig Pen–like uniform, showered and got in the car — never saying a word. To this day the man's a saint — I mean you would have to be in order to be married to the Fruitinator for over 50 years!

So, getting back to Hazeltine, I had to ask Jim to implement the little stroke that he did have. Wielding his mighty softball bat, Jim was able to get me off the assembly line and into a position as an "expeditor." An expeditor was a person who tracked down various parts within the company that individual departments needed in order to fulfill their orders. You see, Hazeltine consisted of ten buildings over a mile radius and there were parts scattered everywhere throughout the various buildings. So every day, my boss would give me a list of what I needed to find for who, and I was off. Are you getting the beauty of this yet? Ten buildings within a ten mile radius? I could be at any one at any time? In other words, my boss never had any idea where I was. And if I told him I was either here or there, he more or less had to take my word for it. Thank God there was no such thing as cell phones at this point or else this scam would have never worked for me. What scam, you ask?

Let me explain. At about nine o'clock every morning, my boss would give me a list of the parts I needed to track down that day. Without hesitation, I would race from building to building, gather all the parts, and usually be done by lunch. Now, my unsuspecting boss had no idea that I was able to find the elusive things in such a short period of time. As long as I had the parts by the end of the day he would be tickled. So, every day at about noon, I would gather my old friend from the assembly line, Hector, who was a Hazeltine vet and close to 20 years my senior. (Hector? Wasn't he of Puerto Rican decent? Why was a racist like me hanging around with him? Hmm?) Anyway, Hector and I would get in my car and head to Aqueduct Raceway, every day, to bet on the ponies. So, while my boss John Gordon assumed I was in Building Four or Building Ten, I was putting ten bucks on the nose of Lucky Pete to win. Believe it or not, my boss never caught on to this. Looking back now I clearly understand that if he did, it wouldn't have looked too good for my dad. On second thought, he probably wouldn't have really cared — as long as there was a game that day.

My point? I understood at an early age what it felt like to go to work every day and feel miserable. I was never going to put myself in that situation again. Sitting on that assembly line day after day made me fully understand that nobody was going to hand anything to me — that if I wanted a better life then I had to work for it. There were no handouts and no free passes in the real world. I was never going back to that assembly line again.

That was until 1999 and wcw.

By this time, my job at wcw had gotten worse than that assembly line ever was — and there was no Hector to escape with to the racetrack every day. There was nothing good about the job — *nothing*. I swear to you, I don't think that George W. Bush himself experienced the stress level that I did at wcw back then. From the politics to my physical well-being and everything else in between — I loathed the situation I was in. And at that time, Eric Bischoff was no help. As a matter of fact, he was probably the straw that broke this writer's back.

I can clearly remember an incident where I knew in my mind I was done with Eric. It was shortly after a *Nitro* where he had once again criticized a segment involving Scott Steiner and a simulated ufc cage. Now again, Eric had seen it all on paper before it even aired, but never said a word until *after* it was televised. This was always his mo and I was tired of it. Whether you're my boss, a consultant or working for me, if you see something isn't going to work, then tell me before we do it, not after. My question: Why wouldn't you? In my mind there was only one answer. You wouldn't tell me if you wanted to see me fail. I remember that day getting off the phone with Eric and literally throwing the phone. I had had enough. I called Brad Siegel and told him to let Eric run the ship. At this point I still didn't know Eric's official role, nor did I care. I was just sick and tired of the criticism after the fact. I would have had no trouble before it, but after it — I just felt that was weak. If he cared so much then why didn't he just sit in with the committee? He was still living in Atlanta at the time — what, he would have to leave his house and travel a few miles? In my mind I just wasn't going to take it any more, not just for my sake, but for the sake of the entire committee. If Eric wanted to be part of the process, then he should have been part of the process. I never would have had a problem with that. But to call it in after the fact — that was hard to swallow.

About a week later, after I washed my hands of it and went home, Brad called a meeting between Eric and me, and I had to fly to LA. At that meeting Brad *still* didn't clarify the roles. I just wanted to blurt out, "Why am I listening to him? Remember, *I* kicked *his* butt at WWF when we were competing head-to-head!" But, out of respect for Eric, I didn't. I knew that there would have been no point in arguing with him. I just wanted to get this thing resolved.

By the end of the meeting, Brad had decided that he was going to give me the ball and let me run with it. He asked me to go back to work and I agreed. I left that meeting with zero confidence — none. I just had a gut feeling that there was much more going on here: a much bigger picture that I just wasn't privy to. Looking back now, I realize that the sale of WCW was already in place. The company had already reached the point of no return and Brad just needed someone to write his TV in the meantime. I don't know if Eric was involved in those business discussions, but in hindsight, he might have been. Remember before Vince McMahon came in, Eric had a buyer for the WCW that he was going to be a part of.

I don't know — I just know that they rolled over too easy and it didn't feel right.

Regardless, I was going back to work . . . again.

My return?

Bash at the Beach.

Bash at the Beach

It's been eight years ... a very long eight years. Never in my wildest dreams did I ever imagine that what happened one Sunday night in Florida would follow me everywhere I went for almost a decade. Never have I been asked the same question so many times. "What *really* happened at Bash at the Beach?" For eight years I've refused to answer that question, mainly because it has been a very difficult memory for me. Much pain came with that incident — pain that I wasn't able to shake until God himself helped me shake it, gave me the strength to forgive, and to forget.

So why now? The answer is simple: I'm going to take a negative, and turn it into a positive. I'm going to take one of the most devastating nights in my life, and use it to illustrate God's glory. I'm not going to lie to you: I needed a hook to bring people to read this book, and this is it. If this story brings you to read this book and witness what God did to change one man's life then my mission has been accomplished.

Before I tell the story — my side of it — I first want to point out that I have no hard feelings towards anyone involved — not one. I understand completely the motivations of the other individuals involved. The fact is, I wasn't shocked or surprised by the outcome; I saw it coming a mile away. But regardless of the consequences, as both a man and a friend, that night I did what I felt I had to do. I did what was right. The important thing is, I came into the situation with my integrity, and I left with it. At the end of the day that's all that ever mattered to me.

I'm going to try to make this as succinct as I possibly can.

It all began after I wrote the script from my home, prior to the

PPV. To be honest, I can't remember exactly the original script, but I believe in the match between Jeff Jarrett and Hulk Hogan I somehow had Scott Steiner involved. Either Hogan was carried out, or he did the laying out — I'm not sure. I just remember that Jeff Jarrett left with his WCW Heavyweight Title. That outcome was vital, because by the end of the night there would be circumstances that led to Jeff having to defend the title against Booker T, and Booker being crowned the new WCW Heavyweight Champion. As I stated earlier in the book, Booker winning the title was something the entire booking committee agreed upon a week prior, simply because Booker deserved it.

Once the script was written, I sent it to John Laurinaitis, who was going to be the agent of the match. Johnny was to call Hulk and get his input. After calling Hulk, Johnny called me back and told me that Hulk hated the way the match was laid out. I said no problem and immediately went back to the drawing board. At that time all I cared about was Jeff leaving the match against Hogan with the belt, so we could get to the Booker scenario. At that point I rewrote the script and implemented a Hulk Hogan King Kong finish. Hulk would clean house and get to Jarrett and Steiner, leaving bodies everywhere, *but* not leaving with the belt. I believe his actions got him Dqed, but honestly I don't remember the exact specifics. Once I came up with that scenario I called Johnny again, who called Hogan again to run it by him. Johnny called me back and said that Hulk "loved" it — something Hulk later denied ever saying. So that discrepancy lies between Hulk and Johnny. I don't know for sure what the conversation was between the two or who said what; I only know what Johnny told me.

Naturally, at that point I figured everybody was happy. The truth is that I wasn't told differently until about two hours prior to the match. While I was going about my business backstage the day of the event, Eric Bischoff approached me to inform me that Hulk didn't like the finish and wasn't going to do it. This was the first time that I was aware that there was a problem. He told me that Hogan was in his trailer and that I needed to go talk to him. So I did.

When I entered the trailer, it was the three of us: myself, Hogan and Bischoff. The first thing I was told by Eric was that he and Hulk had discussed a different finish and that they had called Brad Siegel and that he loved the finish but told them that they had to okay it with me first. At that time Hulk laid out the story. Again, this being eight years ago I can't remember the specifics, but there are two key elements which I will never forget. The first one being that before Hulk laid out the story he said, "Let's do this as if it were a shoot." The second detail was Hulk walking out winning the match and becoming the new WCW Champion. In my mind I knew that couldn't happen, mainly because only days earlier the entire booking committee agreed that it was Booker's time. Not only did I have to stand by their decision, but I also agreed wholeheartedly with it. I felt strongly that Booker needed to leave the building that night the WCW Champion. At the time, in my view and in the view of the committee, that was the best thing for the company and everyone involved.

At this point, time was ticking away — we were less than two hours away from showtime. As Hulk was laying out the story to me, I was already thinking on my feet. My objective was to make him happy, while keeping our plans intact. After Hulk finished his story, I basically told him that that didn't work for me.

I then used his words and said, "If you *really* want to do this as a shoot, how about this?"

Here's the story I laid out to both Eric and Hulk: "If you want this to look like a shoot — let's make it look like a shoot. Let's try this: I walk into the building tonight and I find out that Hulk Hogan is playing his 'creative control' card and refuses to do the job to Jeff Jarrett. Now, if as a shoot that were the case, this is how Vince Russo would react. I would go to Jeff, who is my friend, tell him what was going on, and then direct him to lay down for you [Hogan] in the middle of the ring the minute the bell rang. Being ringside I would then tell you, 'There — you have exactly what you want. Cover him and take your precious belt.' Now you — not having many options — would cover Jarrett and take the belt. Because that's what you really wanted. And then you'd leave. However, in order to work the boys in the back, making *everybody* believe this was a shoot, the story would have to go one step further. You would be so upset that I showed you up that you would go in the back, get Eric — *your* friend — and the two of you would leave the building in a huff."

I explained to Hulk that that part of the story was vital (he and Eric leaving the building), because in order for me to get to the main event between Jeff and Booker I had to go back out to the ring later in the evening and cut a *scathing* (my exact word) promo on him, saying that Hogan can keep his belt, because that belt didn't mean anything. There would be a *real* Championship match tonight, and it would be between Booker T and Jeff Jarrett for the *real* WCW Title. I again made it clear to both Eric and Hogan that them leaving the building was crucial, because if they were still in it when I cut the promo on Hogan — then Hulk would have had to come out to the ring and *kill* me — storyline-wise.

After I laid this out to Hulk — with Eric there — he looked at me wide-eyed and said, "I like it." He then said, "Yeah, and then I could have one belt, and Booker could have the other, and we could go from there." Now again, all I was concerned about that night was what we had written as a committee. Being that I had just come up with this on the fly, I had no idea where we would go with this. So I told Hulk, "We'll talk about where we go with this — I'll call you tomorrow."

From there I found Jeff and I completely worked him. I told him that Hulk didn't want to do the job for him and he needed to just go out there and lay down for Hogan. Jeff was furious; I had never seen him so mad. Man, it was tough working Jeff — my friend — but keep in mind that Hulk, Eric and myself had all agreed that we were going to work the boys in order to make this come off as "real" as possible. So the match went down just like the three of us discussed — Jeff wasn't in on anything. After the 1-2-3 Hogan took the belt, found Eric and the two stormed out of the building. The boys were buying this hook, line and sinker. From there I went out to the ring and cut that scathing promo that Hulk and I had discussed earlier. The whole reason for the promo was to get to the Jeff/Booker match. It was my job to tie it all together and make it all make sense. That's all I cared about; I just wanted to get to the main event, like we had planned, with it all making sense.

Just an aside: If you remember my character in wcw, every time I went out in front of the people I *always* wore a New York jersey. Well, if you remember that night I wore a San Francisco Giants jersey — something totally out of character for me. Again, that was all part of the shoot — being that I didn't have a New York jersey on this time, it had to be real! That's how closely I looked at this angle.

Well, the next day everybody was talking about it, and everybody was believing it. It was incredible. Even I didn't think the boys could be worked like that. The next day I pulled Jeff aside and told him what really happened — I just had a real hard time working him when he was right in the middle of it. It's funny, but Jeff really didn't seem that surprised. Being a veteran of the business and having seen just about everything, Jeff took it in stride and didn't seem shocked by any of it.

If I made a single mistake throughout this entire incident, here it was: I never called Hogan back the next day like I said I would. Why? Because we were at *Nitro* and I had no idea where to go with the story. I just didn't have the time to think it through. In other words, if had I called him, I just didn't know what to tell him, so I just didn't call. My bad. Hindsight being 20/20, I should have.

When we got back to the office from TV I met with Brad Siegel and told him what happened. I also told Brad that I hadn't called Hulk back yet because I didn't know what to tell him. I wasn't sure where to go with this. At that point Brad told me that financially we just couldn't afford to use Hulk Hogan right now so I should just think about going on with the story without him.

So I never called Hulk back. If it were today I would have; I would have been honest with him and told him what Brad had told me. But at the time, I just didn't think it was my place. Was it a cop-out? Maybe. But back then there was no way that I was thinking clearly. The truth is, I was probably on the verge of a nervous breakdown.

You all know the rest of the story. A few days later I was hit with a defamation of character lawsuit by Hulk Hogan, claiming that he had known nothing in advance about the interview that I cut on him in the ring. He claimed that I went into business for myself and he had no knowledge that I was going to do it. I have my theories on why Hulk reacted this way, but again, they are just my theories. I think two things happened: #1: I didn't call him like I said I would, which deeply upset him, and #2: I can only imagine his feelings when he went on the Internet the following day and witnessed first-hand how the fans had bought "the work" hook, line and sinker. I think — again, I *think* — that is where some ego might have been involved, as many of the fans were saying that "Vince Russo finally put Hulk Hogan in his place," and "Vince did to Hulk what somebody should have done years ago." Hulk couldn't have felt too warm and fuzzy reading any of that.

So there you have it. My side of one of the greatest mysteries of all time. In closing, I would just like to add something that I said many times before the incident, and many times after. Growing up, I was a huge fan of Hulk Hogan. The fact is, wrestling would never — *never* — have reached the heights it did without him. That translates into this: without Hulk Hogan Vince Russo would have never achieved what he did in the wrestling business because — in my opinion, anyway — the wrestling business would probably not have existed. Hulk Hogan paved the way for me, and for many, many others. I can't thank him enough for that. I've said on many occasions that I would work with Hulk Hogan in a heartbeat, and I mean that. With the lawsuit, I totally understand where he was coming from. I was never shocked by it because I know why it happened, but I wish we could both put it behind us. I wish that one day I would be able to thank him for making my career in wrestling possible. But that's up to him.

Broken

Through all the trials and tribulations I was experiencing at wcw, one thing that always remained constant was my spirit. Even though I was broken — severely broken, both mentally and physically — at the end of every day I still had my spirit. Regardless of what was hurled my way, I wasn't going to give up; I wasn't going to allow "them" to beat me. That was the only thing I had left. It was me vs. them and they were going to have to kill me to declare victory.

Unfortunately, the Hulk Hogan defamation of character suit stripped me of that too.

The lawsuit was devastating on many levels. Even though it had nothing to do with the money and I was never in danger of losing even a dollar because I was legally covered under my wcw contract, it just completely crushed my spirit. It took the only thing I had left. I was finally broken, for many reasons. I knew in my heart that it was complete BS. I knew that I had done nothing wrong and that Hulk was in on the script from the first page. I knew that I was simply being dragged into a much bigger case that he had with wcw as a whole. Even though I knew it was all about the money, and none of it was personal, it still hurt. To me, it just exemplified everything that was wrong with the business. In order for one individual to make a personal gain, this one being monetary, he would hurt whoever he had to in order to make it happen. Even though I was never chummy with Hulk, this really hurt. Also, I had lived 40 years of my life without getting into any legal trouble. I had never been arrested and never been sued. I had no idea what it felt like to sit through a deposition; heck, I had never even been accused of ever doing anything wrong. This just wasn't me; this wasn't what I was about and I felt very uncomfortable.

I held a grudge against Hulk throughout this entire debacle. Even though I understood that his motives were based on greed and ego — the two things I hate about the wrestling business — at the time I couldn't find it in my heart to forgive him. Was this just a case of a wrestler being a wrestler — and, if not Hulk, perhaps somebody else at some other time? Yes on both counts — but that didn't relieve me of that sick feeling I held in my stomach towards him.

I felt as if I had been violated. I didn't care how many lawsuits he had already been a part of with WWF and WCW; this was all new to me. This wasn't the reason I got into the wrestling business. This wasn't this reason I was calling the former Editor-in-Chief of the *WWF Magazine*, Ed Ricchutti, back in 1993 begging him to give me a freelance story for $150. This wasn't why I used my own money to fund the radio show *Vicious Vincent's World of Wrestling* on 1240 WGBB in West Babylon when I was looking to get my foot in the door. No, this — I don't know how to say it any other way — this was 100%, absolute BS.

I just wanted the whole thing to end and, no matter what, I wanted to be exonerated. I knew I was telling the truth — the *whole* truth — but I also knew that it wasn't just my word against Hulk's: it was my word against Hulk's *and* Eric's. There was no doubt in my mind that in this case one would lie, and the other would swear to it. But even with that — even with that — the entire notion was more ridiculous then a Glenn Gilberti storyline. I cut a fake promo inside a wrestling ring on a wrestling character. At the end of the day, that's what it all broke down to. Never — *never* — at any point had I cut a single negative promo on Terry Bollea the man. Not to any dirt sheet, not in any radio interview, not on any website. The truth is, I never said anything negative about *Terry* — period! Why? Because I never had anything negative to say about him. I had no beef with him — *none*.

Deep down I knew that there was no way this ridiculous claim would ever hold up in a court of law. I mean, what would a judge think? You see, they didn't live in the wrestling bubble like we all did. Whereas this was normal in the wrestling world, in the real world it was about as ridiculous as a Ren and Stimpy cartoon — an *early* Ren and Stimpy cartoon! Dragging out for what seemed an entire lifetime, the entire mess was finally dissolved when a judge threw it out. Hogan appealed, only then to have a second judge repeat the original verdict.

Man, after this abomination, there was just nothing left; I was a mere shell of my former self, just going through the motions with nothing meaning anything to me. Too put it simply: I had lost my innocence. I felt as if I had been raped. What was once my dream had become a sentence in hell.

Planes, Fantasy Baseball and J.J. Dillon

March 26, 2008

On the road again – just can't wait to get on the road again.

Willie Nelson

Even though I am a Willie Nelson mark, no doubt he was high when he penned that one.

Right now I'm in the last seat on a plane, about 36,000 feet above the earth. The fasten seatbelt sign just fired up, probably having something to do with the tail end ferociously wiggling and shaking Shakira-like! Man, I hate to freakin' fly. There's no positives — none! I'm always looking for the glass to be half full, but when you're above the clouds in a metal tube, not only is the glass empty, but you need to order another drink!

I've hated to fly my whole entire life; it's just the finality of it all. Yeah, flying in a plane might be safer then driving in your own car, but when these things go down, they *go down!* Forget *Lost*; that's a television show — if this zeppelin nose-dives we're all cooked! After all these years you think I'd be used to it by now. But how do you get used to it? It's always going to be in the back of your mind; just look out a window and see how far up you are. Bad things are going to happen if this bird decides to belly-flop head-first back to earth.

More than anything, it's my beliefs today that get me through every flight. Knowing that God is in charge of every second of my life gives me the peace I need to hop aboard one of these bad boys every week. And the truth is, before every flight, right before take-off, I say a prayer. But my prayer is never "God, get me there safely"

— I'm not going to tell God what to do — my prayer is "God, if it's in *Your will* to get me there safely, *then* get me there safely." In the past, during my WWF and WCW days, I was scared to death of death. Whereas today, even though the human side of me still views it as an unpleasant subject, I'm at peace knowing that whatever God decides to do with my life, whatever path He chooses to take me down, it is simply designed to make me a better human being, and bring me closer to the Father.

There goes that !@#$ seatbelt sign again!

So, I'm up here in a death trap, sitting in the last seat that doesn't recline, and trying to bang out yet another chapter. What also isn't helping is the fact that at the bottom of each eyelid is a ten-pound dumbbell, looking to draw the curtains so I can peacefully Z-out in dreamland. Why is Mr. Sandman sitting right next to me singing sweet, soft lullabies? I'm sure it has something to do with not having slept in the last 48 hours. You see, the baseball season kicked off in Japan on Monday night, which meant that I had a game to watch at four a.m. MST, Tuesday morning. That game was then followed up by a second contest — same Japanese time, different American channel — Wednesday morning. So now, I'm going to three days of TV, not having slept in the last two. Yeah, come tomorrow I should be about as fresh and pleasant as the screaming and kicking two-year-old in the seat directly in front of my lap. But there are no regrets — none — because with the first two days of the baseball season also comes the start of fantasy baseball '08!

Despite the business I'm in, I don't share the same vices as some — or many — of my colleagues. With my 25th wedding anniversary less than six months away, I am proud to say that I've never cheated on my wife. Whereas adultery is the norm in the bubble, I was never the least bit interested. Yeah, I've worked with some beautiful women over the years, but none were ever worth disrespecting Amy for. So chasing tail: not an option. With that out, let's take a look at alcohol. Let's see — let me get myself hammered, a thousand miles away from home, so I can put myself in a compromising position, in the hopes that something bad will happen so I can regret it for the rest of my life. Yeah, that's a rational decision for an adult. Nope, no drinking. I've never been a drinker — not even before my days of Christianity. To me, there's no worse feeling than not being in control of yourself. And not only is it a bad feeling, it's downright scary. When the show's over, I go to my room — and follow my fantasy baseball team on my laptop. Pitch by pitch, inning by inning, I'm there until the final out of the night is made. That's my vice.

Unfortunately, it has become somewhat addictive. Before I moved to

Colorado, I actually had "Fantasy Central" set up in my man-cave — or finished basement. I had my 60-inch television set fed with Direct TV's baseball package, so I could watch every game from every city, every minute of every day. I would follow my players pitch by pitch, studying every facet of the game, much the same way I reckon that dirt sheet writers following fake Japanese wrestling matches. But that wasn't enough — I had to be multi-faceted. While scoping the action, I would be on my computer dropping those players who were in a slump and adding those who looked like they were about to break out. In a 162-game schedule, I had over 120 transactions off the waiver wire — a record that I am more proud of than any *Raw* rating. The other managers in my league despised me because while they were fast asleep, I was beating them to the punch and acquiring players off the wire sometimes at two, three, or four in the morning. I became so wrapped up that I even began to sleep in the man-cave, only going upstairs to feed my belly. It soon became a sickness as I would find every excuse not to go out with my family while a pitch was being thrown in a ballpark . . . somewhere.

But in the end . . . in the end it all paid off. "Bonds is Innocent" won the 12-team "North Metro & Friends" league last year, bringing home a check for 90 big ones — aside from my kids being born, perhaps the greatest accomplishment of my life. So now, I'm back to repeat with all eleven other teams gunning for the champ. You see how little it takes to amuse me. All the gossip and all the dirt you hear and read about me — and at the end of the day I'm probably in my man-cave, alone, watching Big Papi take his hacks. Life can be so simple if we only let it.

I have to derail myself from the wrestling train now and then just for my own sanity. I don't like talking about the subject, let alone writing about it. The memories sting to this day. The taste in my mouth of rotten eggs still lingers. There are things I haven't gotten to yet in these pages, positive things, things I look forward to — those are the things that somehow get me through writing about the "dark age." There is a happy ending, there is light at the end of the tunnel — but until I get there, I just have to lighten myself up every chapter or two.

Before I get to Russo's last stand at WCW, I first have to comment on a story that old reliable Bill Banks reminded me of yesterday. No doubt I overlooked it because I wanted to forget about it, but it wouldn't be just if I didn't own up to it.

I very rarely went into the office at WCW. There's just something I hate about offices in general. Unless my boss is Michael Scott and I work at

Dunder-Mifflin, I'm going to avoid you like an ice-cold Corona. It's the politics and the butt-kissing and the phoniness. I hate it all. If I can't be comfortable in a place just simply being me, then I don't want to be there. Even when I played the role of "boss," I hated it. I don't like people serving me, or fearing me, or trying to rack up points with me. I get nauseous when I see a superior ask a person they deem below them to get them a cup of coffee. Are you kidding me? That's nothing but a power trip. If you can't get your butt out of your cushiony seat and get your own cup of coffee, then you're an egomaniac where I come from. So in order to not get myself upset, I just try to stay away.

However, on this very unfortunate day, I had to go to that ugly blue building in Smyrna, Georgia, for I don't remember what. Now, being that I rarely made an appearance, it was easy for me to sneak in the back door and remain incognito, so that no one would even know I was there. I could sneak in and out before the butt-kissing or political warfare began — pick your poison. So, I'm sitting in my office, minding my own business, when from a few doors down I hear what I think is somebody in the office ripping the previous *Nitro* to ribbons to someone they are apparently talking to on the phone. Now remember, I had just gotten off the road from working on that show, and this was probably the last thing I wanted to hear. But giving this individual the benefit of the doubt — maybe I was tired, maybe I wasn't hearing right — I decided to go out in the hall and get a closer listen. So, I tiptoed out, positioned myself right in front of this person's office . . . and listened.

Not being noticed by anyone, and the office being full of workers, I perched myself just outside this person's door, and listened in amazement as he loudly criticized me, the show and anyone who had anything to do with *Nitro*. Now this was by no means shocking, because I suspected that this person had already been ice-picking me behind my back, but what was upsetting was that he was doing it in such an open forum. His office door was wide open and anyone on the *floor* could hear every word he was saying. Man, this would surely be a bummer for morale. So I'm standing there, almost in shock, when I realize I have to do something. I realized that before any more poison is passed throughout the halls for everyone to hear, I had to stop it. So I carefully took one giant step sideways and showed myself in the frame of this person's door. Not realizing I was there, he fired a few more bullets until looking up. I'm going to try to describe the look on his face when my eyes meet his. I have to really search my bank here in order to come up with the best comparison. . . .

I got it.

When I was working for the WWF, we shot an angle involving Owen Hart. I can't remember the specifics — maybe it had to do something with the Canadian fiasco — but they're not important. Anyway, based on the angle, we sent Owen home for a while because we were trying to sell the fact that he "legitimately" was no longer with the company. When it was time for Owen to make his return to *Raw*, we flew him in a day early to the pay-per-view so we could talk to him about where we planned on going to next day. Much like Manny being Manny, this was a case of Owen being Owen.

Now keep in mind, Owen was officially off of TV, and the viewers believed he was no longer with the company. So, towards the end of the show, two wrestlers brawl to the backstage area. Remember, this is *live*. Suddenly the two fight their way into an office, which they think is vacant. As the camera follows, the office door flies open, and there stands Owen Hart, clear as day, for the world to see. Now, Owen, realizing that he was caught with his pants down, without missing a beat, looks directly into the camera with a deer-in-the-headlights look on his face and says, "I'm not here."

That was the expression when my WCW basher saw me. So much so that when he realized it was me standing there all he could say was, "I'm on the phone."

The individual was the Head of Talent Relations, J.J. Dillon.

What followed was a verbal barrage of every cuss word I had ever heard. I mean, I didn't cuss J.J. just like a sailor, I cussed him like an Army General, like an Airforce Pilot, like a Marine, like a Boy Scout, like a Pueblo, like a Cub Scout, like a Girl Scout and . . . like a Brownie. Every curse word known to man I hurled at J.J. with the speed of a Nolan Ryan fastball. One after another. I didn't know I had such a vocabulary. Man, it was vicious, it was ugly and at the end of the day, it was wrong.

That was so out of character for me, I had never before, or ever since, gone off on somebody like that — *never*. This was a man just like me, a husband, a father, somebody just trying to support his family. And I spoke to him like he had just killed someone I loved. I screamed at him, stripping him of all dignity and respect . . . and for what? Because he didn't like the show? At that point, I clearly realized that I had lost my freakin' mind. I was psycho, crazy, nuts. I wasn't the same guy who walked into this insane asylum of a business some nine years prior. I had become everything I despised, everything I didn't want to be. I had become one of them.

About a year ago I saw J.J. at a convention I was working, and there was no way I was going to leave before I apologized to him. So with zero pride and a ton of remorse, I approached him. I told J.J. that I was deeply sorry for my actions on that day — no excuses. J.J. graciously accepted my apology, saying that he realized it took a lot for me to walk up to him and say I was sorry.

So, J.J., this is a second apology — only this one is public.

I'm sorry.

Russo's Last Stand

Well, things were spinnin' 'round me
And all my thoughts were cloudy
And I had begun to doubt all the things that were me

Been in so many places
You know I've run so many races
And looked into the empty faces of the people of the night
And something is just not right.

Jim Croce, "New York's Not My Home"

Nothing better describes what I was going through at that time in wcw than those lyrics by the late great Jim Croce. I had no control of what was going on around me — zero. Even though I wielded the mighty graphite at the time, this #2 pencil had no eraser. I couldn't white out the obstacles surrounding me: the hate, the physical pain, the emotional torture, the controversy, the back-stabbing, the jealousy, the greed. The entire atmosphere just reeked of negativity; the only time I ever found any kind of solace was on those rare occasions when I could just hide myself from the world in my man-cave. What really made matters worse was that I just had no idea where this thing was going. Forget planning about the pay-per-view for next month — I was way beyond that. No, I was planning for my own demise — the death of Vince Russo. Whether it be mental, emotional, physical — or all three — it was coming. wcw was going to be the death of me. This wasn't about being burnt out and cooked on the Vince McMahon grill as I had been months earlier; this was about doing permanent damage to my psyche. The only thing I could do at the time was just roll with it. I really didn't care where this thing was going — I just wanted it to move forward in hopes that it would eventually reach its tragic conclusion. At this point, I really didn't care what happened to me. I just wanted it to be over. All I could do was kick it into survival mode and strap myself in for the crash. Little did I know that this ride from hell would end in a 15-foot-high steel cage, in my own backyard.

Just one single ray of light broke through the black, ominous clouds as I stepped off the plane at LaGuardia Airport; the location could not have been any better for what could have been my last hoorah. That Monday night, *Nitro* was scheduled at the Nassau Coliseum in Uniondale, New York. Man, I had spent so many great nights there as a teen making some unforgettable memories. To this day I tell my kids stories of the concerts I enjoyed: Stevie Wonder, Bachman Turner Overdrive, Boston, Elton John, Chicago, the Beach Boys (the *real* Beach Boys: Brian, Carl, Dennis, Al, Mike and Bruce) and yes, even Barry Manilow. However, my greatest memories took place right there on the hardwood floor in Uniondale . . . the court that Julius Erving ruled!

Growing up, I was an avid ABA (American Basketball Association) and New York Nets fan. And the ABA was everything Will Ferrell painted it out to be in *Semi-Pro*: the cheerleaders, the music, the pomp, the circumstance and the never-ending promotion. There were Darnell Hillman afros and nicknames out the wazoo.

And now for your New York Nets starting five: Larry "the Cat" Kenon, "The Whopper" Billy Paultz, "The BT Express" Brian Taylor, "Super" John Williamson and "the Doctor" Julius Erving.

Dr. J was decades ahead of his time — freakin' decades. To this day I'll still argue that Michael Jordan in his prime never did what Julius did in the old ABA days. And it wasn't some legend you read about; I was there to witness it all. Sports were so different back then. As a fan, you actually felt part of the team. I mean, when the game was over, the players would actually leave the arena through the front door of the building. Can you imagine that happening today? And it was there where you really got to know the players, literally talk to them one-on-one. Getting back to the opening words of this book, that moment in time was absolutely Avalon. I can remember one particular Sunday matinee when I had to be about 12 years old, waiting outside the arena doors with the rest of the fans in hopes of catching a glimpse of Dr. J after the game. About an hour after the final buzzer, the Doctor didn't disappoint. He walked out of the Coliseum in full pimp daddy regalia: afro, sunglasses, fur coat, Adidas Americanas, the whole shebang. Snoop who? I waited as the Doctor signed every autograph before I approached him. Even though he made himself accessible to all, all I kept thinking to myself was: This is the freakin' *Doctor!*

With nothing left but air between me and Julius, I cautiously approached him and he signed my program. He then thanked me for going to the game — can you imagine that? Julius Erving *thanked me* for going to watch him play — then started walking towards the *public* parking lot. Yes — ABA players parked in the same lot as the rest of us. By this time the next Nets superstar had come out and the crowd (about 50 loyal fans) gravitated towards him. Never taking my eyes off Julius, I watched as he walked to his car in the parking lot, alone. Again, being only 12 at the time, and being in absolute awe of my idol, I to this day still have no idea how this next sentence stumbled out of my mouth. Calling after the Doctor, I said, "Can I walk with you to your car?" Not even believing my own words, you can believe how taken aback I was when Dr. J replied back to me, "Sure, kid." So there we were — me and Dr. J walking together to his car. Folks, it doesn't get any better then that. That moment has stuck with me my entire life — me and the Doc just strolling to his car and talking about the game that day.

Unfortunately, this day some 30 days later — this day was going to be no stroll in the parking lot with my idol. This day was truly the beginning of the end.

Going in, I knew that this was the last bump I was going to take for a while. Week after week, *Nitro* after *Thunder*, the shots to the head just kept piling up. Blow after blow, I felt worse and worse, going to the neurologist every chance I had between TVs and writing. The doctor kept telling me that one more blow could be dangerous, but I wasn't listening. Regardless of the implications, I had to see this thing through. And if the end was indeed near, I was going out New Yawk style, in the same arena where I saw my Nets win their first ABA title 26 years ago.

Looking back now, I have no idea how we got to that point, but at the Coliseum I was scheduled to face Booker T for his WCW Heavyweight Title. You know what? Writing that last sentence — to even myself it reeks of ego, but I assure you it wasn't. On the surface if they were going to beat me, then they were going to beat *me*. Remember, at that point I didn't trust anybody with anything, so if they were going to see to my demise they were going to have to literally go straight through me. Subconsciously, I wanted this thing to end. And in writing this book and really sitting back and analyzing the situation, I think I purposely kept putting myself in harm's way. Remember at that point, I didn't want to quit — I was way beyond that point, in way too deep. But, if I was hurt, if I was injured . . . that may have been my ticket out. Again, this wasn't what I was thinking on the surface, but somewhere in my psyche I now believe that this conversation was going on without me even knowing it.

Throughout the day I had rehearsed the match with Booker and everything went off without a hitch. It was easy with Booker; always was, still is. But what an egomaniac he had to think I was, because not only was I wrestling him for the title — I was winning it! To this day I feel my reasons were valid. You have to remember — forget your tainted Internet/dirt sheet opinion for a second — at the time, with two shows a week and twelve pay-per-views a year, we were writing 116 shows a year. 116! How do you make 116 shows different without each show starting to look like the one before and after it? You have to shake things up, even if you know the wrestling "smarts" are going to blast you for it. You have to take chances, try new things. You can't play it safe as a writer because if you do, you'll lull the audience to sleep. And remember, the goal is always to get new viewers, always to grow your audience. My theory is — and will be to the day I die — wrestling fans will watch the show as long as the word wrestling appears somewhere even near the name of the show. You will always — *always* — have those viewers. You have to go out and capture the everyday television viewer — those who aren't wrestling fans. And what captures them is spectacle, drama, controversy and everything that has nothing to do with wrestling. Hey, don't hate the player — hate the game.

Unfortunatley, whereas Booker wasn't my concern, Bill Goldberg was. The end of the match was all him, as he was written to enter the steel cage, then spear me out through it, thus awarding me the title because I technically left the cage first (again, written as a "that wasn't supposed to happen" moment). Knowing what physical condition I was in at the time, I laid out this finish with precision, trying to ensure that I wouldn't get hurt. My plan was to have Goldberg spear me through the cage onto the runway between — again, *between* — the two steel barricades that outlined it. Again, *between* the steel barricades. During rehearsal that day, I went over this numerous times with Bill, and time after time he assured me that he literally would lay me down on the ramp between (there's that word again) the barricades. Even though I had some reservations and may have been a bit concerned at the time, I never thought about changing the finish. Again, for those regular viewers watching at home and not those smarts who were going to blast me the next day, I thought that finish was the most entertaining and unpredictable we could come up with — almost as good as the David Arquette one, which I'll get into later.

The match between Booker and me went according to plan. Again, looking back now, Booker must have hated the thought of being in there with me — his boss, this egomaniac — but being the pro that he is he just did his job. As the finish Goldberg came down to the cage and walked in. As we had played this out a dozen times during the day, I then got myself in position against the part of the cage that was gimmicked to break away. So far so good. Goldberg then gets in position, sets up the spear . . . and comes at me full force. The impact explodes me through the cage as I feel the air deflating from my lungs. Now in complete control of my body, Goldberg follows through on his finish, only to crash me *head first* into the guardrail. Not *between* the guardrails, but *head first* into the one on the right. Luckily, not trusting him from the beginning, I was wearing a hockey helmet, which may have protected me from serious injury. I always went into the ring with as much protection as I could put on. Remember, the boys had this thing about a civilian stepping into their world, and I wanted to be as protected as I could be. But to get back to the spear, helmet or no helmet, I felt the impact full force. I remember being both dazed and confused as security and an EMT crew came over to check on me. Even though this was all part of the script, for a short period of time I wasn't acting. Fortunately, by the time I was carried to the back I had regained my senses.

Did Bill Goldberg mean to hurt me? I'll never say that. The fact is, I'll never know. Was it just a miscalculation on his part? Probably. Did I have any business putting myself in harm's way like that? None. Was I an imbecile? Most definitely. At that point in time I knew that my in-ring career was over, and I was happy. Physically I was in no condition to take that kind of head trauma again. I honestly didn't know what kind of permanent damage one more severe blow to the coconut may have caused. Not even the hockey helmet was getting it — even with all that protection it still hurt. Hey, maybe I'll try to shield myself in a Pope-mobile next; nobody will ever get to me that way — read all about it in the next chapter.

Anyway, knowing I was done, on the following *Thunder* I did an interview where I relinquished the WCW title, stating that I had "nothing more to prove." It's ironic that even before the match with Booker took place, I had already written my finish without any knowledge of how it would end.

Without knowing that I would once again get my bell rung, this time courtesy of Bill Goldberg. Looking back now, I can only believe that the story was already written, and somebody was trying to tell me in advance. Why God wrote it that way — to this day I have no idea, I just know He wrote it. And I also know that at this point He was just about to wrap up the entire wcw book . . . a book that would change my life forever. A book that even though I wished I had never picked up, I knew I had to. I didn't understand the significance at the time, but I would years later.

Turning Over the Keys

The only one who knew it was going to be my last show was me. The way this whole thing played out was ridiculous. The ground work was laid out in my hometown, but my last day would take place in my second favorite city in the world, San Franciso. Home of my beloved Giants, I loved 'Frisco the moment Amy and I set foot on the wharf in the mid-'80s. To this day I have never been in a city with so much character. Pier 39, those fruit baskets performing on the street, Alcatraz, that crooked street, Ghirardelli chocolate and Candlestick Park — the closest we'll ever get to heaven while living on this planet. Avalon again. I had subconsciously picked this place to end my WCW run, or should I say it was picked for me. And I was going to go out in style — again, a stunt the smarts would hate, but the non-obsessive, normal fans would love.

With ol' reliable Jeremy Borash at the wheel, we drove straight into the Cow Palace in a Pope-mobile. Knock it, hate it all you want, but throughout the entire history of the business it had never been done before, and has never been done since. How many things in wrestling can you honestly say you have only seen once? It was a great stunt, one I am still very proud of. Why a Pope-mobile, you ask? Simple — Bill Goldberg wasn't going to get to me this time, no matter what. There weren't going to be any mishaps or mistakes, and more importantly I wasn't going to get hurt. Now, mind you, Bill could have pulled JB out the driver's window and had his way with him — I was cool with that, no problem — but me, I was hands off. Not even Goldberg was going to be able to break through four layers of Plexiglas.

Later that night in the same show, I symbolically handed the keys over to the head of the Natural Born Thrillers, Mike Sanders. He's perhaps the second most misunderstood individual in the business behind yours truly. Man, maybe he's more misunderstood than me — Mike just rubbed people the wrong way. To those who didn't know him well he came across as both brash and arrogant. However, those who did know him knew his critics were totally mislabeling his confidence. Mike was a confident individual, which is a rarity in the wrestling business. He knew he could wrestle, and he knew he could talk and he just wanted to earn his merit on those facts. But getting back to those keys, that was my way of saying, "Here you go; I'm done. Do with this place what you want."

The next day I put the nail in the coffin when I turned my back on going on a wcw tour in Australia and instead made the easy decision of going to Pac Bell Park to see the Giants play the New York Mets in the 2000 mlb playoffs. Shortly after that, when everybody returned to the States, I told Brad Siegel that the Molotov cocktail of my post-concussion syndrome combined with the stress I was suffering on the job was physically, mentally and emotionally killing me. I told him that while the crew was in Australia I visited my neurologist and he advised me that it was time for me to take time off due to my condition.

Guess what? I lied. I was bailing out on wcw because wcw had bailed out on me. By this time it was a known fact to everyone in the company that the nameless and faceless brass were doing everything they could to sell the wrestling division. I was going to be damned to give the same effort I had been giving since the day they hired me, putting my health on the line with every situation, when those in charge couldn't have cared about any of us or our families. Pardon my language here, but screw that. I had put everything I had into this company, even my own well-being, and at the end of the day, nobody cared. So I sat myself home in the comforts of my man-cave and waited for the inevitable to happen.

Looking back, there was no way that I could have been at that last show — no way. To see Shane McMahon gloating, and to give Vince McMahon the satisfaction of having me in the palm of his hand after I left his company . . . no way. Nothing good was ever going to come out of that. The only thing I regret about the whole situation was when I heard that Kevin Nash had told somebody that I "bailed on the boys." It hurt, because it was true. And to this day, I respect Kevin Nash perhaps more than any other athlete I ever worked with. I respect him simply because he always told the truth, just like he was doing there. Kevin opened my eyes because I never looked at it that way. I never took into consideration that I was quitting on the guys I cared about most: the hard-working individuals who made it possible for me to make a living in this business. To me, I was bailing on the suits, those individuals who didn't know us and didn't care to know us. Those were the individuals who killed wcw.

This book is called *How WCW Killed Vince Russo*, because every bit of that is true. I walked away from that situation a different animal. My heart had been ripped out, and a business I once loved, I now hated more than hate itself. I had lost hope, I was depressed, I wasn't even looking at myself the same way anymore. I felt like a failure, stripped of any confidence that I had built over the years. I no longer trusted anyone. And even though the doctor didn't tell me to walk away at the end, to this day I am a step behind the man I used to be. My focus isn't there; words and ideas don't come as easy as they once did. I don't need a doctor to tell me that I left part of my mind on wcw's mat. wcw had beat me — something that I swore I would never let happen.

So now, with so much lost, one question loomed large: what next?

David Arquette

Ahh, my favorite chapter.

The thing I love most is that due to this fiction (David Arquette never actually beat anyone for a fake wrestling belt — I just wrote it that way), I've been labeled clueless, a moron, a jerk, an idiot, an imbecile, stupid, dumb and just flat out ignorant. Now, while all that might indeed be true, what is also true is that here we are, eight years after the fact, and to this day — you're all still talking about it! Amazing! Every time I'm interviewed, the first question always concerns one of two things: David Arquette or Bash at the Beach. Now, what's ironic is that that my intention in the first place was to get people talking! But I have to be honest, not even I expected that you would still be having a love-fest with it some eight years later. But it's not only you. A couple of months ago I saw David on *The Tonight Show* with Jay Leno and *he* was still talking about.

Not bad legs for such an atrocious story, huh?

I'm always asked if I regret it — regret putting the belt on David Arquette. Are you kidding me? I'd do the same thing tomorrow, in a New York minute. *Eight years* of people still bashing my David Arquette storyline with everything else going on in the world — gas prices, presidential races, Britney. It's money, I tell ya — money! But I can't take full credit for it. Because actually, it wasn't my idea. Yeah, I get blamed for it, and I have no problem with that because I ultimately was responsible by giving it my stamp of approval. But actually, on the day it happened, the thought hadn't even crossed my clueless, empty mind.

The one match that would kill the wrestling business forever pitted Jeff Jarrett (the WCW Champion) and Eric Bischoff against Diamond Dallas Page and David Arquette with the title on the line. Whatever man scored the pinfall would be the new WCW World Champion. If you forgot how it came to an eccentric, bad dresser but all around good guy and actor David Arquette stepping into the ring, it all started when Arquette used a number of wcw wrestlers in his movie *Ready to Rumble*. Even though it's one of the only two movies I've ever walked out on in a theater (the other was Bo Derek's *Bolero*, which I went to see as a teen because I thought she'd be naked), the boys still enjoyed the experience — especially working with Arquette. For weeks Page was telling me we should use Arquette, and why not? I mean, the guy was a professional actor, he knew what to do in front of a camera and would no doubt portray a character better than 99.9% of our talent could. Well, one thing led to the next, and we were at this tag match.

Originally, with the title on the line and Jarrett the WCW Champion, we were just going to put the heels over. In Wrestling 101 that was the thing to do, so we never thought twice about it. We discussed the match at the production meeting, laying all the details out to those who needed to know, and then we broke for lunch. To this day the only good thing about production meetings is that lunch immediately follows. Having been to literally hundreds of them over the years, to me it is the most tedious part of the job. For starters, I already know the show inside and out because I wrote it; secondly, as I stated before, I hate details; thirdly, I can't sit still for 45 minutes. I guess that's another reason why I've always enjoyed Disco in those meetings. While the producers, directors, lighting guys, sound engineers and agents were busy hashing and rehashing what had already been hashed and rehashed 100 times before, Disco would entertain me by writing his ridiculous thoughts on the top of my run sheets — a practice he still does religiously to this very day. Anyway, after the meeting broke, Tony Schiavone, wcw play-by-play guy and a man I greatly admire, approached me and asked if he could talk to me for a minute. Always having time for Tony I said, "Sure — what's up?"

Following came the line that would kill the wrestling business forever. This one line, this one sentence would take everything that was built for almost a century . . . and crush it. The wrestling business as we knew it would never be the same again. From Georgeous George to the late great Tojo Yamamoto, they would all be flippity-floppin' over in their graves. This one line would spit in the face of visionaries like the great Vince McMahon Senior. Not another single ticket would be bought, not another single wrestling show would ever make air, no more rats; the boys would have to go out and get "real" jobs, "Dirty Dutch" Mantel would have to enter the professional world — bullwhip and all. Oh, I tell ya — this was the end for us all!

Tony said, "Hey, Vince, what if David Arquette wins the tag match and becomes the WCW World Champion?"

Blasphemy, I tell ya! Blasphemy! How could you, Tony? How could you? You'll set the business back 50 years — everything they worked for; the "Love Brothers" Hartford and Reginald, Abe "Knuckleball" Schwartz, the Yeti, Bertha Faye, the Mountie for cryin' out loud! What about the Mountie? You'll kill it — kill it all! Shame on you, Tony Schiavone!

Now, there is no doubt that a good majority of you reading this book may have looked at it that way, but of course . . . not me. My whole life has been outside the box, so why change? Tony's suggestion caught me so much off guard that that was the one thing that stuck. Throughout the booking of the match, throughout the production meeting, the notion of Arquette winning that match and becoming the WCW World Champion had never even crossed my mind. I guess that even in the wrestling business, that was unthinkable. But once I had time to digest Tony's idea I realized that if I, the writer, never even had that thought cross my mind, then the same would go two-fold with the viewer.

Knowing full well how far-fetched this idea was, I recalled the troops, and opened the topic for discussion. I threw out Tony's plan and was ready for any feedback, whether positive or negative. Everybody was there — everybody — including all the agents, Johnny Ace, Jimmy Hart, and yes, even Eric Bischoff. After some discussion and deliberation, the consensus was unanimous. The entire crew said go for it. So Vince Russo . . . me . . . I went for it! Not one person, not one single voice objected to the idea — not one. Everyone, in unison, wholeheartedly gave it a thumbs up. But yet, when the negative feedback came from the wrestling purists, not one of those individuals grabbed a stick, pounded the mud off their cleats, stepped into the box, and went to bat for me. Not one. All the heat went on Vince Russo. That's just the way it was at wcw: 100% brotherhood.

Not for one second since that infamous match have I regretted it — not one. My main goal was to get people talking about wcw; I didn't care if it was David's wife Courtney getting the pinfall. And speaking of Courtney Cox, let me tell you how she came into play. Not only was there a picture of David Arquette pinning *Eric Bischoff* — not Jeff Jarrett the WCW Champion, but Eric freakin' Bischoff — on the *cover* of the entertainment section of *USA Today*, but David Arquette flew with the wcw title to Hollywood to be with his wife on the set of a movie she was filming. There, along with fellow actors Kurt Russell and Kevin Costner, Courtney shot a vignette with David and the WCW Title, for *free*. You couldn't pay for publicity like that, and that's what the wrestling smarts do not and will never understand. WrestleMania 24 just made a trillion dollars and do you think people actually bought it to see Triple H/Cena/Orton? Get a clue — Vince paid Floyd Mayweather a reported 20 million dollars because he knew the masses, the non-traditional wrestling fans, would slap down their hard-earned $54.95 just to see what would happen. For the same reason he signed the Trumpster one year earlier. It's the spectacle, the promotion and the entertainment that pulls in everyday Americans, not arm drags and Hakuna Matatas!

So thank you, Tony Schiavone, for the great idea! And more so, thank you for being bold enough to even suggest it.

9/11

With the sale of wcw becoming official, there was only one thing I was concerned about: was I going to be paid for the remainder of my contract?

Getting back to whether or not wcw would fulfill my contract after being sold to the wwf, I was called into the office and asked to sign some papers. I forget how the fine print read, but one thing stood out in big, bold, black ink: wcw was going to make good and I was going to be paid the remainder of what I was owed. I have to tell you, it felt like the weight of Yokozuna had been lifted off my back. I can't even describe to you the feeling of glee — absolute *glee* — as I drove my Jeep back home that day. It was over — done. The two-year nightmare had finally come to an end. Even though I wasn't born again at that time, I literally fell to my knees and thanked God. At 39 years old, the worst period of my life was over.

I felt like I was done with the business for good. I had no desire to go back to Vince McMahon — none. Had I decided to return, nothing would have changed; not a single thing would have been different. It would have been all about Vince making money, with everything else important in life taking a back seat. No, it was time for me to move on. But I was faced with a dilemma that all of us in the wrestling business have to own up to at one point or another. Where do I go from here? The day I signed up to work for the wwf, I knew I was painting myself in a corner simply because in the wrestling business back then, you had two choices:

I just went online to find the date of the last *Nitro*. The search came up with a "tribute to Vince Russo" on YouTube. Out of curiosity I had to click on it. Up came some insane multi-level cage match with all the top stars of WCW . . . then I made my way to the ring. The significance of me telling you this? No, not to put myself over. Just that watching it, I didn't remember a single second – not one. There was a lot of action, I took a bunch of shots from everyone, and I don't remember it at all. I can't explain any of that. Was it my physical condition at the time, or was it all psychological? Did I just block out everything about that time? I honestly don't know.

After watching that clip there was another, with Mike Tenay interviewing me during the early days of TNA. Man, I can't put this in a nicer way than this: I just flat out raped Mike. If I was him I would have just gotten out of that chair and slapped me across the face. Yes, it was part of the show, but the inferno that was burning inside me was real. I never had a personal problem with Mike – never – but the anger I had built up inside during my WCW days had to make him think that I despised him as much as he despised me. At that time Mike didn't like me, and who'd blame him? I was truly unlikable. Aside from showing the pain of my scars to anyone who would even glance at me, Mike and I were just two different people with two different backgrounds and two different philosophies on the wrestling business. Watching that video it was real easy to see why people hated me – and still do. I would have hated myself. But again, it was what the business had done to me. I was going through those trials and tribulations because it was all part of a storyline – one that I wasn't writing, one that would be played out later.

WWF or WCW. There was no place else to go. It wasn't as if you were working for a computer company, or a mobile phone distributor, where there were literally hundreds of other options in your field. This was professional wrestling — where were you going to go? For me, the natural progression would have been Hollywood, but I had two huge strikes against me there: my age, and the fact that in Hollywood professional wrestling is a joke. It has no credibility whatsoever. That's why Vince was never able to crack it, as badly as he wanted to. He eventually had to start his own studio in order to produce really bad movies featuring his WWE "superstars." Hollywood, before Darren Aronofsky's *The Wrestler*, wanted nothing to do with wrestling.

Man, this is by far the worst thing about the business: where do you go afterwards? You work in a profession — at that point it was nine years for me — and when your run is over there is nowhere else to bring your skills. (Who am I, Napoleon Dynamite?) And it was only nine years for me, and writing and producing does give you a bit more opportunity than bouncing off the ropes for 25 years. I'm not going to cry here because the boys have it three times as hard as I do. Where do they go when age catches up with them, or they're released from the company they worked for? They're wrestlers, and the craft is the only thing many of them know. They've been doing it since their early 20s, late teens for some. After wrestling, where do they go? That's the most difficult thing about this business. Even when you are ready, willing and able to walk away from it all, in what direction do you take your first step? Why do you think so many of the boys wrestle long after their prime, or work the indies when their time in the "Big Show" is over? For some, it's ego. But for many it's simply a case of having to support their families. And, keep in mind, many of these guys don't have a nest egg to fall back on. Living on the road in the manner they're accustomed to, many of them squander it all. That was the only thing that saved me. I hadn't thrown my money away on a lavish, unnecessary lifestyle. Remembering the words of the great Lou Gianfriddo, "Every day in the wrestling business could be your last," I saved and invested every penny I made.

Knowing that it would come down to this the minute I started working for Titan back in 1993, I had no other option but to open my own business. And that was fine with me. I loved being in business for myself back in the mid-to-late eighties when the video industry was just starting to blossom back on Long Island. Yeah, it was hard work and you busted your butt 80 hours a week, but at the end of the day you had something to show for it. Plus, you were working for *yourself*, not some greedy boss who never appreciated what you sacrificed in order to make him successful. So, after doing some research I decided to open a CD Warehouse in Marietta, focusing on something I both knew and enjoyed. I would offer my customers everything and anything they were looking for to escape their daily doldrums. From new and used CDs, DVDs and video games, to vintage cassettes and vinyl, to every kind of gimmick and collectable you could imagine — I had it all. The store was no doubt a reflection on who I was, easy to tell by the Ricochet Rabbit bobble head doll that called the front desk at the computer home.

So I took some money from my savings, a bit over $100,000, and I went into business. The thing that stands out the most about starting CD Warehouse was that I had to fly for training to Oklahoma City. The date? September 11, 2001. I can remember as if it were yesterday, waking up with the eagerness and anticipation of a first-grader getting ready for his first day of school. The first thing I did, as I always do, was turn on the TV. Once I got past the hotel info channels, there was Katie Couric reporting on some poor idiot who just flew his plane into the Twin Towers.

Then a second plane hit.

These were no ordinary idiots.

Moments after Katie reported on the second plane, she threw to a reporter live at the Pentagon. During that live report, an explosion could be heard in the background. The United States of America was under attack. At that point all I could think of was my family: Amy, Will, VJ and Annie all at home, alone. I immediately called to touch base with Amy, just wanting to hear her voice. We watched the reports together, but some 1,000 miles apart. I told her I would be in close contact all day, as I was scheduled to be at training in a short while. What seemed like just moments after I arrived at the CD Warehouse headquarters, I was told that both Twin Towers had come crashing down — they were no more. In my mind I just couldn't contemplate that. Growing up on Long Island, I had been to the top of those buildings many times. And the people inside — how many people were inside? These were innocent men and women who just got up and went to work in the morning. Their kids would never see them again. It all seemed surreal. This just wasn't happening. At that time more than any other I felt like a New Yorker. I felt like that was my home and those were my people. And now, my people were being attacked.

That night I got back to my hotel room and immediately turned on the news broadcast. I remember sobbing in my room alone, as all those people were looking for missing loved ones. You knew they all were gone, and you knew that the people looking knew they were gone. It just hit so close to home, because it was home. I stayed in constant contact with Amy, just wanting to be reassured, to know that the kids were okay. I honestly felt like this was the start of the nuclear war that analysts had been predicting for years. I felt like it was the end of life as we knew it. Things would never be the same again.

I remember going through the next few days of training, and almost losing it on the last. Compared to this, my drama at WCW was a joke. All I could think about was family, family, family, and I just wanted to get home. Because no flights were getting out, I had to rent a car and drive non-stop from

Oklahoma to Atlanta, mostly through the night. Listening to the radio broadcast in that car, I just had no idea where this thing was going, or how it was going to turn out. It was the first time in my life I can honestly remember being scared — for all of us. Driving home that night had to be the longest drive in my life. I was just waiting for that next attack to come, and all I wanted to do was get home before it did. The hours felt like days until I finally walked through my front door. At that point I was with those I loved more than anything else in the world and nothing else mattered.

In the days that followed, and as things cooled down a bit, I prepared to open the doors at CD Warehouse. Can you imagine the timing? But what could I do? The store was built out, the lease was signed and I was in business. All I could do was make the best out of the cards that were dealt. At that time, losing the CD Warehouse investment wouldn't have killed me, because I had other money saved. However, as each day passed, and as the market dropped to record lows on a daily basis, it was only a matter of time before I lost my nest egg. Not going with my gut and pulling out early, I stuck with the advice of my financial advisor who told me to ride out the storm. Oh, I rode it out all right, and following the fallout of 9/11, when all was said and done, I cashed out, losing over $200,000. All I had left to my name was my new business. It was make it or break it time, and there was no room for error.

BitchSlap

Before I continue with life after wrestling, I'm going to backtrack for a second and tell you the story of a television project I pitched with Jeremy Borash following the crash and burn of WCW. The show was called *BitchSlap* and the Federation that surrounded it was Sports Entertainment Xtreme — yes, the same Sports Entertainment Xtreme that was used by TNA (Total Non-Stop Action) less than a year later. The brainchild of Borash and me was inspired by my teenage love for *GLOW* (Gorgeous Ladies of Wrestling). A show that was decades ahead of its time, *GLOW* offered beautiful, sensuous and sexy female wrestlers (with the exception of the 300-pound Mount Fuji) with hugely over-the-top characters such as the Farmer's Daughter, Lady Godiva, Tiffany Melon, Tina Ferrari, the tag team of Hollywood and Vine, and Vicky Victory. You can only imagine the impact that this show would have on a fourteen-year-old just sliding into puberty.

Based on this general concept, JB and I were going to take women's wrestling into the 21st century. Inspired by the "Attitude Era" of *Raw*, we were going to launch these bodacious battling babes to a place they had never dared to venture before. And it was going to be crass — and there was going to be nudity. That's why JB and I pitched it to the execs at Direct TV as a weekly pay-per-view show, long before TNA was presented to them in the very same format. To this day, just to entertain ourselves, we pull out the *BitchSlap* pitch and read it aloud until tears of laughter begin to flow down Jeff Jarrett's face.

Here's a sampling of the *BitchSlap* roster, with descriptions of each character.

(God forgive me. I wrote this before I was saved, but it's too funny not to share.)

Toxic Shock

Many of the superstars of *BitchSlap* wrestle with no strings attached; however this is not the case with the very volitile Toxic Shock. Like a dog in heat, this stuck-up, temperamental temptress uses the pads of the BitchSlap ring to the max. While she tends to turn men off with her moody demands, she claims she can make gay men menstruate. Always craving chocolate, she rides her own cycle, as she only shows up to wrestle once a month.

Homeless Heather

"Nice box," commented a young boy to his loving father as they walked by Homeless Heather's place of residence on the sidewalk just outside the *BitchSlap* Arena. The only BitchSlap competitor who wrestles for food, Homeless Heather is the she-god of the shelter. Not only does she compete in the *BitchSlap* rings, but Heather also serves as cleanup crew, as she wheels her shopping cart around the arena in search of aluminum cans during the show. Burning her bra for heat, in the twilight of the September sky Homeless Heather hits the soup kitchen before dusk. A riot around the ladle, Heather is loved by her fellow bums, but it's no laughing matter when she steps into the ring.

Kentucky Love with Pappa Woody

Get your raincoats, kids – Kentucky rain is falling! To say things are a little different in the Kentucky foothills is an understatement. Kentucky Love, a bluegrass, bosomy, bodacious bimbette, is the envy of every farmer's eye. However, for Kentucky Love, there won't be any sowing wild oats. With shotgun in hand, Kentucky's father Pappa Woody holds a very special place when it comes to his divine daughter. You see, Kentucky Love is Pappa Woody's forbidden fruit. However, though she attempts to keep her fondling father in line, Woody is hell-bent on bobbing for his daughter's apple!

The Ass Pirates: Blackbeard and Treasure Chest

Ahoy matie! Like the swashbucklers of the Caribbean, Blackbeard and Treasure Chest, the Ass Pirates, have buccaneered their way to the seas of BitchSlap. Sword-fighting a specialty, the Ass Pirates force their opponents to walk the plank while taking no prisoners. Through their revealing denim shorts, the Ass Pirates invite rump-wrangling to those seamen who lust after them. Action heroes to the pre-teen audience, Blackbeard and Treasure Chest are among the ten most wanted in every elementary school in America – no, not for prematurely causing cannons to fire, but rather leaving blue balls behind.

Birdy Hole-For-One

A PGA legend, Birdy Hole-For-One claims she doesn't need wood to win in the rings of *BitchSlap*. Nicknamed "Butch" by her fellow competitors and sporting a rock-solid 28-24-36 figure, Birdy's sexual preference has been in question since the day that she refused to stroll through Tiger's woods. Handicapped by a mean streak, male officials of *BitchSlap* beware: keep your balls away from Birdy Hole-For-One. *Fore!*

Beastie Ally with Her Little Dog Scroat

Wanted by the humane society in 48 states (apparently it's legal in North and South Dakota), Beastie Ally and her little dog Scroat have brought their act to *BitchSlap*. Posted on Alpo cans across America, Beastie Ally brings new meaning to the term "puppy love." With his eyes not the only thing bulging, let's not forget that Scroat is the innocent victim, being held against his will. But, Beastie beware: every dog has its day and it may be only a matter of time before Rover takes over!

Moose Knuckle and Camel Toe

Much like Oscar and Felix of *Odd Couple* fame, Moose Knuckle and Camel Toe came from two different worlds. From the mountains of Ozark, Moose Knuckle is a bosomy lumberjack who wields a wicked ax, while Camel Toe is a highly ranked officer of the Iranian National Army. Together, this unlikely duo has wrought havoc among the ranks of *BitchSlap*. But there is a problem: after a night of passion with a crew of young, innocent American sailors, both Moose Knuckle and Camel Toe have suffered a social disease which has disfigured their most intimate of areas. At press time, Moose Knuckle and Camel Toe are in search of the cure and on their quest to finding it they will take no prisoners!

MBP (Missing Body Parts): Stumpy and Gimpy

Park in their space and you better be ready for both a fine and a fight! Stumpy and Gimpy, collectively known as MBP, are two handicapped heroines who have learned to use their disabilities to their advantage. Walking tall and carrying her wooden leg, Gimpy will literally stick one foot in her mouth while inserting her wooden peg in your !@#$. Stumpy, sometimes referred to as the One-armed Bandit, has one of the most devastating combinations in the business today. When she hits you with a right, and then a right, and then another right, you'll most likely be down for the count. Can you lose to a one-legged woman in an !@#$-kicking contest?

You may if you are in the ring with MBP!

Nurse Hershey with Doctor Proctor

Bend over and say "Ahhh." The team physician of BitchSlap, Dr. Proctor, is known to be a real !@#$man within the locker room. Assisted by the lovely Nurse Hershey, Dr. Proctor feels his way around the superstars, assuring that each and every one of them has a clean bill of health. Anally retentive, the popular Dr. Proctor has become so overbooked that the robust Nurse Hershey has been forced to increase her role. Now the physician to the male management team of BitchSlap, Nurse Hershey lets her fingers do the walking while her rectal thermometer does the talking. Ouch!

Grandma Gas

Constantly blowing her own horn, it is methane madness when Grandma Gas steps into the ring at BitchSlap. Fueled by a flatulent fanny, this queen of brown wind uses her deadly gas to gag her opponent into submission, leaving revenge on their minds and skid marks on their bodies. Riding a Geritol high, this walking wind tunnel will catch you off guard with her finishing maneuver – the colon cleansing !@#$ blast – she *Depends* on it!

The rest of the *BitchSlap* roster was filled out with various other superstars such as: Terry Springer, Britney Shears, Fleminem, Yenta the Jewish-American Princess, Lorena Choppit, Jenny Knockersville and Q-kumba (you can only imagine).

Amy is going to kill me for including this, but I think it's relevant when laying out my journey. I dread that my mother-in-law will now be introduced to *BitchSlap*, but no chapter of my life should be omitted. Even though they, and many of you reading this, might find *BitchSlap* cruel, offensive and vile, that's not what Jeremy and I were after at the time — not at all. Keep in mind, we wrote *BitchSlap* during the final days of wcw. A time that was just so dark — so ugly and negative. Together, I think we were just looking for a little humor. I also think we just wanted to allow our creative juices to flow, due to the stifling restrictions that were put on us by Turner censors. Looking back, *BitchSlap* was a great outlet. I don't think I ever expected it to see the light of day, but it was much needed therapy for a writer who felt like he was laying on a bed of nails.

Today, the most enjoyment I get out of *BitchSlap* is when Jeff Jarrett pulls it out during one of those brain-freeze moments of our creative meetings, and starts reading the character descriptions aloud . . . mostly the characters that I wouldn't dare write about here. Jeff's laughter is contagious, and when his face turns red as he tries desperately to get out the words between laughing fits, that's when I know that *BitchSlap* served its purpose and was worth every second of my time.

Rocky Mountains = Rocky Marriage?

April 12, 2008

> When the husband honors his wife and she submits to her husband's leadership, God's formula for happiness is in place.
>
> 1 Peter 3:1-7

> If your marriage is rocky, it is likely that one or both of you have tried to modify this formula. God can restore brokenness and bring blessing out of pain, but you must be willing to obey God's formula in order to receive restoration.
>
> Dr. Michael Youssef, founder and pastor of the
> Church of the Apostles, Atlanta, Georgia

For the first time in our 25 year marriage I left home without saying goodbye to my wife. Through all our trials and tribulations, that is one thing I had never done.

I left for my flight to Boston for a TNA pay-per-view a two o'clock Saturday afternoon. The plane took off at about four and landed around ten at night. Amy called my cell shortly after I landed and I decided not to take her call. I went to bed that night and woke up not having spoken to her for nearly 24 hours. Throughout our entire marriage we had never gone that long without talking.

I thought about her, and the entire situation, throughout the four-hour flight. I was never mad at her . . . just scared. I was being faced with a situation that was foreign to me. My wife wasn't being the person who I had become accustomed to for over a quarter of a century. Something seemed different about her — foreign. It was as if I didn't know her anymore.

On that four-hour plane ride, I turned the situation over to God.

It is now two days later and I'm sitting with Tennessee Tuxedo's Chumley to my left, and Mr. Peabody's Sherman to my right, crammed in a middle seat on my way to Orlando. Yesterday, 26 hours after I left home, I called Amy and spoke to her. Why?

Believe it or not, and as ridiculous as this may sound, all I could think about was one of my favorite movies, *The Breakup*. Gary and Brooke lived together and loved each other. They had a fight. There were numerous chances for both parties to communicate with each other, but both sides were too proud to take the initiative. No words soon led to a deafening, crippling silence. The relationship soon became non-repairable. Brooke led a vote that got Gary kicked off their couples bowling team. Gary and Brooke soon broke up for good shortly thereafter.

These were the thoughts that were actually running through my head. Divorce? Outside of our first year together — the "feeling out" process — the word had never even been considered, let alone brought up. But on that flight, it found its way into my thoughts. It had nothing to do with my feelings towards my wife, but everything to do with the actions of this stranger who I was sharing a bed with.

The first 20 years of my marriage, even though I was a believer in Christ, I wasn't a *believer*. If you were to ask me if I believed in God, I would have said yes. But I had no relationship with him: zero — none. No prayers, no cards, no letters, no phone calls. Did I give him a jingle when the Giants needed to break that five-game losing streak? Absolutely. But beyond that, I wasn't a very good friend. Amy on the other hand had been on his T-Mobile top five since she was able to walk. A devoted Baptist her entire life, God was always Amy's top priority. That's what got her through the first 20 years with me. She prayed, and prayed for me, not on a daily basis but on an hourly one. In her heart of hearts, no matter how hard my shell became on the outside, she always knew that my soul was there. She just had to allow God the time, the love and the patience to make His way towards it.

Man, I can remember Amy inviting her pastor over to our house in Connecticut when I was working for Vince. Aside from J.J. Dillon a few years later, I had never been ruder to any human being. But even that didn't rattle Amy's cage. She went on believing, having a faith that I had never seen before or since. And all along she played the role of the submissive wife better than any Academy Award actress ever could.

But Amy wasn't acting — it was strictly her nature. And, even though I was Godless, I never dishonored my wife — never. Being that she was the human being she was, I always wanted to respect her; that was always the most important thing to me.

So how and why did that bond become broken? How did a rope that was once twined so tightly suddenly become frayed? What link in the chain became weak? What made Amy question me after all these years? What has put me in this God-awful position?

It was 1983 when I first set foot in Boulder, Colorado. Growing up in the Northeast, New York always was my home. At that time I had no reason or desire ever to leave. The truth is that I thought I would die there, be buried in the Farmingdale Cemetery right next to my beloved grandparents. But that day in Boulder, at that very moment I was overcome with a feeling of "why don't I live here?" I can even remember saying the words out loud. I don't know, there was just something about the place. Something that just made me feel closer to something . . . or somebody.

Over the years throughout my travels in wrestling, I have been everywhere you can imagine in the United States, from the armpit known as Poughkeepsie to the painted mountains of Utah. From the charisma of the City by the Bay to the saddened weather of Detroit, from the lights on Broadway to that desert stretch between Las Vegas and Los Angeles where I had no idea where I was. Coast to coast, sea to shining sea, I had seen it all, but, no matter how gross or grandiose the sights, that feeling that I had in Boulder never came back again. Through my 20s, into my 30s, ahead into my 40s, the way Boulder Canyon made me feel never left. I don't know how to explain it other than it was just calling my name. I don't know why . . . but I was supposed to be there.

> "He was born in the summer of his 27th year, coming home to a place he'd never been before."
>
> John Denver, "Rocky Mountain High"

"Coming home to a place he'd never been before."

That was it. Nothing will ever say it better. It was home, but still it was foreign to me. My job in wrestling has had many stops along the way, from New York to Connecticut to Georgia, but from U-Haul to U-Haul, in my heart and in my mind, Boulder, Colorado, remained the place I wanted to be my final desination. Oh, there was always a reason not to go there: distance from family, we can't move the kids again, snow, it was unrealistic, more snow, what if we get attacked by a bear — you name it, there were a million reasons why it shouldn't and wasn't going to happen. But through all that, it just never left me. Man, I swear to you, as ignorant as this may sound, every John Denver song spoke to me. Even though I had never met the legend, and even though he is now dead, it didn't matter. He was speaking to me! "Yes, he'd rather be in Colorado"? Who else was he writing that for? But, it never became an obsession. I never forced it to happen, simply because I didn't need to; it was going to happen. I didn't know when, but it was. It was all in "the plan."

On August 1, 2007, it happened.

After a year of our house being on the market, it finally sold. So I packed the wife, three kids, two cats and Yogi, and we were gone. Yes, we were going to be in Colorado! Only one slight problem: I was the only one who wanted to go. The order of struggle went like this: Amy first, because the hardest thing for her was starting over (and I don't know why — being married to me for the past 25 years should have given her plenty of practice); Will second, because he was leaving not only his high school sweetheart, but his soulmate who he lived directly across the cul-de-sac from for the past eight years; Annie third, because she was being separated from her pack of middle-school divas; and vj fourth, because he really doesn't care about anything. Give vj a "deep" DVD and his iPod, and he'll move to Afghanistan without missing a beat.

The only one who seemed to want to go was Yogi; you see, being my faithful, canine companion, he goes wherever I go — no hassles, no objections, no talking back, no headaches. If only the rest of them could be like him. But they couldn't. They were more content with not only biting, but ripping the flesh from the hand that fed them.

It was a bad situation, basically because while they had no problem living in Atlanta, I hated every passing tick of the clock. For the past eight years I had despised the place. The reason was two-fold. First being, a northerner in the south fits in about as well as a nun at a gentlemen's club. I mean, everything was foreign — everything! From the pace, which is slower then a Tim

Conway old-man walk, to the people, who all dress in flannel and wear base-ball caps, to the culture — NASCAR — right down to the language. Let me ask you this. What does it mean when you're "fixin' to go to the store"? I don't get it — everybody's fixin' to do this or fixin' to do that. All the *fixin*'s just seem to drive you crazy after a while — that's why I was *fixin'* to get the heck outta there!

But the driving force to leave Atlanta behind was the heart-wrenching memories of WCW — the place just stank of it. Everywhere I turned were bad reminders of the damage the entire episode had done to my psyche. No matter what I tried, I just couldn't shake it, couldn't leave it behind. Amy never understood this. While she was digging in deeper and deeper, I was looking for an escape route in the middle of the night. One of the perks Amy had in Atlanta was that her mother and sisters lived only six hours away in Evansville, Indiana. So on those occasions when I just became too unbear-able for her, Amy would just pack the car and go. Knowing how sensitive Amy was to meeting new people, and knowing the trauma that another move could have on my kids, I sucked it up, and just kept sucking it up, until I could suck no more.

So now I live in Broomfield, Colorado, a quaint little town right smack between Boulder and Denver. From the small home office I can see the mountains — the view that I always dreamed about. Unfortunately, right around the corner from that is usually the sight of a depressed, isolated wife who just about hates my guts. Every second of every day, Amy reminds me of how much she hates the place. From the people to the weather to the schools to the price of milk at King Sooper — it all stinks!

I've got to be honest with you. I knew it would be bad — I just didn't think it would be *this* bad. I know Amy better than anyone else I know; I understand living her entire life in a small town where everybody knows everybody, it's difficult to graze in other pastures even if they might be greener. But in Amy's eyes, not only didn't she want to graze, but the pasture was dead — while I was looking at God's majestic landscape, she was seeing brown, burnt fields of hay! But at her very core, even though she was human, and no matter how she felt, she was questioning my leadership after all these years. That's what I was struggling with.

For now, Amy and I seemed to have talked it through. While she needs to trust in her faith, and rediscover her trust in me, I need to be more sympa-thetic and understanding. But that's the way a marriage works — and that's *why* it works. Man, in the circles I run in, marriage means very little to very many. If there's that one hot stripper on a pole, everything and anything goes, even your vows. I guess that's what makes me solid when it comes to my relationship. I've seen the other side time and time again. No 25 minutes of passion is worth 25 years of the greatest relationship of my life. No, it hasn't been Disneyworld every minute of every day, but nothing is. It's just life. Times are hard; they get better, and then they get hard again. That's the way the world turns. You either go for the ride . . . or you get off. Me? I'm sitting in that front seat of the rollercoaster and I'm taking every dip and doodle that life has to offer.

I wouldn't have it any other way.

The Dawgman Cometh

"How ya doin'? I'm the Dawgman." He handed me his business card and he was right: the name inscribed there was, sure enough, "Dawgman."

As a writer there are two things I love the most: good dialogue and interesting characters. The greatest dialogue in any motion picture ever made? *Glengarry, Glen Ross*. Greatest character: Dustin Hoffman as Ratso Rizzo in *Midnight Cowboy*. My love for the spoken word is what I feel separates me from anyone else who has ever written for wrestling. I thrive on making the characters speak like real people, all the while penning verbiage that you haven't heard 1,000 times before. In wrestling, that becomes both difficult and very frustrating. No matter how different you try to make the words and the characters, the backdrop will always be a wrestling ring. It gets extremely challenging to avoid repetition — to not repeat the same obvious monotonous promo over and over again. I work very hard at being different and keeping the characters and the words as fresh as possible.

But this Dawgman dude — bro, I had never witnessed anything like him before. Sporting a short-cropped mane featuring a long bleach-blond tail in the back, and standing (on his hind legs) at an imposing six-two, and weighing in at a robust 300 pounds, never had I come across a gimmick such as this — not at the wwf, and not at wcw. Why? Simply because this was no gimmick, no make-believe character. This was the real Magilla! His real name? As the great Rock would say, "It doesn't matter what his real name is!" No name could be more fitting than the one he gave himself. Why Dawgman, you ask? The answer is both obvious and simple: he was both obsessed and possessed by his beloved Georgia Bulldogs. Now, when you live in the south and you talk about Georgia Bulldogs, you're talking about only one thing: SEC (Southeastern Conference) Football.

Every Saturday afternoon was a ritual for Dawgman: he would take his only possession, a brand new white Ford pickup truck that he couldn't afford, and dress it headlight to taillight in Georgia Bulldog gear. From the huge car door magnets on both the passenger and driver's sides, to the flag that waved ever so proudly from high atop his antenna, the Dawgman bled red and black with every ounce of blood pumping through his gargantuan veins. Now, I understand that they say that a dog is loyal to his master, but a college football team? I had never — *never* — seen loyalty like this before, and remember, this is coming from a guy who couldn't sleep until the San Francisco Giants game was complete — on the west coast, which usually meant about two a.m. So what did all this mean? If you know me, the answer is simple: I had to hire this guy to manage CD Warehouse.

"Dawgman — bark at me."

That's how he answered the phone every time it rang at my store. The greeting became legendary, as grown men — even grown wrestlers — would call just to her his unique greeting. But again, knowing me, the greeting wasn't enough; I had to take it one step further. For starters, outside the door I posted a "Beware of the Dawg" (I had changed the spelling with a Sharpie) sign. Granted, this was bad for business as some customers were afraid to enter because they thought there was a *real* canine inside, but you can't let business stand in the way of a good joke. From there, if you had the Spaldings to enter, you would experience the whole Dawgman aura, from his massive black spiked collar, to the rubber tug-of-war toy he had hanging on the wall behind him, to his tip bowl full of dog biscuits which lay adjacent to the register. Obviously I had a terrible need to amuse myself. Remember, this was a grown man we were talking about: 30 in human years, 210 in dog.

Dawgman stories soon became legendary in Marrietta, and I'm not talking about the one where he claimed that *his* dog ate the store keys when he lost them. The one that rated top gem you almost had to witness yourself to believe. One day, when minding the store solo, Dawgman began to track a suspicious looking 14-year-old, who appeared to be acting uneasy in the rap section. Picking up a scent of mischief, the Dawgman slowly walked to the suspicious lad, sniffing trouble. As he approached, the kid became nervous and sprinted towards the door. Once outside, the chase was on. Keep in mind, we're talking about a 300-plus-pound man, or Dawg, hoofing it after a scared 14-year-old African-American. Not only did Dawgman's chances not look good, they looked downright hopeless. As the kid quickly gained distance between the two, the Dawgman had an idea: he'd jump in his Ford pickup, which would enable him to make up some time. So the Dawg got in his truck and proceeded down the road. About half a mile later he caught up with the young thief, who had indeed stolen a used CD which I had purchased for approximately 50 cents. Did you grasp that last line? I said 50 cents. Why is that relevant? Because throughout the 15-minute chase — the Dawgman had kept the store open — and unattended!

Yes, the important thing was that the Dawgman got our fifty-cent CD back. After apprehending the villain, Dawgman not only called the cops, but took a picture of the kid sitting in the back of the patrol car. Where he got a camera, I have no idea. From there, he proudly posted the picture of the kid behind the counter with the header reading, "Caught by the Dawgman — Crime doesn't pay!" About three months later the poor kid called the store crying, begging me to take down the picture because all the kids at school were making fun of him.

Obviously my preoccupation with the Dawgman meant I was bored out of my mind working behind a counter 40 hours a week. Yeah, it was my store, it was fun, it was easy, and I was making money — but it just wasn't me. Having experienced the excitement I had over the past six years, slinging CDs just wasn't going to do it for me. All of a sudden the wrestling business wasn't *that* bad . . . was it? At the same time the ratings for *Raw* weren't just sinking, they were free-falling. What Ed and I had built into consistent mid-sixes were now very low fours. Just like I had told Vince, the writers following us had ridden the wave, and now they were crashing *head first* into the shore. I knew that if I made that one phone call that Vince would take me back in a heartbeat. But did I really want to make that call? In my heart of hearts, I knew that nothing there had changed. I knew that Vince was still the same guy — always and forever only looking out for Vince.

During this time Disco would call me on a daily basis, saying, "What are you doing? This is ridiculous, you and the Dawgman over there. When are you going to call Vince?" It went on for months, with me holding off the temptation as best as I could. Finally, one day I told Disco, "All right — if the ratings drop below a four, I'll call," I never in my my wildest dreams thought they would. The next installment of *Raw* drew a 3.9. Disco called immediately.

To be honest, I didn't know what to do. Was this fate? Was I supposed to be with Vince? Was I never supposed to leave the WWF for WCW in the first place? So many questions and emotions ran through my mind, but the one outweighing factor was that going back to Vince meant going back to the east coast, a place that I know my kids — as well as myself — longed to be. For the past two years I had tried to sell my house to get out of Atlanta and nothing — no bites — nothing. I guess people just weren't dying to move to the beautiful Peach State. In the back of my mind I knew that if I called Vince, *he* would buy my house, then sell it himself, in order to get me back to Connecticut ASAP. He would own me again, sure, but at the same time I would be out of the miserable, godforsaken hole I was in.

But I had to consider Amy. I knew she would be vehemently against moving again — going away from her family *again*. No matter what spin I put on it, I knew she wouldn't want any part of it. I was at a crossroads. I couldn't even pray about it, or turn it over to God, because at that point He hadn't come calling. No . . . good, or bad, I had to make this decision on my own.

Then the phone rang.

It was my old friend Double J, Jeff Jarrett. And then he said he was starting his own wrestling promotion.

An Old Friend Calling

I didn't know how long it had been since I last spoke with Jeff, but hearing his voice it seemed as if only 15 minutes had passed. To me, that's the measuring stick of a real friendship. No matter how long it's been since you last saw or spoke to someone special, that connection was never severed. In many ways it's hard to explain. You just know that for whatever reason, you were destined to be in each other's life.

I always considered Jeff my closet confidant in the business, and the reason is easy to explain: he has a heart like no other I have ever been associated with in wrestling. Through all the deceit, dishonesty, paranoia and ugliness running rampant in the backstage locker room, Jeff was always the blond-haired, blue-eyed babyface, standing tall above it all with a smile. Even though he plays a convincing heel on TV, the truth is that Jeff doesn't have the makeup to be a real-life bad guy. Maybe his beautiful wife Jill and his three angelic daughters Joslyn, Jaclyn and Jaryn had something to do with it. His family was his shining light, and he just seemed to carry them with him everywhere he went. So when Jeff called and said he was starting his own wrestling promotion and he needed my help, it didn't take me long to roll up my sleeves and jump in head first.

Jeff envisioned a weekly wrestling show, broadcast on PPV, that would be an uncensored, unrestricted and unadulterated spectacle. It would ooze with attitude, a style he knew I was very familiar with. It would be cutting-edge, different and daring — very daring. The familiarity of it was shocking — for what Jeff was talking about was *BitchSlap* with male wrestlers. He asked if I could come up with some outlandish characters that would be the stars of the show: characters with no boundaries, only unique flaws. I immediately got together with Disco and we came up with a roster that mirrored *BitchSlap* to a T. The one team that stands out in my mind as I write this is the Jew Tang Clan, a group of bad!@#$ Hasidic thugs. You get the picture. At that time I also came up with the company's name — TNA — but it didn't stand for Total Nonstop Action, though we later had to say it did. During all this, Jeff and I never talked job, or money for that matter. I was just happy that I could help him, while freeing my creative cuffs. The prospects seemed promising until Jeff mentioned one very small detail: his father, Jerry Jarrett, was going to be his partner in the endeavor.

Now, I had previously worked with Jerry Jarrett for a short time while under Vince, and to be honest, I genuinely admired him. Like the legend who gave me my first break in the WWF, Cowboy Bill Watts, Jerry was a pioneer in the wrestling business. He was a staple in the Mid-South, selling out the Memphis Coliseum week after week, while putting up astronomical TV numbers in the local market — "local" being the key word. But like many promoters of that day, I also knew that Jerry carried the one trait they all hauled around: stubbornness. With many promoters from that era, it was their way or the highway — and not much room in between. While I respect that in theory, and have been accused of it myself, the one flaw in it was that things weren't the same in 2002 as they were in 1972. Times had changed, the business had changed, but those who paved the way fought the change with everything they had. Do I wish it was still 40 years ago? Absolutely! Do I wish that the original *Batman* was still in production? Yes. Do I long for Julie Newmar to still look like Julie Newmar? Without a doubt. But I'm also realistic enough to know that's just not going to happen.

On top of that, there was always something else that bothered me about the Jeff and Jerry Jarrett dynamic. When around his dad, Jeff always seemed to just fade in the background; he just seemed to lose self-esteem and confidence. Without getting into detail, I knew this had a lot to do with their relationship growing up, but nonethless, I didn't care for it. When Jeff called me and said that *he* was starting a wrestling promotion, there was no doubt in my mind that Jeff could be successful. Working with him for all those years at both the WWF and WCW, I knew how smart he was; there was never a question over his ability and capability. But this meager Jeff while Jerry was around — I flat out hated it.

Once Jeff told me his father was involved, I knew that I was going to have to have a conversation with the elder Jarrett. I had to know, first-hand, where he was at. So Jerry and I had a telephone conversation that seemed to last hours — did I mention that the pioneers like to talk as well? Without going into detail, one thing rang loud and clear. Jerry Jarrett wanted to be in charge . . . of *everything*. And you know what? I didn't have a problem with that. It was his money, his son and his right. But I also knew that I had no place in that equation. Jerry wanted to write the TV — he made that clear to me — and when I mentioned that I had the utmost confidence in my writing ability and that I still felt I was the best in the game, he later told his son that I was "delusional." You know what? Maybe he was right. But I wasn't delusional enough to think that this three-way dance would work.

On a side note; Jerry Jarrett recently wrote a book where he buried me; I refuse to reciprocate. Jerry Jarrett did some great things in his career, and even though I may not like the type of human being that he is, it's not for me to judge him. At the end of the day, we're just different people, that's all. Different ages from different eras with different philosophies and different beliefs. And one more thing: different hearts. Very different hearts.

Being that I had now put my toe back in the water, I was now ready to sink or swim. Knowing that things weren't going to work with Jeff, there was only one place left: back to the evil emperor himself, Vince McMahon.

There Ain't No Going Home

There was no question that when it came down to who I'd rather work for — Jeff Jarrett or Vince McMahon — the fair-haired, blue-eyed country boy won, hands down. It was no contest, George Foreman vs. Joe Frazier circa 1973. I was only 12 years old, but I can still hear Howard Cosell bellowing from the top of his lungs.

"Down goes Frazier! Down goes Frazier! And Foreman is as poised as can be in a neutral corner! He's as poised as can be!"

A vicious KO in the second round — man, that was flat ugly. Maybe a harsh comparison, but in my opinion just as hideous is the contrast in personality between the Henderson, Tennessee, native and the Greenwich millionaire. What it really comes down to is this: one has heart — one doesn't. Now, I'm not saying that Vince is a bad guy — because he really isn't — what I'm saying is that money, for Vince, supersedes everything else. If you're making money for McMahon he loves you; however the second that cash cow drops some manure, it's on to the next side of beef. In all my years with him, Vince just never treated people like people. Jeff — Jeff genuinely is a southern gentlemen who sincerely cares about not only those who work for him, but people in general. Does he have a mean streak, a business side? Sure he does, but he's never "ice-cold" or "you're dead to me." Jeff has compassion, and I'm just not sure Vince does. He certainly didn't show it when without missing a beat he told me to hire a nanny to take care of my kids so I could have more time to make more money for him. That conversation would have never taken place with Jeff. Family is more important than anything else to him. It's called heart. The other promoter's lost somewhere in a black hole of greed.

Still, the last thing I was going to do was come between a father and his son. The Vince Russo/Jeff Jarrett/Jerry Jarrett triangle was never going to work, as much as I might have wanted it to, so I was left with no other option. If I wanted to get back into the ring then it was going to have to be with Vince McMahon.

Even though there were major trepidations, there were reasons why a move "back home" seemed logical. Again, Vince would buy my home in Atlanta and get me back to the east coast where I thought I belonged. Secondly, it would give me the opportunity to explain to Vince, face to face, why I left him in the first place — something I had always longed to do. For over two years I had looked for that closure and just couldn't find it. So after some deliberation, I called Vince. He was eager to take my call. No surprises there: his business was down — *way* down. So I flew in for a clandestine meeting with the WWE Chairman at his mansion. From the first second I stepped in the palace, things were the same — after waiting nearly 30 minutes for his grand entrance, he came downstairs. I gave Vince a hug, but to be honest, the response was stiffer then a Kurt Angle uppercut. After exchanging plastic, meaningless pleasantries, I got right into it and explained why I left his company for his competitors. I remember telling Vince that part of the reason was that I had grown so attached to him and his family — and I wasn't sure if the feeling was mutual. I asked Vince, "Was I just the cash cow — or did you really care about me and my calves [family]?" I'll never in 17 billion years forget the words that made up Vince's emotionless answer.

"Vince, when you work as closely with someone the way I worked with you . . . then you *have to* care about them."

Two years and that was it? My closure? That was the answer I was searching for? You work with somebody for a long time and you *have to* care about them? No, you don't! I worked for years with people who I *never* cared about! Vince just couldn't find it in his heart to tell me that as a human being, as a person, he genuinely cared about me — not that he had to but that he genuinely did. The truth? He didn't lie; he was honest; he told the truth. In his own words he just confirmed everything I had expected. He cared because, and only because, I made him money. You know what? If that's what it takes to be rich with money, then I'll die a poor, caring slob.

After that first meeting, there was a second, where I laid down an entire year of creative direction. My main story was that Vince would hire Eric Bischoff as the GM of his company. Working off a somewhat shoot, Vince would torture Eric with glee now that he had his main competitor as an employee. Eric, being Eric, would take everything in stride, taking everything Vince had to dish out, until the boss started to become quite fond of his moxie. Once he had Vince's trust, then Eric would kick into action his plan to overtake Vince McMahon and the mighty WWE, but this time from within. While Eric was working Vince the way that no one else could, the only one wise to him would be Vince's son Shane. Of course, when he confronted his old man, Vince would accuse Shane of being jealous, and pay him no mind. Once it was too late, and Eric's plan worked to a T, Vince would lose power. Only his son was left to try to win it back. There was more detail to it, but that was the gist. Through it all I wanted to play off of Eric's previous relationships with WCW talent, and his new employees now working under him from the WWE.

Needless to say, Vince loved the idea. Previously he had had no intention of hiring Eric, and I think he was taken aback when I suggested it. Hey, but why wouldn't I? Eric was a smart, good-looking TV personality who *got it*. He was a great on-air character. So, after agreeing on my position (I would oversee *Raw* and *Smackdown* while working under daughter Stephanie — I guess, it was never officially said to me) and salary, I asked Vince how he was going to break the news to the creative team. In his matter-of-fact voice, Vince told me that he wanted me to show up at the upcoming pay-per-view that weekend, and he would notify the troops then. In *my* matter-of-fact voice I flat out said no. I told Vince that that was the wrong way to go about it and it certainly wouldn't have been the best way to announce my return. With that feedback Vince suggested that I stay overnight and that he would bring me to the creative meeting the following morning at the TV studio, and make the formal introduction there.

The following morning before the meeting I met Shane McMahon for breakfast. No doubt Shane was thrilled to hear that I was coming back because he knew I was always his biggest supporter. To this day, I'll go on the record to say that Shane was one of the best on-air personalities that I ever worked with — yes, even better then his old man. In my opinion over the course of the years Vince McMahon has become a parody of the Vince McMahon character. Again, the "big gulp," when Vince gets scared or intimidated, is always what kills it for me. I feel that Shane just brings much more credibility to his character. During my breakfast with the "Prince," Shane wasn't shy about asking me what my thoughts on his character were. With Shane not being on air at the time — I had no idea why — I confidently told him, "My plans? To get you back on TV where you belong."

From there I headed over to the TV studio where Vince met me outside. Before even setting one foot in the building, things felt strange. For starters, why were the booking meetings now at the TV studio? When Ed and I were writing TV, the meetings were held at my house in front of my 46-inch Mitsubishi television — that way we could work and watch the *Jerry Springer Show* simultaneously. The stodginess and confines of writing TV in the office just wouldn't have worked for us. Man, I had smelled this before . . . the stench of corporate was gagging me as I walked in the door. Once inside, Vince walked me over to a conference room where he opened the door and walked inside with me in tow. I remember this as if it were yesterday: the impression of my first glance at the WWE brain-trust left a lasting imprint more significant then any Ric Flair chop I had ever taken at WCW. It was so powerful that I literally had to take a step back.

What I saw was a room chock full of kids . . . children, all bright-eyed and bushy-tailed, while looking scared to death at the same time. And at first glance it appeared that there was a sea of them. I've never been to a Star Trek convention in my life, but I swear to you, this is what one surely must look like. They were marks; that's all I can say. I felt it then, and I feel it now. They had no business being in that room, writing that TV. Vince had groomed me for years before I ever got the pencil; what had these kids ever done? Who had they ever beaten? The only familiar faces I remember were Michael Hayes and Paul Heyman. And to be honest, I wasn't quite sure if they were part of the committee, or just babysitting for a few hours.

After Vince made the formal introduction, he exited the room and left me alone with his tenth-grade class. Over the next three hours I laid out the TV for them for the next year: storylines, characters, plots and twists that were way beyond their comic-book realm of understanding. The looks on their faces were priceless. I mean, jaws weren't just dropping — they were crashing to the carpet. To this day I have never witnessed a group of "professionals" so afraid of losing their jobs. And you know what? They should have been. At that time the writing was atrocious. They had taken the masterpiece of a painting that Ed and I had perfected over three years, and they had graffitied it with their Crayolas in less than two. Shame on them — shame on them all.

Heyman and Hayes said nothing — absolutely nothing. Now, even if you aren't in the business, it's obvious to see from the description that what I was doing was absolutely burying myself. Taking the shovel and just heaving the cold, hard dirt all over myself. The insecurities in that room were more obvious then an Ashlee Simpson nose job. "If this guy is hired, what do they need us for?" They might have well just said it out loud, because they were screaming it with their blemished faces. And even though I knew that none of those kids had the Spaldings to bury me to Vince when he returned, Hayes and Paul E. had decades of experience to do it for them. But you know what? I didn't care. If Vince had me there to try to help his sinking ship, then that's what I was going to do, no matter what anybody was going to say and do after I left that room. The reason was simple: in my heart of hearts I knew that if they buried me to Vince, they would eventually all lose their jobs because their inability to achieve would catch up with them at some point. In taking me out they would sooner or later cut their own throats, because at the end of the day I was the only one who could help them.

Now, you're probably wondering, "Where was Stephanie during all this?" Well, Stephanie wasn't there. However, during a break I was summoned to an empty office. Stephanie wanted to talk to me via speakerphone. Obviously, one of her stooges had already called her, filling her in on the gist of the meeting. Now understand this: while she was a creative director in training, Stephanie would attend the creative meetings with Vince, Ed and me, and never say a word. She was listening and learning as she should have. So imagine how shocked I was when this disembodied voice spent ten minutes talking down to me not only like a red-headed stepchild, but a red-headed and *freckled* stepchild. Stephanie treated me with no respect — *zero*. Could she have been as insecure as the rest of the class? Maybe — but she was the *boss's daughter*, for cryin' out loud! I began to wonder if Vince had even wised her up that I was coming in.

I left Stanford without seeing Vince again, and maybe that was a good thing. As I pondered the day during my return flight, I came to one very quick conclusion. There was no way, no how this thing was ever going to work. And, not only from my end, but from the McMahons' as well. It was as clear as Saran Wrap, the only one who wanted me there was Vince. He knew what I did for his company, he knew what I could bring to the table, and he also knew that if the WWE was ever going to get back to the height it was when I left, that I was probably the only guy to do it. Even though I understand that sounds like I'm blowing my own horn, it was the truth.

I remember going home and my boys being all excited to get the news. Remember, a move back to Vince meant a move back to Connecticut, and that's all they cared about. I couldn't even look them in the eye. I had to get Amy alone to explain to her that as much as I wanted this to happen for the sake of getting the family back "home," it just wasn't going to work. Amy looked at me and said, "Well, maybe that's why Vince was trying to call you while you were flying home."

There's no question that Vince was feeling the exact same thing that I was: we were the only two wanting this thing to happen. And that's understandable; we both knew the magic we created together when we were in our own little world, and it was small, and it was manageable. No one knew better then us exactly how well we did work together. And you know what? Nobody cared. Nobody cared about where the company was going because all they cared about was their own job security, including Mrs. Levesque.

Let me just publicly say it, and this is just my opinion: Vince McMahon made the single worst decision for his company when he put his daughter in charge of creative. And even though I don't think Stephanie is qualified for the job, that in itself really has nothing to do with it. The problem is, Vince can never replace her — *never*. Replacing his own daughter and leaving egg on her face is not an option. First and foremost, Stephanie is his flesh and blood, and even though Vince is as heartless as the Grinch at times, he could never do that to the apple of his eye. And I applaud him for that. But if anyone else without the last name of McMahon was responsible for basically cutting the ratings in half over an eight-year span, where do you think they'd be now?

It was too late to call Vince that night, so I called him when I woke up the following morning. His first words to me: "Vince — this isn't going to work out."

My first words to him: "Why, Vince? Because the second I left that room all your minions buried me to you?"

From there the conversation got a bit ugly, not because I was upset by Vince, not because I was upset with his tenth-grade class, but because I was upset with the veterans in that room — and you know who they are — who didn't have the guts to bury me to my face. I remember telling Vince during the conversation, "You talk about bravado all the time, Vince — what happened to yours? You're not the same guy I knew two years ago. You and I both know that you want this to happen, but you're going to kowtow to a bunch of people who are afraid of losing their jobs? Where's the bravado, Vince?"

In hindsight, the real reason was Stephanie. The fact that I would be reporting to Stepanie was a ridiculous notion and Vince knew it. So what was he supposed to do? He had no other choice and I understood that; I was just trying to make it difficult for him.

My last line to Vince McMahon was, "Vince, forget business for a minute. From a personal standpoint, I'm telling you: you don't have the people in that room to turn your product around."

That was in July 2002 and the rating was at a 3.7.

Last night's *Raw*, on April 28, 2008 — six years later — earned a rating of 3.3.

Same people; same results. Same daughter; same results.

At this point I'm thinking that the Vince Russo/WWE story is officially finished. To my surprise Vince called back less than 15 minutes later asking me if I would consider coming on as a "consultant." I knew the return phone call came due to my last line. He had to be thinking, "What if he's right? What's my plan to fall back on?" I told Vince that he caught me by surprise and that I would have to think on it. It was Friday; I told him to give me the weekend.

Before I could give Vince's offer even a second of thought, the phone rang again.

"Vince . . . I need you to write my TV," a familiar voice said.

It was Jeff Jarrett.

The Birth of TNA

May 1, 2008

Today is Will's 21st birthday.

Talk about mortality setting in. I can remember his birth as if it were yesterday: hearing that cry as the doctor brought a new human being into this world — my son, William James Russo. I cried like a child; it was by far the happiest moment in my life. I can remember running out and buying this huge, almost life-like My Pet Monster and placing it next to him on the bed. The hideous-looking stuffed toy had to be three times the size he was. Then I had a small T-shirt printed up that said, "Will the Thrill," and placed it over his tiny frame. Yes — my son was named after one of my favorite baseball players of all time, former San Francisco Giant first baseman Will "The Thrill" Clark.

Another moment that is still vivid in my mind is calling my beloved Aunt Mary when I got home from the hospital. The sister of my late grandmother on my mother's side, Aunt Mary was the closest thing I had left to Nana and I absolutely adored her. Some 21 years later, Aunt Mary has long passed, and my baby boy has moved out of the house. Some of Will's friends followed us to Colorado shortly after we moved, and before we could barely get settled Will moved into an apartment with his buddies from high school. Even though I would never let on to it, it broke my heart. Watching him get in his car and drive away, I saw a man. No longer the child I held so tightly as I ran through the streets of New York trying not to miss the start of the Teenage Mutant Ninja Turtles concert at Radio City Music Hall. Or the toddler who used to crawl about my head as I tried to play two minutes — just two minutes — of Nintendo's *Rygar* before I had to go to work. Or the pre-schooler whose feet rested on my shoulder as I stretched his arms in a vertical position forward as I flew him through every mall in Connecticut with the grace of Superman. Or the ten-year-old whose first home run I missed because I was working for a human being who just couldn't grasp the idea of family and what was truly important.

Even though Will is only 30 minutes away, I miss him every day. Maybe *he's* ready to grow up . . . but his father certainly isn't ready for him to.

But hey, if I still pay his car insurance, don't I have some claim?

On a lighter note, big blow-up in the North Metro & Friends Fantasy Baseball League yesterday. The controversy began when a trade a fellow manager and I agreed to was vetoed by the rest of the league. Why? Because the deal would have helped "Bonds is Unemployed" (the name of my team) in the long run and my jealous peers simply don't want me bagging the $90 first place prize money two years in a row. Fortunately, the minute I pulled the ol' Vince Russo on 'em and threatened to take my baseball and go home they saw things in a much different light.

But getting back to Jeff . . .

"Vince, I need you to write my TV" are the words I'll always remember. They struck such a powerful chord with me at the time because I had just left a place that didn't want *me* at all — only the knowledge that I brought. As a friend, Jeff made it clear that he needed *me*, and that was the most significant thing I could hear. I explained to Jeff the fiasco that had just occurred at Titan Towers, and I told him it ended with Vince offering me a spot as a consultant. Jeff asked me if I would be willing to at least come to the next show in Nashville (it was TNA's second) and take a look-see. After all we had been through together, the least I could do was check out his new company.

My next call was to Stephanie McMahon. How strange; I was now calling Stephanie instead of her old man — laughable. Anyway, I called Stephanie and told her that I didn't want her to read it in the dirt sheets so I wanted to tell her myself: I'm going to check out TNA, and I'll give you an answer regarding that consultant job when I get back. I remember Stephanie being taken aback, as if she wasn't believing what she was hearing. But think about it; at that time what could she do? She knew she was in way over her head and she knew that she needed help. As a consultant I was now no threat to her at all. So, basically having no choice, Stephanie said okay, and that she looked forward to my call when I returned.

Who better to take the four-hour car ride from Atlanta to Nashville with than Glenn Gilberti? All the way up I discussed my dilemma with Glenn, and to be honest, I think Glenn was leaning towards me going to the WWE only because I told him that he would be part of the package. However, I was leaning the other way for one reason, and one reason only: Jeff Jarrett. Comparing Jeff Jarrett and Vince McMahon as human beings is like comparing Entenmann's chocolate fudge cake to the Pathmark brand: there is no comparison. Jeff genuinely cared about you; Vince didn't. It was a simple as that. And with me, that was everything. Face it: there would be no comparison to what Jeff could pay me as opposed to Vince, but that meant absolutely nothing to me. It all came down to looking into their respective hearts. One would have handed you the last peanut butter and jelly sandwich left on the planet, with a smile on his face; the other would have sold you a quarter of it for 50 bucks.

But there was still the "Jerry Factor," remember?

Not only didn't I want to come between Jeff and his dad, but I also knew that Jerry just didn't like me. And it wasn't just a matter of our wrestling philosophies being different — that would have been one thing — but I also feel that in an odd way, Jerry was jealous of the relationship I had with his son. Jeff and I were close, perhaps even closer than the father and son were, and for some reason Jerry made me feel like he was somewhat intimidated by this, like Vince Russo had some kind of power over Jeff Jarrett. Again, these are just my thoughts and my insights — I'm only telling you how I viewed the situation. But those words just kept ringing through my mind: "Vince, I need you to write my TV." The vast differences in talent and production between the WWE and TNA that I experienced while hanging out backstage in the Nashville Municipal Auditorium didn't mean a thing. Even with the indie feel that went with TNA at the time, it didn't matter. Even though one side had Triple H, John Cena, the Undertaker and Shawn Michaels, while the other side had the Johnsons with Mortimer Plumtree, it didn't matter. What mattered was that Jeff was on one side of the fence and Vince was on the other.

When I returned home, Jeff called the next day and basically asked me what it was going to take financially for me to come over to TNA. I gave Jeff a number that was well below what Vince was offering me for the consultant position. Jeff said he could do it, but there is also no doubt that Jeff thought I was merely using him and TNA as leverage to hopefully force Vince to up the ante on his offer. I wasn't; not at all. I had every intention of going to TNA, even though I knew that the upstart company could be out of business in a month. Again, it all came down to Jeff and Vince.

I called Stephanie the next day and declined the WWE position of consultant; needless to say, she was shocked. Turning down the machine for the little train that couldn't was ridiculous — I knew it and she knew it — but she didn't know Jeff Jarrett, or her father for that matter, like I did. I told Stephanie that with all due respect it was apparent that I wasn't wanted at the WWE and I wasn't going to go to a place that was going to make it difficult for me to perform. I also told her that I wasn't going to pay any penance, to anybody, for anything, because I made the decision to leave the mighty empire a few years earlier in the best interest of my family. I thanked Stephanie for the opportunity and then hung up.

Howdy boys!

I was on my way to Nashville.

Sorry, Jack, Chrissy and Janet — Three Is a Crowd!

I think it started with me writing the first couple of TNA shows, and then Jeff handing them off to Jerry for his final say. With that structure in place, Jerry Jarrett was getting the last word. In my heart of hearts, I knew that Jeff didn't want it this way, but I also knew that he was somewhat insecure with the pressures and the responsibilities of starting his own company. He relied on Jerry because Jerry had been there, and I understand that clearly. But in my opinion Jerry had done it decades ago. Sure, some of the principles in professional wrestling will always stay the same — the fundamentals are always fundamental — but how you present them today is radically different from how they were presented in the 70s and the 80s. At the end of the day, however, TNA was Jeff's baby. I was going to respect the way he wanted to go about business even if I disagreed with it.

Fortunately, there was no time for Jerry and me to even get into it because within a matter of weeks TNA's financial backer pulled out. Needless to say, Jeff was devastated. He apologized to me over and over, saying that he knew that I passed up an opportunity at the WWE for him. Not only did I have no regrets, but for some reason I didn't think this was the end of the road for the company. Call it fate, call it whatever you want, but I believed that good things happened to good people — and Jeff was just too good a person to have his livelihood pulled out from under him.

For the next couple of weeks, both Jerry and Jeff did their best to keep TNA afloat as they searched for other financing. The thing I remember most about this time was not getting paid. Why I remember is because on the day that we missed our first paycheck,

Ed Ferrera packed up his desk and headed out. In a way I didn't blame Ed; the minute you miss a paycheck in wrestling you need to fill the tank with gas and point it towards Mexico. That's just part of the business — here today and gone tomorrow. My case was different because I was closer to Jeff and I had faith in him. Jeff told me that even though he had no idea how, he would make up those missed paychecks, and I believed him.

Right around that time, Jeff and his wife Jill invited me and my family out to the lake that sits right off his Hendersonville property. This day was a pivotal one in the life of Vince Russo. Not because Jeff told me that a woman who was doing PR for TNA by the name of Dixie Carter had a wealthy father, a business tycoon from Dallas who he was already scheduled to meet with and talk about possibly backing TNA, but because of a series of events — and words — that happened and were said that afternoon.

To be honest, I'm not exactly sure what brought it on, but in the nicest way that he could, Jeff said that my life was getting out of control. Maybe it had something to do with my two teenage boys running rampant, disrespecting everything and everybody along the way. Or maybe it had to do with me being in my own little world, to the point that you wouldn't even know Amy and I were a couple, let alone married. It could have been a million things, but that day, as a friend was as honest as a friend should be, something happened that was beyond anything I had ever experienced before. Never at any time did Jeff bring God into the equation, but when he delivered the message it seemed like it was coming from more than just a friend.

In the days that followed, Jeff met with Dixie Carter's parents, Bob and Janice, who were indeed the real Magilla. The Carters owned a company in Dallas called Panda Energy, and they had the financial clout that Jeff and TNA needed to stay alive. Much to her credit, Dixie saw something in both Jeff and his company: she saw potential in something that was on life support, to say the least. Jeff and Jerry came to an agreement with the Carters, and TNA was in business again.

And Jeff made up for my lost pay, just like he promised.

This was great news for the company, but not so good for this writer. Now, if there's one magical element that wrestling promoters possess, it's the ability to work people, especially outsiders, who just don't have a clue to the way the wrestling business functions — and Jeff Jarrett is not the promoter that I'm talking about. According to Jerry Jarrett, the only reason the Carters made the investment in TNA was because of him. It was his experience and expertise that compelled Bob and Janice to fork over the greenbacks. Now, even though I didn't believe that for a New York minute, what was I supposed to do, call Jerry Jarrett a liar? Yeah, I guess I should have, but now there was the "Jeff Factor." I told myself that I wasn't going to get between Jeff and his dad and I was doing everything in my power to live up to that. Jerry, now the cock of the walk, even went as far as to say that if he wasn't in charge of creative, that the Carters would pull their money out. Even though I knew that premise was laughable, there was nothing I could do. So, Jerry Jarrett took over creative at TNA.

In my view, the next few weeks of programming were the worst I had ever seen in the history of the business. And we all knew it. But nobody had the nerve to say anything to Jerry.

Until one day . . .

Dixie held a company meeting a few weeks after Panda took stock in TNA. During that meeting, we discussed everything, including creative. All I can say is that my encounter with the elder Jarrett was just barely a shade prettier than the one I had with J.J. Dillon a few years earlier. In the presence of Dixie and the entire company, I told Jerry just how bad I thought the creative was. It was totally out of line on my part — totally — but at that point I just couldn't help myself. The look on Jerry's face? I really can't describe it; all I can say is that he was going to be hellbent on taking me down, somehow, some way, when the verbal smoke had cleared. The thing I remember most about the meeting is looking towards the end of the table in mid-rant and seeing the smirk on Ron Harris' face. No doubt I was saying what everybody else at that meeting was feeling.

From there, Jerry shut me off completely. I remember felling really bad about it and apologizing to him later. Soon thereafter Jerry, Jeff and I all met at Jerry's "estate." I was now in the exact same spot that I dreaded being in: sitting right between father and son. Knowing I put Jeff in a very horrible position, I said my piece and then tapped out. Jerry was going to be in control — total control — and I was just going to be idle on the sidelines. That night, Jeff and I went out to a very late dinner — I think it was IHOP — and for the very first time we felt extremely uncomfortable around each other. I knew how difficult this was for Jeff, and at that point I just wanted to keep the friendship intact, because had it been two other people, it would have been irreparable.

The thing that frustrated me the most was that I knew that on his own, Jeff could make this thing work. I had all the confidence in the world in him, but out of respect and perhaps fear of the unknown, Jeff sat back while Jerry took control. Back then Jeff was just a different guy in Jerry's presence, just not himself. I know it had everything to do with the unique nature of their relationship. Jeff grew up in the business under his promoter dad. Still, I realized it was something Jeff could only get through himself. You couldn't talk to him about it because Jeff's just not that way. To this day I have to pull his true feelings from him, even though that has changed drastically, since his wife Jill passed away.

One thing that really stands out about this time took place on a bus ride from the airport in Orlando to Universal Studios. Jerry Jarrett was holding court at the front of the bus, telling a story about when Jeff broke into the business. He said Jeff's first job was to drive the King Jerry Lawler from town to town. According to Jerry, every time Lawler would get in his son's car, the first thing he would do was change the radio station to his favorite. Over time this began to annoy Jeff, and rightfully so. It was, after all, his car! So one day, the younger Jarrett finally had enough and cut a scathing promo on Lawler, telling him to never touch his car radio again. From there, Lawler went to Jerry. In Jerry's own words, here's what happened: "You know what I did? I fired my son!"

Jerry laughed about it like it was the greatest thing he'd ever done. I'll never forget that moment. How on earth do you not only fire your own flesh and blood, but go on to tell a busload of people who work for him, and then laugh about it? Will and vj did some stupid things while working at CD Warehouse . . . but to fire them, and then boast about it?

This was only the tip of the iceberg in the Jerry/Jeff saga.

So yeah — I tapped out. What else could I do? I was there if Jeff needed me, but that was it. Unfortunately, the writing was going from bad to worse, and Jeff knew it. Finally one day he picked up the phone, called and said, "Vince . . . remember that Sports Entertainment Xtreme thing you used to talk about? We need to do it."

SEX
(Sports Entertainment Xtreme)

July 1, 2008

It's been a while since I've written — a month, maybe two. During that time two things occured which once again put everything into perspective, especially my age and my mortality.

I took Will to Las Vegas for his birthday and some father–son bonding time. Who am I kidding? *Bonding* . . .

I knew it was probably one of the last times I'd ever get to spend quality time alone with my son. He's growing up at such a pace that only Harry Chapin's "Cat's in the Cradle" can describe how I feel. The time we spent together meant everything to me. Certainly more than he'll ever know. Being with him for four days . . . I could just see so much of me in everything he does. I was *him* when I was that age, some traits good, and some not so good. Aside from him being perhaps the cheapest human being I know — besides myself — Will has a tremendous, tremendous heart. Maybe one ventricle can be attributed to me, but the other three go to Amy. No doubt.

Highlights? There was spending the day with the great Professor, Mike Tenay, at a sports book not too far from his Las Vegas home. Will bet on the NBA semi-finals, while I stuck with my passion: hardball. The time with Mike was great, truly great. If you would have told me five years ago that Vince Russo and Mike Tenay were going to spend a day off *together*, I would have accused you of being on the rum candy again. As you'll read soon enough, there was a time when Mike Tenay and I were about as close as Batman and Mr. Freeze. But fortunately, with time and experience we grow up; I certainly did. And getting to spend time with Mike in Vegas was like spending time with Elvis smack in the middle of his heyday at the Hilton. Mike is simply Mr. Sports Book in that town, and it was quite an experience to see him in action.

But the highlight of the trip? I took Will to see Tom Jones at the MGM Grand. It was the first time that I had ever seen my first idol live and in person. Yeah, even though I knew Will was taking it as a total goof, it meant a lot to his old man. And Tom didn't disappoint. Man, there is something about entertainers that fascinates me. From Liza Minelli to Sammy, Dean, Frank and Tony Bennett, it's a kind of lost art. Now, even though I wouldn't put Tom Jones in the same category as the Rat Pack, there's always something about seeing a performer hold the audience in the palm of his hand. And even though the night started with giggles from Will, when TJ walked off the stage that night, my eldest son was wowed. Instead of seeing what he envisioned as some 70-year-old man holding a walker with one hand while holding a mike to sing "Delilah" with the other, Will saw an honest-to-goodness entertainer. Me? I cried. What can I tell you? Tom got me early — maybe second song in, "Help Yourself." Yeah, I'm a freakin' sap.

An added, once-in-a-lifetime bonus? I got to meet and shake hands with the great Tony Curtis. Tony freakin' Curtis — perhaps one of the last, true, Hollywood icons. As I shook his hand and said, "God bless you, Sir," all Will could do was look at me and ask, "Who was that?" I know, many of you are asking the same thing right now. Let me put it in a language you can understand: Google him!

Next? My youngest son, VJ, graduated high school a couple weeks later. Two down; one to go. (Yup, more tears.) You know, at 47 I find myself crying a lot — more than I ever did as a younger man. I guess that comes with knowing it's more than half over. The ride that started so long ago is now closer to the end than it is to the beginning. I guess it started to become clear when I turned 40. I look at Will and VJ, 21 and 18 now, and I just can't remember when they were young. I know they were once; I was there. But I just can't remember. The truth? I don't know.

Is it that I can't remember, or that I just don't want to?

I know you want me to get back to wrestling again, because none of this means anything to you. Trust me: someday it will.

Anyway, let me spell it out for you: S-E-X.

Sports Entertainment Xtreme.

It was the concept that was going to change the business forever. At the time it was hip, cutting-edge, ingenious, dangerous, but perhaps even more importantly, different. That's what I felt the business most desperately needed at the time: just to be different. It was towards the end of 2001 and the wrestling business had gotten into a rut. Everything on Vince's TV was the same old same old: been there, seen it — a million times. Wrestling had just stopped evolving; it had gone back to being safe, doing just enough, what it always knew how to do — two guys in a ring, following an outline that was written 50 years earlier. It was not only boring, but predictable and most often downright silly.

Sports Entertainment Xtreme was a concept that I wanted to first try almost a decade earlier, at WCW. Even though the formula was still rough, and really needed to be fleshed out, I truly believed then — as I do now — that the concept could take the business into the 21st century. The rules were simple: there were none. Everything you saw in the ring would be done spontaneously — simply put, true reactions to true circumstances. With the key word being "reaction." You see in the wrestling business there are a lot of *bad* actors; in my opinion I'd say for every good one, there are four who can't cut it. Again, not their fault — wrestlers are trained to wrestle, not act. That's something else that needs to change, drastically, *now*. Bad acting is what makes the product, at times, unwatchable.

In SEX, I would be the catalyst. I would hit the ring and nobody on the show would know I was coming — especially Mike Tenay. What this was meant to do was simply make the players play off the circumstances. But you had to be on your A game, because I could come at any moment, at any time. Unfortunately, this is also where the concept would falter. Many of the wrestlers and other performers just weren't seasoned enough to pull it off. I'd do the run-in, and they would pull the old Ralph Kramden: stand in the middle of the ring and mumble, "humina-humina-humina." Except Mike — he was a pro. Mike's reactions were so true to form that he actually had me believing on more occasions than one that he was about to lay me out, square in the middle of the ring.

To break down how this would work is simple: I would spend the entire TV day at Jeff's house, usually yenta-ing with his wife Jill, and at the appropriate time I would get *the call* from Jeff who was at the building. Jeff would tell me what time to come, and who was going to be in the ring — that was it. There were never any directions on what to do — I would just *do*. So, I would arrive at the building at Jeff's call time and be met at the back door by the Harris Brothers. From there I would hit the ring, and simply react to the situation. Jeff usually picked a spot where Mike Teney was center stage, knowing that Mike had the experience and skill to think on his feet. He was dead on: the look on Mike's face every time I interrupted was pure genius. Man, the guy is such a pro.

I'll never forget this one time during the height of SEX. It was a Hallowe'en special and AJ Styles and I were dressed as Jason Vorhees and Freddy Kruger and spent the entire night in the crowd. Nobody — *nobody* — knew it was us. At one point during the show, Mike and Don had an on-camera and AJ and I stood right behind them — on TV the whole time. During the entire stand-up I kept poking Don West in the back of the neck with my Freddy razor claw. Don was getting hotter and hotter because there wasn't a thing he could do because we were live. As soon as the stand-up was over, Don called over for security and pointed AJ and me out, stating that there was going to be "a problem" with those two fans. As the show went on, AJ and I would saunter over to Mike and Don — just irritating the base-ball card salesmen to the point of almost instigating a fight. Finally, the end of the show came: AJ and I jumped the rail, hit the ring and then revealed ourselves. Don looked like he'd been had like a man had never been had before. It was priceless — and that's what SEX was all about.

Another incident that stands out had to be the most impromptu thing in the history of professional wrestling. I'm not exaggerating. The incident would have been talked about for decades — if the fans actually knew what was going on. But even when I explain it to you now, you're not going to believe it.

It was supposed to be yet another impromptu run-in. As I waited outside the back door of the old Asylum for just the right moment to hit the ring, I was getting mentally prepared to raise all kinds of !@#$, when I heard a sound that was very familiar to me. As a matter of fact, it was a sound that's familiar to any wrestling fan: bagpipes. And that could mean only one thing: Rowdy Roddy Piper was in the house. I couldn't do anything but smile. Jeff had gotten one over on *me*. While I was outside waiting for my "impromptu" entrance, Double J one-upped me by bringing out Piper — something that I knew *nothing* about. So, I'm standing right outside the door and I'm lis-tening to Roddy go on with some diatribe about dead wrestlers. As out-of-place and inappropriate as I thought it was, at the same time I found it very amusing. That is, until my name was thrown into the mix.

He said: "Vince Russo killed Owen Hart."

***

Not only couldn't I believe what I was hearing, but to be honest, those words made me literally lose my mind. It wasn't because Piper was accusing me of being a murderer; that's not it. It was because he had no idea — none whatsoever — how much I truly loved Owen Hart. I mean, I *loved* Owen like family. Perhaps more than any other wrestler I had ever worked with. To this day, I still haven't gotten over his death. I see Owen every single day; whenever I take my eyes off my keyboard I see him looking at me, courtesy of his one and only WWF magazine cover. I was completely devastated when he died, and here was this !@#$% telling anyone who would listen that I killed him! You know what? Whether it was a shoot or a Roddy Piper work, I didn't give a !@#$. All I knew was that somebody had to shut him up.

Without even thinking, my feet started going. As I made my unannounced entrance through the Asylum backdoor, nobody saw me coming, not even Piper himself, because all eyes were on the legendary lunatic ranting. I remember stepping between the ropes and simply standing in the corner of the ring. Piper's back was to me and my first instinct was to just take him down from behind and gain an advantage before he even knew what hit him. Don't get me wrong, Roddy Piper can kick my butt any day of the week — with his hands tied — heck, with no hands — but I was running on full adrenaline and not thinking sensibly. Fortunately, my brain kicked in at just about the right moment. Before I could make the kind of ridiculous move I would regret for years, the Hulk Hogan lawsuit popped into my mind. Regardless of the trash and nonsense that was coming out of Piper's mouth, I wasn't going to put myself in a position that would waste years of my life with legal depositions.

As all these thoughts were racing around my head, Piper turned and saw me. His expression was one of shock, to say the least. Now, with his you-know-what in his hand, Piper had to do something. Folks, I promise you — this was not part of the show. At this point I'm nervous, not really knowing Piper that well, even though I had worked with him before. I had no idea if he was really a schizophrenic, or it was just all an act, but I was about to find out. Not knowing what to do, Piper walked towards me and more or less called my bluff, asking me what I was going to do. At this point I'm on the other side of Ralph Kramden's "humina-humina-humina." Since I was choosing to do nothing, the ball was in Piper's court. And realistically, what was he going to do, hit me? Piper may not think straight at times, but he's by no means a stupid man. I'm sure at that moment he fully understood that his bank account was a lot bigger than Vince Russo's. So, having to do something so I wouldn't seem to have shown him up, Piper gingerly pie-faced me and walked out of the ring.

Being out of harm's way, I was racing on adrenaline and just realizing what had just happened. Remember, this was a live pay-per-view. Anyway, at this point I was saying to myself, Screw this show, screw Jeff, screw TNA. If Jeff wants to play ha-ha (an ol' Pat Patterson term meaning to do something for one's own amusement), then I'm going to play ha-ha. I decide that I'm not leaving the ring and that the *live* show is going to come to a complete stand-still. Ladies and gentlemen, even though those watching didn't have a clue as to what was really going on, this was television at its best.

Firmly holding my ground, it wasn't long before one of the Harris Brothers came from the back and got into the ring. Even though I wasn't sure which one it was, it didn't matter. He said to me, half serious and half laughing — let's face it, this was all very entertaining — "Jeff wants you to get out of the ring." My reply was, "You tell Jeff !@#$ him, !@#$ his show; I'm not !@#$%ing going anywhere. If he wants to !@#$ing play, then we'll !@#$ing play."

So the Harris Brother — not sure which one it was — left the ring to deliver the message to Jeff, who was watching from the back.

About a minute later a Harris Brother — still not sure which one it was — came back out, only this time not smiling. "Vince, Jeff said that if you don't leave the ring, then I should kill you."

Now you have to understand, to the Harris Brothers kill actually meant "kill." There was no in-between. These guys were pit bulls — cuddly, loyal and loving if they liked you, but if that order was given at any time, they would rip out your throat, chew on it a while, spit it out, then go back for whatever was left.

Without saying another single word, I got out of the ring.

The Piper situation clearly put a strain on my personal situation with Jeff. The fact that Owen's name was brought up by Piper was something that I just couldn't get by. This wasn't a rib to me — it was serious. A few days later I went into the TNA office in Nashville and Jeff and I had a sit-down. It was very uncomfortable for both of us. I remember telling him that I had already contacted Stephanie McMahon and I was contemplating going back up north. It was a bald-faced lie. The older I got, the less and less Vince appealed to me. By far this was the low point of both my professional and personal relationship with Jeff. We had reached rock bottom. And I never imagined we could get any lower . . . until a few short weeks later.

**

October 3, 2008

Reading through my first draft, I realized that I forgot to include a pivotal story about something that Jeff and I debate to this day. Since this is my book, I'll tell my side. If Jeff wants to state his case, then he needs to write his own book.

There is no *fair* in wrestling!

Kidding aside, let me first preface things by stating up front: I brought the entire situation on myself.

I may not have clearly understood it then, but I most certainly do today.

You see, during the height of SEX, when I would literally hit the ring and verbally and at times physically shoot on unsuspecting wrestlers, I made the case to Jeff over and over, that the talent needed to get more "snug" in their in-ring work. I just couldn't understand why the boys couldn't *really* hit each other without hurting each other. My goal was to make the action look as real as possible, and it was my belief that the guys should be professional enough to work real contact.

When I pitched this kind of stuff to Jeff he usually said nothing. He had been doing this wrestling thing since he was a teenager, and it *was* a work. Ultimately, he showed me a form of respect with his deafening silence, not commenting on my innovative idea rather than burying it.

But on the night the script called for me to attack Double J, I went into business for myself. I was going to put my new concept into motion, without telling Jeff first. In my mind, for the first time in the history of TNA, there was *really* going to be a fight. At this point I think it's important for me to educate you on my background as a fighter. When I was about 16 years old, a kid by the name of Billy Reyes put me in a headlock. As I went down to one knee, I threw a right uppercut, catching and bloodying Billy's nose. That was my first bout. Then, at about the age of 20, I was cold-cocked square in the jaw by an Indiana Sate University of Evansville basketball player, who didn't like a few things I had to say about his coach in the student newspaper. That contest was even shorter then the Reyes/Russo bout, simply because I never expected — or saw — the blow. Anyway, despite my lack of experience, with this SEX thing going on, I was actually starting to believe I could take these guys. I took down Ron Killings with not much of an effort, right?

Okay, he was working and I was shooting. I actually believed that I gave the Harris Boys a run for their money . . . Jeff? Heck, I could take *him*. He was from *Hendersonville*, for cryin' out loud!

In the weeks leading up to my brawl with Jeff I began working out, hard: 30 minutes of cardio a day. In my feeble mind, I actually believed that that would be sufficient for me to go with a guy who had been doing this for a living for the past 20 years. Do you really comprehend how out of my mind I had become? This was no joke — I was going to prove to Jeff that a "controlled" shoot could work in a fake wrestling world.

Which brings me to that unforgettable night in the Asylum. The story was laid out that I was to attack Jeff during his interview, and that he and I were literally going to fight from one end of the building to the other. So here I was, waiting outside the back door of the flea market waiting for my cue. Jeff barely got a word out of his mouth when I hit the ring with the vengeance of Hurricane Katrina. I speared him from behind, taking him down, and then rolled with him from the middle of the ring to the arena floor. Once on the concrete, it was my time to shine. Without hesitation, I grabbed a steel chair and started lambasting Double J. No, I wasn't working the chair — I didn't know how to — I was swinging it! After a few Albert Pujols–type cuts, I quickly came to the realization that I was blown sky high! A few weeks of cardio clearly wasn't enough. I was sucking air more frantically then Dennis Hopper in *Blue Velvet*. My heart was racing like the Energizer Bunny on speed. I couldn't breathe. So much for me laying it in — I didn't have enough stamina to stand on my own two feet, let alone exchange blows with a world champion.

Jeff saw this as clear as the Boulder sky, and he quickly understood that he was going to have to carry me through the brawl. At that point he took over, beating me from one end to the other of the Asylum just like we had planned.

The end of the fight called for Jeff to beat me almost into a state of unconsciousness, then bind me at the wrists and hang me, hands over head, from an overhead railing. Then he was to pick up a steel chair and beat my lifeless body like a 200-pound piñata until security made the save. As Jeff picked up that chair and stared into my eyes, I heard him loud and clear, even though he never uttered a word. With every vicious swing, Jeff was saying, "You want this to be real? Well it's real, New Yawker. You want it snug? Well, it's snug. Now do you understand? Now do you get it? This is why I do what *I* do. And you do what *you* do."

Jeff swung that chair again and again, holding nothing back. I was defenseless, with no way of protecting myself. Never in my life had I been hit that hard. The expression on my face went from "What the !@#$ are you doing?" to "Please stop . . . *please!*"

Following the assault, I walked to the locker room area and crumbled onto the cold concrete floor. I had learned a hard lesson, from a teacher who had tried to teach me the right way. But when I failed to listen, he had no other choice but to show me. I got it, loud and clear — and the truth is that unless Jeff did what he did, to the extremes to which he did it, to this day I would still be suggesting that the fake fighting could be real.

These are the things that the dirt sheet writers and the smarts will never understand. Unless you've been in the game you will never in your lifetime understand. I know I didn't, until teachers like Jeff gave me the knowledge and the wisdom — even if they had to do it the hard way.

To this day, Jeff still hears it from me concerning that incident. His reply has never changed. "I did what I would have done to any other 'wrestler' in that situation."

I hope you get that, because I did . . . and I still do.

Rock Bottom

After bringing the last chapter to rest, I just want to point out that following the "Owen Incident," I worked with Roddy Piper on one other occasion. By that time I had turned my life over to Christ. There was no animosity towards the Hot Rod — none. To this day I consider him one of the greatest personalities in this business, an individual who made it possible for me to even be doing this. Back then, I couldn't help but to take the Owen comment to heart — it was about the worst thing that anyone could have ever said about me. I like to think that in his heart Roddy didn't believe what he said for a second; I'd like to think that he was just trying to sell T-shirts.

At this point, my relationship with Jeff had hit bottom. It was John Lennon/Paul McCartney "Let it Be" sessions strained. As much as I tried to put myself in Jeff's shoes, it was difficult, because at that time in my life it was all about *me*. "What about me, Jeff? What does that do for me?" Man — what a schmuck. I had no idea what Jeff was dealing with at the time, being caught in the cross-fire between his dad and a good friend. Time and time again Jeff told me that he knew what he was doing, that it was all going to work out. But as our relationship wore down, so did my patience. In my mind, the "Piper Incident" was the last straw. Whether it was Jeff's idea or Jerry Jarrett's, I blamed Jeff for Piper's comments. I just couldn't get past it; the words cut straight to my heart.

During this period, the only one I could find solace in when it came to what was going on between myself, Jeff and Jerry, was Jeff's wife Jill. Let's just say that she wasn't a big fan of the elder Jarrett either. You have to understand — and I really don't want to get too deep into this because I don't want to offend Jeff in any way — but not speaking for Jill at all, I was never a big fan of Jerry's because of the way I saw him treat his son, a way that my father never treated me, and a way that I never treat my two sons. To put it as simply as I can, Jerry just treated Jeff like a child — a 35-year-old child. He had Jeff convinced that he couldn't do anything without him. Now, whether that was the truth or not, it was my perception at the time. Jeff just lacked confidence around Jerry — he just wasn't the same guy when he was in Jerry's presence. He was always second-guessing himself, always seeming to look for his dad's approval.

No, it was none of my business — and still isn't to this day — but what was just so frustrating to me was that I knew Jeff could do it on his own. There was no doubt in my mind that done his way, TNA would be a success. He didn't need Jerry Jarrett. And he certainly didn't need Vince Russo. Jeff was a student of the game — he had been studying all aspects of it ever since he was a kid. From wrestling to production to promotion, Jeff had a PhD in professional wrestling. And to be honest, I think that Jerry Jarrett knew that. Heck, to give him his props, he was the one who taught Jeff "the ropes"! But Jerry would never — *never* — let Jeff know that. You never saw Jerry give Jeff any credit. I think that Jerry was afraid to let his son know that he didn't need him to run TNA. I think Jerry's insecurities came knowing that Jeff was fully equipped to run the company without him. Okay, enough; I have Dr. Philled you to near death — let me move on.

My first book, *Forgiven*, kind of began at this point. With our relationship about as strained as Eddie Van Halen's and David Lee Roth's, I really started to contemplate my future. This Jerry/Jeff/Vince triangle was never going to work, so what was I going to do if I had no choice but to move on? I still had CD Warehouse back in Atlanta, so worst case scenario, I'd go back to working with the Dawgman. When my TNA run was going to end, or how it was going to end, was a mystery, but knowing the business, I just knew that the end was near.

It was around this point that Jerry Jarrett called me into his office and told me to sit down. Jeff was already in the room, and by the look on his face, I could tell that he was very uncomfortable. Jerry went round and round as he always did, until he finally got to the point.

"Vince, we have decided to bring Hulk Hogan into TNA, so we need to send you home. Now, don't worry — we'll pay you while you're at home. But you need to get home."

Man, this dagger went deeper then Piper's. *Hulk Hogan?* Are you freakin' kidding me? All I could do was look at Jeff — in my mind this now wasn't between Jerry and me, it was between Jeff and me. Jeff was red-faced and quiet; no doubt he knew how I was going to receive this news, but in the wrestling business, business is business. And you know what? That's absolutely true; you can't let personal issues get in the way of dollars and cents. But this wasn't just about personal issues — this was about Hulk Hogan!

The entire Bash at the Beach soap opera started simply because Hogan didn't want to do a job for Jeff, period! Knowing that was absolute BS, I stood up to Hulk because I wasn't going to allow him to treat my friend — Jeff Jarrett — that way. I got dragged through the court systems for well over two years of my life because I took a stand for Jeff, and now *Jeff* was bringing *Hulk Hogan* — the same Hulk Hogan — into TNA? And I was going home to boot?

Jeff sat there and said nothing; Jerry did all the talking and I knew that he was loving every minute of it. Jerry hated the fact that Jeff and I were close — to this day he blames me for them not talking. Man . . . this was his Avalon. At that point, I was so disappointed in Jeff that I couldn't even speak. Even though I understood that he knew this would hurt me, I really didn't think he understood how much. I despised everything that Hogan put me through following Bash at the Beach — despised it. Being questioned over and over again — being treated like I had raped or even murdered somebody — when all I did was cut a make-believe wrestling promo. Looking back, I guess I went into shock when Jerry hit me with the news. I say that because I sat there and calmly took it. At that point in my life, that wasn't me. At that point in my life I should have cut an obscenity-laced promo on the guy — one even worse then the one I cut on him a few chapters back. But I didn't; I sat there and I quietly took the news. I realize now that part of my behavior was due to shock, but the other part was also due to the respect I still had for Jeff. A few months earlier in a public forum I was disrespectful to Jerry, and I shouldn't have been, because whether I disagreed with him or not, he was still Jeff's dad. I wasn't going to let that happen again.

So, I went home, and I got paid, just like Jerry said. Unfortunately, when I was back at CD Warehouse and had a lot of time on my hands between customers, all I could think about was Jeff, and the meeting that took place days ago. With each passing second, as I had time to digest it, I grew insanely mad — I mean *insanely* mad. To this day I've never been more upset over anything. At this point I can remember being in my back office of CD Warehouse and on the phone with TNA President Dixie Carter. I was screaming like I don't even know what — I'm searching for the word right now and I can't even describe it; it just doesn't exist. I buried Jeff to Dixie — absolutely *buried* him. I had never buried anyone more before, or since. I called him every name in the book, and ones that hadn't even been put in the book yet. At that point in my life, I hated Jeff for what he had done to me. I didn't want to hear excuses, I didn't want to hear logic, I didn't want to hear about business — I *hated* Jeff!

Then, the strangest thing happened.

The second after I slammed the phone down following my verbal tirade with Dixie, I heard a voice as if someone were standing in the room next to me.

"Look at you, look at what you've become. You once loved this man, and now you hate him like your worst enemy. Look at what you've become."

That's the part where I turned crazy, right? Heard voices, had a religious experience. I don't know what else to say. It was clear, and it was audible. I don't do drugs — never have. There were no customers in the store. It couldn't have been Dawgman because the voice definitely didn't speak redneck. No, it was loud, it was clear, and it took any shred of non-belief I ever had in God away instantly. But you have to understand, it wasn't just the voice, it was the whole experience. In that instance there was a blanket of calm thrown over me. I felt at peace, absolute peace. Never in my entire life had I ever had an experience like that. Everything that was black, everything that was negative, everything that was ugly just seemed to have left my body in an instant. Right there, at that very moment, in the back of my CD Warehouse, Vince Russo was simply no longer Vince Russo.

I never thought I would be one of those people who "found religion." And let me make one thing clear: I didn't find God . . . God found me. I've replayed that day over and over in my mind a thousand times trying to understand. Why then? Why me? I think the latter is a bit easier to understand. Throughout my entire life I always had a good heart. I may have been a bit rough around the edges, due to necessity caused by the business I was in, but when it came down to it . . . I really was one of the "good guys." I was always honest and sincere, much to my own detriment. I never had a cut-throat attitude, I never hurt other people and I cry when I watch movies — especially *Field of Dreams*. But following the Hogan deal with Jeff, my heart had turned pitch-black. I was at a place that I had never been before. I mean, I sincerely *hated* Jeff at that time for what I felt he had done to me and our almost decade-old friendship. I had never, at any other time, had such harsh feelings towards anyone. I truly feel that when my heart turned black — when I hit rock bottom — God stepped in. There just is no other explanation. On that day I became a believer and I haven't looked back since. From that moment to this very day, I am not the same creature.

Obviously, now floating on a cloud of peace, every ill feeling I ever had towards Jeff left in an instant — they were just no longer there. I was now seeing everything clearly, and I now totally understood the decision he had made. Knowing that Jeff was a Christian himself, I couldn't wait to tell him of my experience. Knowing me as well as he did, I knew that he might have a hard time believing me, but I also knew that my actions would speak louder than my words. I had changed, and I couldn't even help it. After I shared my experience with Jeff, our relationship suddenly, and almost magically, turned around. Nothing mattered anymore — not Jerry, not Hulk — everything about our past had become trivial.

It's ironic how things turned out from there. Within a matter of weeks the Hogan deal fell through — surprise, surprise. So I asked Jeff if I could return to TNA and deliver an in-ring promo on the next week's show, explaining the change in my life — within the boundaries of a wrestling show. Jeff knew how important it was to me and he gave me his blessing. Later that week in front of a live audience and the "hundreds" who were watching on PPV at the time, I told the world that I had truly been forgiven. I knew that those watching at home thought it was just another Vince Russo full of New Yawk BS promo, but it wasn't. It was the most important message I ever shared in my entire life. I nearly broke down in the ring as I publicly declared that Jesus Christ was now my Lord and Savior — without blatantly saying it outright. When I came to the back, something happened that meant everything to me, something that I will never forget. Jeff was waiting for me, and without saying a word he embraced me. I'll never forget that moment because the significance of it for me was that Jeff knew I was sincere. This wasn't an act, this wasn't another Vince Russo storyline — this was *real*.

In the weeks that followed, some amazing things began to take place. One that stands out far from the rest is when Jeff informed Sting that "Yes, Vince Russo has become a Christian." Even though I had worked with Sting at WCW, I hadn't really worked that closely with him. So the only Vince Russo he knew about was the brash, trash-talking big mouth from New Yawk. Upon hearing the news, Sting literally tracked me down at the old Asylum at Nashville and asked me if it was true. After I told him it was, he went on to poke and prod a bit to see if I was indeed being honest. Again, I knew that my actions were going to speak louder then my words because, again, I just couldn't help myself. A few weeks later, Sting took me behind our production truck and recited the Lord's Prayer with me. Suddenly, everything I had every done in the wrestling business, the good and the bad, was all starting to make sense. There was a reason for it . . . all of it. It was a journey to bring me to where I was right here, right now. My life suddenly not only had purpose, but more importantly, meaning.

Saying Goodbye to TNA

An important part of my writing for the past dozen years has been to walk the tightrope between fact and fiction as often as possible. The reason is simple: if there is a shred of reality to the storyline, not only will the talent be able to sink their teeth into it, because it won't require acting, but it will come across as real to the audience, because it's real to the performer. With that philosophy in mind, I wanted to use what was happening in my life, and play it out on TV.

Now, understanding that Christianity is a sensitive subject to say the least, I wasn't the least bit interested in banging anybody over the head with a Bible. I wanted to take a lighter, more mainstream approach, one that people would understand. I simply wanted to play the part of bad boy gone good, by giving a chance to those wrestlers who had never been given a chance before. I wanted to have faith and belief in the younger generation, the underdogs so to speak, and simply give them opportunities. The message was simple: we're all capable of change and change can be a good thing.

So within the boundaries of the storyline I was going to take a young Wildcat Chris Harris and turn him into a champion. In order for this story to have worked, I felt that at the conclusion of it Chris would have to become the TNA World Champion, beating Jeff for the title. I pitched Jeff the story and he gave it his approval. Unfortunately, on the night we were to switch the title, Jeff told me that he had changed his mind. Even though I disagreed with it at the time, it was Jeff's baby and at the end of the day my job was to do what he wanted. On the surface, it seemed like no big deal, but I had a notion that it might be the end of my TNA stay, for more reasons then one.

The booking team (man, I hate that term — I even hate typing it; I don't book, I write) at the time consisted of myself, Jeff and Dutch Mantel. To put it as succinctly as I can, to know Dutch Mantel is to love him. No question that two of the most creative minds in the history of the business belong to Dutch Mantel and Jim Cornette, and both have a wit like none other. I swear to you, if they hadn't chosen professional wrestling as a career, they both could have been successful stand-up comics. The thing about Dutch is that he doesn't have a hateful bone in his body, and is about as much of a threat of taking your spot as the Johnny Rodz was to taking Bruno Sammartino's WWWF Heavyweight Title! Dutch is harmless, and that's rare in a world where everybody is jockeying for position and will stoop to any level to leapfrog the guy in front of them. Not Dutch; his main objective is always to put a smile on your face.

Dutch is famous for coming up with sayings that you've never in your life heard before, even though he thinks everybody has. Here's a couple of "Dutchisms," as we call them: "He's deader than Kelsey's nuts" or "He's about as over as Adam's housecat." Does anybody out there have a clue as to what either means? Well, not only does Dutch have a clue — but he'll give you a 30-minute lecture on the origin of the phrase! He's nothing short of brilliant, and a man that I will always admire.

Here are a few more Dutchisms, simply for your reading pleasure:

Scott DeMore (former member of TNA booking committee): "I talk about back in the day, but hell Dutch, you lived it!"
Dutch: "Not really . . . I just drove through it."

Dutch: "You know, instead of bringing a blood test to the pay-per-view, they ought to bring a psychiatrist."

Dutch: "Never interfere with your enemies while they're in the process of destroying themselves."

Dutch: "He doesn't drink, smoke, do drugs . . . anything? Hell, what's he doing in the wrestling business?"

Dutch: "He talks about how he's been abandoned before — his mother left him the day before he was born!"

Jerry Jarrett to Dutch back in the day: "Dutch, are any of the boys [in Memphis] on steroids?"
Dutch: "Steroids? Hell, we're not even on food!"

Dutch (In reference to a recent match he saw): "They could have followed grass growing, and it still would have sucked!"

Dutch (In reference to a ten a.m. creative meeting): "Make a note that I was here at ten-ten."

Dutch: "Poverty has a way of changing your attitude."

Scott DeMore (to Dutch on solving a booking issue): "Dutch, you look like you could use a bottle of Malibu rum."
Dutch: "Hell, we could get drunk and we still wouldn't solve it . . . we'd just feel better."

Dutch: "It's like a proctologist . . . they're always behind in their work."

Jeff Jarrett (to Dutch on laying out a match): "Executing that is going to be the tricky thing."
Dutch: "Executing them? I'm all for that!"

Dutch (mocking a former TNA talent): "I have the heart of a warrior and the brain of an imbecile."

Dutch: "He couldn't draw you a fresh breath!"

Dutch: "First thing you got to learn if you get married is how to say, 'Mmm hmmm . . .'"

Jeff, Dutch and I gelled well. We genuinely liked each other. I was, however, getting to a point of frustration — a place I wasn't interested in visiting — when it seemed like every time I headed back to Atlanta after our booking sessions, Jeff and Dutch would change things without letting me know until I arrived at the building on the day of the show. Now, they had every right to do this, especially since they were always working together and I was about four hours away, but it got to the point where I felt I wasn't even needed. If they were going to change what we spent hours writing, why did I even have to drive to Nashville every two weeks? In other words, it started to feel like a total waste of my time.

Not being the least upset about it, I asked Jeff if I could bow out of the creative, and just let him and Dutch do it. Jeff gave me his approval. I was simply going to be a character on the show. With my absence from creative, Jeff and Dutch booked me in an angle with Dusty Rhodes over who was going to be the DOA (Director of Authority). Man, this was a huge disconnect for me. At the time it meant so much for me to tell my story of change on TV, now I felt I was in just another wrestling angle with Dusty. No disrespect, but I just loathe wrestling angles. In my opinion they're fake, boring, silly, unbelievable and have been done a million times before. But I knew in my heart there was more to the way I was feeling about the entire situation. As a Christian, I was now seeing the wrestling business for what it really was. All the negatives now seemed to be magnified; it was starting to become something that I didn't want to be a part of. Something or *someone* was telling me that it was my time to leave. I was finding it more and more difficult to stay true to God while working in a business that I just couldn't find many positives in at the time.

For weeks I tried to fight the feeling, but it soon overcame me. With nowhere else to go other than back to CD Warehouse and the Dawgman, I gave Jeff my two weeks' notice. Jeff was shocked, to say the least. There was no heat between us at all at the time; it was just something I had to do. Towards the end of our conversation, Jeff looked at me and said, "Vince . . . this is a really bad time. We found out a few days ago that Jill's cancer has returned."

Those words were a devastating blow. A few years earlier while at the WWE, Jill had gotten breast cancer only to beat it and be cleared . . . now it was back. Man, I was torn. I knew how much Jeff needed me, but I also felt I was being told by a source much greater than the both of us that it was time for me to leave. Conflicted and distraught, I assured Jeff that I would be there personally whenever he needed me, but professionally, I needed to go. So for the first time in my career, I walked away from professional wrestling on my own terms. As much as I wanted it to be over, I certainly wasn't declaring it was. Again, at the time, this was something I was being told to do.

I had faith . . . but I only hoped that God knew what he was doing.

Ring of Glory

Without many options, I headed back to CD Warehouse, determined to discover exactly what path God wanted me to walk. I spent several months studying scripture. Man, throughout my entire life I really thought I had a grasp of who I was, what made me tick, why I did the things I did. But the more searching I did, the more digging, the more I peeled layer after layer of skin away from my body. There was no doubt that I was becoming a new creature. Things that once meant everything to me now meant nothing, and things that meant nothing now meant the world.

I went about studying and praying for days; the days soon turned into months. I kept asking myself, "What does this all mean? Why would God place me in a business for almost 15 years only to have me walk away from it? What was the purpose? What am I supposed to do? God, what do you want me to do?" Even though I wasn't getting an answer, man — at the time, I just felt so in tune with God. There was no doubt that an answer was coming, but this time it was going to be on His terms, not mine. This wasn't about me and what Vince Russo wanted; this was about God's purpose for me. It was clear why my life was such a mess up until this point. It wasn't until I turned it over to God that everything became right; everything became clear.

I'm going to pause here because as you read this one of two things is taking place. You're either (a) saying that Vince Russo is a Jesus freak, or (b) skimming through these words to get to the rasslin'. Pardon these words, God, but *screw the rasslin'!* Whether you love me or hate me, I really don't care. I can only be who God created me to be. And He created me to tell you about Him. This isn't about some invisible, mystical ruler who decides who's good and bad, what's right and wrong, who's going to heaven and who's burning in hell. No, this is actually about *life*. The second that I began to put people before myself, that very second — whether it was my boss, my wife, my kids or the mailman — my entire life changed. Once I took the focus off Vince Russo and put it on being a better human being, my entire life changed. Screw wrestling; it's fake — always has been, always will be.

Okay, I'm off my soapbox. Time to move on.

The answer I was looking for came in the form of a customer with a familiar face. There was no fanfare, no trumpets from above — as a matter of fact it was just another mundane weekday.

His name was Andrew Mincy, and I had worked with him at TNA. At the time I remembered only two things about him: he was a friend of Jeff's and a member of the crack TNA "working" security staff. We had exchanged pleasantries in the past, but that was the extent of our relationship. By the look on his face I could tell that he had come to my store to say more than hello. Not having a clue to where I was at that moment in my life, Andrew looked at me and said, "Vince . . . God sent me here with a message."

Think about it for a minute. Chalk it up to coincidence all you want, but we all know that many times that's used as a defensive shield for what this *really* might be. For months I had been studying, I had been praying. During that time I was in contact with *no one* — you hear me? No one! I didn't know Andrew Mincy from Adam himself — and yet he had a message for me?

How convenient.

"Vince . . . the reason you left TNA is because God wants you to start a ministry for Him. He wants you to take all the gifts that He's given you and use them to glorify Him — not Vince McMahon, not some promoter looking to make a buck, but *Him*."

Wow.

Don't get me wrong; I didn't bite right into Andrew's vision. But he certainly got my attention. The one thing that really grabbed me was that I truly felt that God had placed me in the wrestling business for a purpose. What that purpose was I had no idea, but I knew that there had to be some meaning to it. I also knew that everything that I had achieved in the wrestling business meant *nothing*. Great, I made a truckload of money — fabulous — but at the end of the day I was tired, miserable, empty and lost. Everything I did — the sex, the violence, the potty-mouth stuff — was done to achieve ratings to please a person who may have *thought* he was God. What I'd created was created for all the wrong reasons and that's why it finally came crashing down.

Andrew and I spoke for hours in my store. During our conversation I learned a little bit more about him, perhaps most importantly that he had been a member of the Power Team, a group of Christian strongmen who travel around the world sharing the word of God with youngsters. So the wrestling fit was certainly there as Andrew had more or less already walked the walk. I went home that night and thought for hours more about his concept. Was it possible to put on a wrestling show that would glorify God? Heck, I knew it was — I would be the one writing the thing! It didn't take long for me to get back in touch with Andrew and tell him that I was in. The bottom line: I knew that Andrew didn't walk into my store alone.

In the weeks that followed, Andrew and I worked out the details. The problem wasn't writing the show, or even getting the talent for it; the problem was finding a stage for it. Bring professional wrestling into a church? Man, we had to find a Pastor who didn't just think outside the box, but was ultimately and truly *out there!* Of course, with his past experience on the Power Team, Andrew had met hundreds of pastors and he knew just the one. His name was Jamie Chant and he was the pastor of a church called Covenant Life Worship Center, right over the Georgia border in Chickamaunga, Tennessee.

Growing up a strict Catholic on Long Island, I didn't think there was such a thing as a hip pastor. The only thing I experienced every Sunday morning was a boring priest who talked way over my head. Jamie — man, he talked the talk in a language you could understand. He was a real guy, with a real family and real issues, and it didn't hurt that his young son Noah was an avid wrestling fan. Jamie was in tune to what it was going to take in order for non-Christians to hear His word. And whereas many of them would never be caught dead in church, they sure as heck would come watch rasslin'! All we needed was for Jamie to understand that — and we would do the rest.

Once we had the house, I had to bring in the performers. In putting together the card, what I was looking for was two things: those who had good hearts, and those who I felt could benefit from a show such as this. Throughout my years in the business I've known so many men and women who've had great hearts; however, being in the business they were in, they became victims of their own circumstances. I knew this . . . because I was one of those people. Ring of Glory, as the historic event would now be called, would enable those good-hearted individuals to just go out there and do what they did best, no BS attached. It would give them the stage to take the talents that God had given them and use those talents to not only glorify

Him, but hopefully to bring those in attendance closer to God as well. But Ring of Glory wasn't just an outreach program; God was also looking to touch those from the inside: wrestlers who were just having a hard time of it in their lives. That aspect of ROG was just as important to me as spreading the word of God. Throughout the years I have seen so many wrestlers struggle with so many issues: addiction to prescription medication, alcohol, steroids, family issues; in hindsight I was hoping that ROG could be something of a safe haven for them.

On Febuary 20, 2004, Ring of Glory was officially born. About 500 people packed the Covenant Life Worship Center and witnessed a miracle. Never throughout my entire wrestling career had one event been so meaningful. I had never been so moved in my 43 years on the planet. And even though it was about the people who came to see what ROG was all about, to me it was also all about the boys. By the end of the evening all of the boys had come out and surrounded the ring as Andrew extended the Lord's olive branch to His people. As hardened as the business made them, the boys were in tears. Just like myself, they too had been moved by the event. It was something that none of us had ever experienced before in our lives. It was special and not just another wrestling show — no, this one meant something.

In that instant I understood my purpose. Whether it was to touch a hundred people that day or one, I knew in my heart that God's message was delivered, not only loud and clear, but in a language people could understand. This little show at a little church in Chickamaunga was bigger than any WrestleMania I had ever attended. Why? Because we did it for all the right reasons. It wasn't about the money, because the boys did it for a minimum and Pastor Jamie, the church and myself didn't benefit one thin dime. It wasn't about sex and violence, because there were no ratings to achieve for a greedy promoter. It was about God. It was about taking what He gave us and using those gifts to glorify Him. Some of you reading this will never, and could never, understand that. Honestly, I feel sorry for you, because you are missing a much bigger picture.

From there I was on fire for both God and Ring of Glory. If it was left up to me, I would have been doing a show every week in a different city, but it wasn't up to me — it was all in God's hands. For whatever reason, only He knows why, our biggest cross to bear became the churches themselves. They just couldn't comprehend putting church and wrestling in the same sentence. Perception is reality, and those who really don't follow or understand our business simply look down their nose at it. It is beneath them; it is silly,

X-rated and vile. At Pastor Jamie's church we actually built the ring on the altar — nobody could have achieved that but God himself. Unfortunately, as we tried to move forward, churches wouldn't even allow us to get the ring in the door! And to be honest, much of it was also political. I mean, what would the financial patrons, donors and contributors of the church have thought if the head pastor had made the decision to bring "that rasslin'" into "their" church? Would they have pulled their money out? So like everything, it came down to dollars and cents. It wasn't worth the risk of the pastor to bring ROG into his church no matter how much he may or may not have believed in it.

So, in wanting ROG to move forward, I put Plan B into effect. I would rent out an arena myself, try to get some outside help from the churches in the area, charge just enough for tickets in order to cover my overhead, and move on. So the second ROG was held at the Rome Civic Center in Rome, Georgia. This was the first time I ever attempted to promote an event on my own. I recruited a good friend of mine, TC, and we spent day and night shaking hands, kissing babies and papering the town with flyers. TC is one of those true blue-collar guys, a man's man who grew up on the mean streets of Boston. With a heart of gold and a unquenchable love of wrestling, TC gave everything he had to help me get the word out. At the end of the day, the results weren't too shabby: over eight hundred people showed up to witness Ring of Glory II: The Great Commission.

The results of the second Ring of Glory were even more rewarding than the first. There was no doubt in my mind that God Himself had His hands all over it. I can say that because I've run literally hundreds of wrestling shows from the production end, running around like a man who just broke out of a psych ward on each and every one . . . except the two Ring of Glory shows. They simply ran themselves. I was never more at peace in my life. There was no yelling, screaming, swearing or sweating — just tranquility. There was actually sanity to what we were doing. In Rome, hundreds of those in attendance raised their hands in wanting to find out more about God, and at the end of the day that's what it was all about. The boys once again loved the experience as they were just able to go out there and do what they did best. Jeff made it to both the Ring of Glory shows and that meant the world to me, especially knowing of Jill's condition and what he and his entire family were going through. To take time out of his schedule for this . . . that's what real friends are.

Despite the success of The Great Commission, I had to be both sensible and realistic. After adding up all the expenses from the show, I had spent almost $10,000 of my own money. The God's honest truth? I didn't care one second about the cash — to me it was simply an investment in God's Kingdom. But the harsh reality was that I couldn't afford to keep financing the shows myself. Trying to keep the concept alive, I continued to canvass churches for support, but it just wasn't there. They just couldn't envision taking a product that I'm sure many of them had seen on Monday nights and transforming it into a spectacle that would spread God's word. Not even my own home church was interested. When my own pastor from my own church told me "Ring of Glory isn't for 'us,'" not only was I devastated — I was also defeated.

Today, as I look back at Ring of Glory, I ask myself, "What if?" What if I continued to go forward? Where would we be now? On the other hand, I fully understand that where I am now is where God wants me to be. Ring of Glory accomplished what it was supposed to do. God is in control of everything; He knows the big picture, and I still don't have a clue.

The Return of David Arquette

The scary part about faith is believing in what you don't see. After dedicating almost two years of my life to Ring of Glory, I now found myself back where I started: at CD Warehouse, working side by side with the Dawgman. Even though I had no idea what God wanted me to do next, I never questioned Him. I just looked forward to hearing from Him again. I know you probably think I've lost my mind, but I guarantee you that is not the case.

How do you hear God? It's real easy. Listen to your heart . . . that's where God resides. You have to have faith in what you don't see; if you don't, then what are we doing here? Going through our day-to-day lives, getting our Starbucks, playing fantasy sports, eating dinner, watching *The Office*, going to bed? Is that what it's all about? You can choose to live your life believing that, but not me.

So, even with CD Warehouse dying a slow death, with everybody being able to download everything from their computers, I still wasn't worried. I knew that God had my back. Even when I had to let Dawgman go in search of redder hydrants because I couldn't afford to pay him, I wasn't concerned. It was all part of His plan.

September 4, 2008

It's 7:20 a.m. MST and I'm pumped! No, it has nothing to do with my caffeine intake, but everything to do with tonight being the official start of my fantasy football career! After declining an offer last year from the official TNA Fantasy Football League because of my lack of expertise in the game, I decided to accept this year due to my current success in the make-believe fantasy baseball world. If I excel in hardball, I certainly can dominate in pigskin; it's just a matter of getting to know the players well — about as well as I know my wife.

Fantasy sports are my weakness. What can I say? I don't drink, I don't do drugs, I don't go out with friends, I sit in front of my computer and manage my teams like I'm the second coming of Billy Martin. I don't know, I think the appeal is the cut-throat competition — who's going to outmaneuver who, who's going to get up the earliest, or stay up the latest to grab that next big sleeper off the waiver wire. Yes, my past venom is alive and well when it comes to competing in fantasy sports.

But hey, it's not just me — you have to see some of the heroes in this TNA league. I don't know who's more crooked: them or the New Jersey State Athletic Commission! The problem starts at the top: two co-commissioners, one being Showtime Eric Young, who's only concerned with drinking beer, and the other being senior referee Rudy Charles. Now let me tell you about Rudy Charles, who is about as crooked as a C.C. Sabathia slider. Last year Rudy saddled everybody with playing in a mediocre league that nobody ever heard of . . . and why? Well, it could possibly have something to do with his buddies having founded the league a few years back. Can you say "kickback," boys and girls?

So, upon my arrival, my first point of business was to oust Rudy and the beer-guzzling Young. Well, Eric went away quietly, not wanting anything to interfere with his buzz, but Rudy fought like a jobber trying to keep his spot. In looking for some help to overthrow the cheating zebra, I recruited one of TNA's young turks, a go-getter from the office named Matt Conway. A new addition to the creative staff, Conway was young and savvy, while I was old and tired. The truth is, he reminded me a lot of myself back in the day. Well, one late August night in Orlando, Florida, Conway tricked the unsuspecting referee, Charles, into giving him his personal password into the league. Upon hearing that news, I gathered the young Conway and the two of us went into the "kayfabe" part of the league, and basically typed the commissionership away from Rudy and into the hands of Matt. Upon finding out about this, the scheming Charles made the decision to hold the league dues ransom until he got his commissionership back. But no way; we got him out — he was staying out. It soon turned ugly until Conway used the stroke of his old man, a big-time agent in Nashville, and scored two Hanson tickets for Rudy and his young bride as compensation for his ruthless ousting.

But the chicanery doesn't end there. How about TNA announcer and last year's fantasy winner Don West bringing a ringer to the draft to advise him on his picks? Or, get this. How about Jeff Jarrett getting the #1 pick — because the draft is held at his house? I tell you, as good ol' JR would say, tonight business is about to pick up!

Back to the store with no customers.

So, CD Warehouse is dying on the vine. I tried every advertising and promotions trick in the advertising and promotions book, but nothing worked. "All right, God . . . now what? Close up shop and do what?" I was at the same exact point I was when I left TNA two years earlier, only this time I couldn't rely on my store for income because very little money was coming in. It wasn't before long after that the Great Magician struck again.

Out of the clear blue I heard from a Hollywood agent who I hadn't heard from in years. She was just making a service call to see what I'd been doing. Somehow, the topic came around to *Rope Opera*, a script I had written seven years earlier. Still showing interest in the project, I asked her to reach out to an old friend, David Arquette, who now had his own production company with his wife Courtney Cox. To be honest, I really thought nothing of it, until she called back a few weeks later and told me that David wanted to meet with me to talk about my script.

Never having expected this, I thought for sure that this had to be some kind of sign. If it indeed was, then I was going to open up *Rope Opera* to all doors, in order to see where I was supposed to land next. That would mean contacting two other people: Jeff Jarrett and Vince McMahon. However, before I ventured down those roads, I was going to meet with David first.

I didn't have to wait long for my appointment with David, who booked the meeting for a week following our initial contact. I was excited about flying out to Hollywood not only for the meeting, but because I was also going to get the opportunity to spend time with my closest friend in the world, who was also in on the project; his name was Jeff Iorio.

Half Italian, half Puerto Rican, Jeff was far and away the closest person to me besides Amy. I had known Jeff for over 30 years, as we grew up together in Farmingville, Long Island. Jeff was a brother to me; we had come so far in our friendship and were always there for each other, even though the times we got to spend together were years apart. For his entire life Jeff's dream was to become an actor. At 45 years old he was still chasing that dream. Whenever I had any kind of a nibble from Hollywood, the first one I would call would be Jeff. I think I wanted to see him become more of a part of the la-la land scene than he did.

Jeff and I had *everything* in common, with our strongest thread being the world of entertainment. For over 30 years we would recite the same Hollywood lines, from the same Hollywood scenes, over and over to each other. Our favorites were easy: *Rocky, Saturday Night Fever*, any Marx Brothers movie and television's *Odd Couple*. Jeff was far and away the funniest human being I had ever met. His main objective in life was to make me laugh as loud and as often as possible. From eighth-grade chorus, to talking his oldest brother Anthony into taking us to our first X-rated movie when we were about 15, to my lowest points with Vince McMahon, Jeff was always my personal clown who had a heart like no other I've ever known.

Jeff and I were so close that when we were 16, and I was going out with one of my first girlfriends, he let me borrow his car, since I didn't have one, to take her on a date. The catch was that Jeff would ride in the trunk in case anything happened to the car. Well, of course within five minutes into the date I kept hearing this sound, as did my unsuspecting girlfriend: "da-da-da-da-da-da *charge!*" Over and over again: "da-da-da-da-da-da *charge!*" It didn't take me long to figure out what the sound was, but not wanting to stooge off my friend — who was in the trunk — I just ignored it. Finally about three or four lights in, my girlfriend turned to me and said, "What is that sound? It sounds like it's coming from the trunk." Of course I told her she was hearing things, but a few da-da-da-da-da-da-*charge*s later, she insisted that I pull over and open the trunk. Having no other choice, I did. To her absolute surprise, tucked away comfortably in the trunk is a half Italian, half Puerto Rican teenager playing a handheld version of Mattel's *NFL Football*. Without missing a beat, and Jeff simply being Jeff, he looked up at the both of us and said, "What? You never saw anybody playing a video game before?"

The meeting went great with David. Jeff was on his A game that day and we both did our best to sell David the ring, corner posts and all four turnbuckles. The former WCW Champion was interested, but he told us that he had just signed on to do a pilot with ABC. The timing couldn't have been any worse. He told us that he'd keep *Rope Opera* in mind and if his latest project fell through, he'd be back in touch with us. In Hollywood, that's a polite way of passing. I wasn't at all disappointed with the news, because I was never expecting anything to come from the meeting in the first place. Hollywood is all hurry up and wait, and I've never really had the time or patience for it. At that time I was really more interested in seeing where God was leading me. If this was supposed to go somewhere, then I was going to exhaust every opportunity I could. The next one would come in the form of a phone call to Vince McMahon.

It had been about five years since I last had contact with Vince, and that experience was an absolute car wreck. But at this point, I didn't care — all I was interested in was to see what God had in mind. So out of the blue I called

Vince; a few days later I heard back from him. I opened up our conversation by asking him how he and his family were, and the minute he didn't reciprocate by asking me about mine, right then I knew it was just the same cold, callous, money-motivated cyborg Vince — just a different day.

Knowing right from the start what I was dealing with, I got right down to it. I told Vince that I knew he had just started a WWE motion picture division, and I wanted to talk to him about *Rope Opera* — it was, in fact, a project I'd pitched to him many years earlier. I told him that I had met with David Arquette to discuss the project, and now I wanted to meet with him. Vince's response was, "Well, I really don't have the time to meet with you." At that very instinct, for a second, the old Vince Russo reared his ugly head. My mind was telling me everything I wanted to say.

"Now, let me get this straight — you don't have five minutes to meet with me? The guy who gave you everything he had when your company was about to go belly-up? The guy who put you before his wife and his children to help make *your* company a success? The guy who is partially responsible for you being able to fund a movie company in the first place? That guy you don't have five minutes for?"

But it was my heart that was holding me back.

Nothing had changed about Vince. He was being about as arrogant as he was seven years ago when he told me to hire a nanny to take care of my kids. But being a different creature, I said nothing. The truth is I actually felt sorry for him.

The next thing Vince said was, "What makes you think you can come back here and write anyway? The same people are here who were here when you were going to come back the last time." It soon became apparent to me that he wasn't hearing a word I said. He was simply getting his rocks off by thinking he was turning me down for a job. So, again, I explained to Vince that this had nothing to do with writing *Raw* or *Smackdown*; this had to do with an original movie I was interested in doing with him. He then went off on an arrogant tangent about how his film company was only looking for "quality" projects. At that point I just wanted to New Yawk go! Was he kidding me? Did he watch any of the disasters he produced featuring Kane, Austin or John Cena? Nothing against the performers — you're only as good as the script — but those films had to be written by either children or monkeys. Quality projects? *Child's Play IV* was an Academy Award winner compared to those bombs. But again, I said nothing. Vince's last words: "Send the script in; I'll have somebody look at it." Right there I knew that I would never talk to Vince McMahon again. I finally had the closure I'd been looking for for seven years. There's no good way to say it: Vince wasn't even a human being anymore — he was just some pompous, cocky guy I didn't even know . . . or want to know.

If you take anything away with you from this, make it this: don't treat anybody like Vince McMahon treated me during our last conversation. Nobody deserves that — nobody. In this world, no one person is better than the next. We are all different, with different gifts and different purposes, but we are all one and the same. Money, fortune, fame and power do not separate one person from another. Because I promise you: you are given those things from God to see what you do with them. Whether you use them to help others or look down at others is your prerogative, but when all is said and done, we all leave this world with the same thing: nothing. And then, based on what you did with those gifts you were given during your lifetime, you will be judged.

At this point I couldn't wait to talk to Double J. I knew that, no matter what trials and tribulations that Jeff and I had gone through, he would treat me with honor, dignity and respect. Again, the difference between Jeff Jarrett and Vince McMahon is simple: one has a heart, the other's the Tin Man. That's always been my attraction to Jeff, and the attraction for everybody that works with, or for him: his heart. Jeff is just a "real" guy — period. He can separate business from pleasure when he has to, but he never makes you feel less of a human being then he is. Vince McMahon on the other hand: he gets off on that.

So I called Jeff and it was pleasant. He told me that the TV network Spike was looking for TNA to develop some new projects and maybe *Rope Opera* could be a part of that. So in the next few weeks I worked on some original programming for TNA to present to Spike. It was great collaborating with Double J again, and, despite any problems we had with each other in the past, there was still a bond that couldn't be denied. At this point of our working relationship there were never any discussions about me coming back and writing for TNA. Again, I left all this up to God. Whatever He had in store for me, that's the road that I was going to travel.

For the next couple of weeks as I began to reacquaint myself with TNA employees. I soon found out some things that Jeff wasn't letting on. His wife, Jill, was becoming much sicker then I had been led to believe. Up until this point every time I asked Jeff about her, the conversation was upbeat and and she was always on a comeback. Even the couple of times that I called her from CD Warehouse it was all good; Jill probably had more faith in God than anyone else I'd ever known. But others in the company, some close to Jeff, were painting a much bleaker picture. I couldn't comprehend what they were saying. I just couldn't accept that Jill wasn't going to beat cancer again; she was so young, so strong, so determined. In hearing this news I flat out asked Jeff about Jill's health, but to me he painted a picture of hope, a picture that I had no reason not to believe . . . because I knew Jill. From that point forward I turned to God. I prayed and prayed for Jill's health and the word I soon received from God loud and clear was: "Your friend needs you."

It had to be about a month later when I received a call from Jeff on a Friday night — again, out of nowhere — and he brought up me writing with him again at TNA. I knew where this was coming from, and I knew who was conducting the orchestra. Jeff needed me, and God was sending me his way. This had nothing to do with TNA; this had nothing to do with ratings — the picture was much bigger than that. Later that week I went to Nashville and met with Jeff. I was thrilled when he told me that he had to go to a meeting and that he would catch up with me later at his house. He told me to go and spend some time with Jill.

I'll tell you what — in my eyes she looked great. Jill just always, always had this glow about her. That time we spent together meant so much to me, because Jill really taught me about faith. Despite her condition, she had faith in God and she believed in him unconditionally. When anyone else would have been asking, "Why me?" Jill praised the Lord. It was a conversation that I will never forget.

In a few short weeks there we were together again: me, Jeff and Dutch. There were things that needed to be ironed out at the beginning, and unfortunately the honeymoon was almost over before it began. Jim Cornette was working for TNA, and to put it mildly, he hated my guts. I had some concerns about working with Jim because I knew just how much he despised me. Even though Jeff told me he would handle it, I pushed the issue, asking him, "How?" I wasn't showing any faith in Jeff at all, and he lashed out, to the point that Dutch left the room. At that time, I heard the old Vince again loud and clear in my head, "Go, right now, get up and go — you don't need this again." But a funny thing happened; my body just could not get up from the chair I was sitting in. Literally, I tried to make the move to stand up and leave, but I was paralyzed — I couldn't move. Again, think what you want, but God was in full control of the situation. He put me here; this is where I was supposed to be. And I wasn't going anywhere.

Jeff and Dixie:
Two People, Two Philosophies

It immediately became apparent that in getting back to work with Jeff and Dutch, the situation that caused the group's breakup two years prior had now been completely resolved. Whatever we had agreed on as a team during our creative sessions didn't change one iota when I boarded my flight, now back to Colorado. Prior to my return, Jeff had promised that the ways of the past would change — and to this he kept to his word. I had kept mine as well, promising Jeff that I would no longer be at times difficult to work with. The change was an easy one for me because I now completely accepted and understood the fact that TNA was Jeff's baby, and I was there to support him 100% in any way I could.

However, whereas the creative dynamic may have indeed changed, some things still remained the same.

Now the story becomes a bit dicey, and suddenly this writer is in a tough quandary. You see, I want this book to be received by TNA with open arms — and when I say TNA I'm saying Jeff Jarrett and Dixie Carter. I want them to be able to promote it proudly on *Impact!*, on the TNA website and wherever else they see fit. I want the entire company to be proud of this book, to be able to openly discuss it. Let's face it: this is the *factual* account of an amazing Cinderella story. I was there, I lived it, and I know how it all went down. But in my heart of hearts, I know that it hasn't all been a good night's sleep on a cozy, comfy wrestling mat. To be quite honest, at times, it's been much the opposite.

From the moment they began working together, there has always been a difference of business philosophies between Jeff and Dixie. The good news is that it isn't personal, nor has it ever been.

But the bad news is, it still exists to this day, up to this very minute. Now, what I'm about to write here is simply my analysis of the situation, my *opinion*. It's what I believe, based on spending a lot of time with both individuals. I try my best to stay in the middle; there are times when I agree with Jeff, and times when I agree with Dixie. They both come from two totally different schools; Dixie graduated from the school of entertainment, public relations and promotions, Jeff graduated from the school of wrestling. Let me make this clear: both are the best at what they do, but based on their backgrounds, both of their approaches are completely different.

In my opinion, from where he's coming from, Jeff believes TNA needs to be run like the wrestling business. On the other hand, because of her experience, Dixie believes TNA should be run like a company. Thus the clash. Since the two came together, they have never been on the same page; it's usually Dixie, and not Jeff, who says that they are, but anyone who works at TNA will tell you . . . well, let's just say that's not completely accurate. What works against them in this situation is that they both are very stubborn and set in their ways. What makes it even worse is that they are both two very intelligent individuals who can both state a convincing case as to why their way is right.

At times it gets really difficult to choose sides. Unfortunately, many in the company are often forced to do just this. On Jeff's side, he's absolutely right about one thing: you can't treat a wrestling company in any way other than a wrestling company, and you can't treat a wrestler in any other way than a wrestler. Wrestling is wrestling, period. If you've been around it as long as I've been you'll understand that. It is a unique animal and needs to be treated as such. In my opinion, Dixie feels that TNA should be run like an entertainment company, and I really do understand her train of thought as well. The wrestler replaces the actor, or the singer, and it's no different than Sony Records or Universal Pictures. Sounds great on paper, and it should work that way . . . shouldn't it? Impossible. A wrestler is a wrestler is a wrestler and has to be treated as a wrestler. So, yes, conflict. What makes it even worse is that the company is clearly divided by the two different philosophies. The wrestling people go with Jeff, the office people go with Dixie. It's the Jets and the Sharks.

Though I want the support of TNA, I still need to maintain my integrity here, and I have to honestly say this conflict has been the main factor in holding down the growth of the company. You just can't have the two people on top, who are respected by those who work for them, going in two separate ways. There has to be one vision and one vision only. That is the why Vince McMahon has been so successful: throughout his entire reign as leader of WWE his vision has remained the same. It's *money*. Make as much of it as you possibly can. One man; one vision. With Jeff and Dixie at times it appears as a competition: whose way is the right way, and who is going to prove the other person wrong first.

How does this thing end? Being right smack dab in the middle of it on a daily basis I can only tell you this: I haven't a clue. However, one thing I do know is this: throughout my entire professional career I have never worked for two individuals with bigger hearts than Dixie Carter and Jeff Jarrett. They are both special human beings who first and foremost care about the people who work for them. To me, this is *by far* the most important element in the story. Their differences are professional, not personal. Big, big difference. Deep down, I know Jeff and Dixie care even more about each other than they do about those working for them. As time goes by, with mistakes and successes made by both sides, they will separately come to a better understanding of each other, thus enabling their respect for one another to grow.

So with that being said, and as both of you read these words, please take what I said to heart and help me . . .

Promote this book!

Nuff said.

Respect

Getting back to the TNA locker room was a great experience for me. Whether or not I like to admit it, this was the most comfortable place for me; this was home. I think what had changed the most for me throughout the years was the issue of respect. At TNA I now had it, and no longer had to prove myself. When I started writing at the WWE it was always, "Who was this guy, and who has he ever beaten?" I constantly had to prove myself, over and over again. At WCW, it was much the same. Even though I had proven myself at the WWE, I never had the respect of the Flairs, the Hogans and the Goldbergs. And no matter what I did, I was never going to get it.

But now, seven years removed from all that, it was different. Most of the guys on the TNA roster were younger than me; it had been their first time to the dance and they knew that I had been there and done that with the Austins and the Rocks. Whether they agreed or disagreed with me, they always showed me respect. The same went for the veterans. When you sit back and think about it, it's really interesting to see that the veterans who currently work at TNA are the ones I talk about with "good hearts"; the ones who just couldn't work another day under the Vince McMahon regime; the ones who got smarter with age and deserved more; the ones who treat people like people no matter who you are or what your role is. I'm talking about the Booker Ts, the Kurt Angles, the Team 3Ds, or Kevin Nash and one of our newest acquisitions, Mick Foley. These are special people who need to be treated like special people — not like sides of beef.

Add Sting to that mix and I truly consider these people friends

— something I never had at either WWE or WCW and something I didn't care to have. I truly love all these individuals . . . even Christian Cage (you try dealing with him!). All kidding aside, there isn't anything I wouldn't do for any one of them, and the same goes for the younger guys who are up next. Samoa Joe, AJ Styles . . . I consider these guys family. It all goes back to the company being a reflection of the people who run it; it all goes back to Dixie Carter and Jeff Jarrett.

Now before I get all sappy here, it's not always the first row at Yankee Stadium. Sure, I get frustrated at times with the younger guys; sometimes they come at you like they know more then you'll ever know, but I never take that personally, I understand that that's the generation. It's a different time in professional wrestling right now, and as the business changes, so do the wrestlers. But again, to me, it's more like a father–son relationship. I treat them the same way I treat my own family. I am there to help them grow and be the best they can be at their craft — that's all that really matters.

After WCW I never thought that I could ever again find happiness in the wrestling business. I left there with the taste of rat poison in my mouth — I never thought that it could be like it is now. But it can, and it is. Despite the few issues you will find with any company, TNA is what professional wrestling is supposed to be. I've been on the other side and it's just a totally different animal. Vince is Vince, and Jeff is Jeff, and Dixie is Dixie. That's it; that's the difference.

Things You'll Never Know . . .
But Need to Know

Perhaps the only person who has more untrue crap written about them on the Internet than myself is Jeff Jarrett.

Let me tell you something about Jeff Jarrett. Something you'll never read about in the *Torch* or the *Observer*.

When I returned to TNA, Jeff, Dutch, myself and Jeff's faithful assistant and crooked fantasy football co-commissioner Rudy Charles, would write TV in the basement of Jeff's house. Now even though Jeff is a very private person and I don't think he'd want me writing about all this, it needs to be said. Every other week, while we were writing downstairs, Jill would be upstairs being tended to and cared for. It was apparent to all of us by now that Jill was much sicker than Jeff was letting on. At that time, Jill and Jeff both believed in trying to find Jill's health through natural and holistic avenues. Jill didn't want any form of chemotherapy and Jeff agreed and supported her wishes. So while the downstairs of Jeff's house was serving as TNA Creative Central, it was also doubling as a natural supplement supply company. The entire kitchen counter was lined with bottle on top of bottle of nature's best. Along with the bottles of pills were various holistic liquids that Jill had to take via injection. Throughout the course of our meetings, Jeff, while trying to stay focused on what we were doing, was constantly preparing Jill's vitamins and also mixing the various holistic liquids that he would give Jill at various times during the day. This ritual went on for months. Whenever Jill needed Jeff's help, which was often, Jeff would stop everything he was doing and run up the stairs to be by his wife's bedside. He'd make the journey up the stairs as many as two dozen times a day.

I'll never forget one booking session where I watched this ritual continue for two straight days. At the same time we were going through a crisis or two in booking, but Jeff kept his balance and saw us through. On my drive home from Atlanta that week there were a million things concerning the show that I could have been contemplating throughout my four hour drive. But something strange happened; every time a wrestling thought came up, God would immediately put a vision in my mind: it was Jeff taking care of his wife. It dawned on me why I was back by Jeff's side; I knew God was showing me first-hand a man's unconditional love for his wife and his family. On that day Jeff was put on an unreachable pedestal for me. Never before had any man shown me, truly shown me, what it meant to be a real man. I pulled my car to the side of the road and I bawled my eyes out. I got it; I understood. This is the side of Jeff Jarrett that no one talks about. His love for his three girls, Joslyn, Jaclyn and Jaryn, is a love that, as a father, I had never witnessed before. Every time we book, one by one, trip after trip, all three girls find their way to TNA Creative Central, and no matter where we are, or how engrossed we are into the "next big angle," Jeff stops everything to give those girls his undivided love and attention.

I wish that I could be that kind of a father. I wish that I could be that kind of a man.

The Angels Go Home

It had to be around Christmas 2006 when I saw Jill again. We were downstairs booking when she was helped through the back door by the woman Jeff had caring for her. I couldn't believe my eyes. She was so frail and hunched over, looking like she was just going to snap before my very eyes. My wind was just taken from me. I wanted to weep, but I knew that I couldn't. This couldn't be the same Jill. When I first meet her she was so strong, so vital, so healthy; this couldn't be her. But it was . . . and the one thing that gave it away was that glow — it shone brighter than it ever had before. That day Jill lit up the entire downstairs, displaying more faith then she ever did before. I had never been in the presence of anyone like this in my entire life.

Coming to fully understand how grave Jill's condition was, I began to accept that it was only a matter of time. Every time I left Nashville and went back to Atlanta, I'd become physically ill when Jeff's name would appear on my cell. I just didn't want that call to be *the* call. Day and night both Jill and Jeff were on my mind. I tried to comprehend what he must have been going through, but I couldn't.

What if that were Amy? What would I do?

I wasn't getting much sleep those days either. I tried to pick up the slack in TNA as Jeff spent more time with Jill. I just wanted to be able to do whatever I could for my friend. Nothing mattered to me more than Jill's condition. I wanted Jeff to spend as much time as possible with Jill and the kids.

Despite my fears, when the phone rang I would pick it up immediately. I knew it would be one of two things: either Jeff needed me, or . . .

I thought I had a moment to get my mind off of things when my father called from Florida. I love my phone conversations with my dad; making him laugh is one of my greatest pleasures in life.

But this time, he wasn't laughing.

"Vin . . ." he began, his voice cracking. "Jeff passed away."

I couldn't understand what he was saying. Why would my father be calling me about Jeff?

"What? What are you talking about?" I said.

"Jeff . . . Jeff Iorio. He died last night," he answered.

It still wouldn't sink in. I had spoken to Jeff twice the day before. Here I was waiting to hear the news concerning Jill, and my father was telling me that my best friend in the world, my brother, Jeff Iorio, was dead at the age of 47. I couldn't react — I was in complete shock.

"He had a heart attack . . . he died instantly," my father said.

"But Dad, he can't be . . . I spoke to him yesterday, twice."

"I love you, Vin," my father said, and then he hung up the phone, unable to speak another word. Jeff Iorio was a son to my father, and having to break the news to me was too much for him.

I knew Jeff was having heart problems; it was a condition he had had since birth. He had told me a few months earlier that his doctor told him that he may have to eventually have open-heart surgery. In an effort to make him feel better I told him it was no big deal: open heart surgery was like getting your tonsils out these days. But Jeff was afraid — I could hear it in his voice. I don't know, maybe I just didn't want to accept it at the time. I mean at 47, Jeff was something like a ninth-degree black belt and the picture of health . . .

He'd be okay.

Just the day before Jeff had called. I was on the other line so I told him that I'd call him back in a few minutes. Fifteen minutes later he called again. I asked him jokingly how many times he was going to call me — I promised that I would call him back as soon as I hung up. When I called him back, he brought up his heart again. He told me that he'd been feeling some discomfort after his workouts. Not wanting to face the issue, I told Jeff that I'd been dealing with some stress issues myself; are you sure it's not that?

Jeff answered, "No, Vin, it's my heart."

Then the conversation went in another direction . . . a direction that I'll never forget.

"Hey Vin, I'm working on a new script. It's about this guardian angel.

You know why I'm writing this? Because my whole life I always wanted to come back a guardian angel after I died."

Later that night, Jeff was gone.

To this day I am shattered. I loved Jeff with all my heart. That night Jeff had a karate exhibition where he was going to receive an award. He gave his performance as planned, received his award, then went down the line and shook everybody's hand. After the last handshake he fell to the floor and died. Looking back, I wondered why the two phone calls? Why the story about him wanting to come back a guardian angel? Throughout our 30 years of friendship he had never mentioned anything like that to me before . . . never. I think, when he called, Jeff somehow knew it would be our last conversation.

It goes that quick. One day you're here . . . the next day you're not. That's why we all have to live every day like it's our last. Know what's important . . . and more importantly, who is important.

After flying to New York for Jeff's funeral, I flew right back to Nashville to be with Double J. I believe that I was scheduled to be there for two days. After the first day, I went back to the hotel to try to get some rest. The emotional roller coaster I was riding was just getting to be too much for me. Then, in the middle of the night, my phone rang. It was Jeff.

"She passed," was all he said.

These are the times when any human being would question God. "Why?" The answer was simple. Two angels had gone home. When I understood that, I was able to deal with my grief. It was a gift from God that both Jeff Iorio and Jill Jarrett were in my life. Throughout the years both of them had taught me so much about life and about love. But the truth is, they never belonged to me; they belonged to God.

All I can do is dedicate this book to their memory.

Jeff, Jill, I love and miss you both very much. I thank God that He put the both of you in my life, and I will never forget what I learned from you. All I can say is thank you, and I look forward to the day when I see you again.

Movin' On

September 6, 2008

It's 6:45 a.m. I've been writing for the past four hours. Sometimes I can only write a sentence a day; others days I'll go on a good run. Before I get to the tail end of this book, I thought I'd bring up an update concerning my personal life.

October will mark a full year that the family has been in Colorado. I think we've made great strides since I wrote about the trouble Amy and I were having. Recently she got a job at an elementary school working as a para-professional for children with special needs. I feel that Amy has a purpose now, something that she had been searching for since we moved here. Being a man, I just find some things hard to say to her, and I know that's ridiculous. But I'm really proud of her for what she's doing: helping those who need help is the greatest gift that anyone can give. I'm proud of her . . . and now she'll know it forever.

Will, 21, is back in college. He's in his third year and going to the University of Colorado. Since I'm paying his tuition, that makes me an honorary Buffalo and I'm proud of that. He too is starting to find his way as he pursues a career in film. Man, the kid is so much like me it's scary — although he may be a bit cheaper than I am.

VJ, 18 and now a high school graduate, just started community college. This kid is smarter than his old man will ever be. I mean, he loves to read. He'll read books for hours on end. Shakespeare, philosophy, poetry — where did he get that from? The kid's got a heart of gold, and it will be that heart that brings him to the right place.

Annie, 13, is now a full-time diva. Thirteen has to be the worst age. Can you believe that in her 13 years on this earth she has already learned more than I have in 47? Oh, yeah, she knows it all. And all of a sudden, she's wearing makeup — what's that about? I dread the day that she hits 16 — absolutely dread it.

Yogi. Well, Yogi is just Yogi: my friend, my confidant. At almost three, I just taught him how to sit . . . okay, he'll sit about 50% of the time. He's the only one who gets excited when I come home from the road. Amy says it's because he doesn't know any better.

As for my mother, Fruitsy, she's as crazy as ever and still an active member of the ailment of the month club. The list now goes something like this: eyes (can't see anything but people who aren't there), ears (can only hear what she wants to hear), neck, back, knees and feet. Oh yeah, she still claims she has a 47-year-old pain in her @#$!

Jim, my dad, is still taking commands from Fruitsy and still playing softball three days a week at 77. The guy actually calls after every game and boasts about how many hits he got. Did you get that? He's 77, and most of the guys he plays with are older. That means that some of them are in wheelchairs, even blind. Do you know how long it takes a guy in a wheelchair to track down a ball in the gap?

So where is TNA today, and what is the future of the business?

You know what? I don't honestly know. But, I can tell you that the business as a whole has changed dramatically since I broke in 17 years ago. The biggest difference I see is in the young kids. Many of them just have no clue as to what it takes to be a star. They work indie shows in front of 200 people chanting their name and they think they hit the big time. No, that's not the big time — that's an indie show where 200 people are chanting your name. The big time is when the world is watching every move you make, every week. *That's* the big time. A lot of kids today just don't know how to be stars. They put together these matches with spectacular move after spectacular move, but after the fans have seen all their spectacular moves, then what? That's why the psychology will always be the backbone of every match — the theatre, the drama, the pulling the audience in for the ride. And I'm not talking about a few bozos chanting, "That was awesome, that was awesome." Remember, they'll be chanting the same thing when you're lying on the concrete floor with a broken neck. I'm talking about the *masses* — working for the masses. That's what's missing today.

The Internet has really poisoned the mind of the young kids breaking into wrestling. Their match gets a four-star review online and in their minds they think they're over. Guess what? You're not. You've over when you can walk down the street and every other person recognizes you — that's when you're over. But I will continue to be a teacher . . . because I love the business and I want to see it thrive once more. Back in the "Attitude Era," I know why we achieved what we did — and it wasn't luck. It was about professionals who went out in that ring every week and knew what they were doing. They knew how to get cheered, they knew how to get booed, they knew how to get over.

As far as TNA is concerned, let me first say that I'm with a company that has made me the happiest I've ever been. Every single arm of the organization is a joy to work with. From the office, to production, to the ring crew, to the boys — I consider them all family. Right now we are all experiencing different degrees of growing pains, but I can confidently tell you, we're getting there. However, in order to be successful we need to bring the "old guard" and the "young lions" together in the same arena, because right now they're often playing in two different gyms.

As I write this, there's a storyline playing out on TV where the veterans are objecting to the disrespect of the younger guys. Ladies and gentlemen, boys and girls, this ain't just another storyline — it's the truth. I know the kids see it differently, some feeling that the vets don't want to move over and let them shine, but in my humble opinion they're flat out wrong. On this one I clearly side with the "established" stars.

What the veterans are really PO-ed about is the fact that the young studs just don't want to listen. They think they know more . . . and then some. Look, I worked in WCW where the veterans *blatantly* held back the young guns, but that's not the case — at all — at TNA. The vets are doing their part to help the younger guys, and everybody has played their part. From Sting, to Kurt, to Booker, to Christian, to Team 3D, to Kevin Nash — they have all done the right thing. But now it's time for the kids to do the right thing: shut up and listen. Don't take that the wrong way; I love and respect every single one of them, but the only way they're going to get better is if they let others make them better. Remember, somebody's got to make you before you get made.

There is no question in my mind that it will all work out because in TNA the boys honestly and sincerely care about each other — that's what separates us from the competition most. Everybody wants to see everybody else succeed. There are no politics holding anybody down. Being a part of creative I can say that with a very clear conscience. From Abyss to Black Machismo Jay Lethal, to the TNA Knockouts, to Mick Foley, TNA is an equal opportunity employer. But remember, we can only take you as far as you'll let us.

Fire Russo!

Let's end the book on an up note: the chants I hear loud and clear at the Impact Zone and at pay-per-views from time to time: "Fire Russo! Fire Russo! Fire Russo!"

The one thing that I really don't understand is this: aren't you people, the ones who chant "Fire Russo!" — yeah, you know who you are — either *paying* to get in to the event, or when it comes to the Impact Zone, waiting in line for hours to enter the building? Why, for heaven's sake, are you wasting either your money or time to get in to a show where the writing is so lousy that you want one of the writers fired? That would be the equivalent of me paying, then waiting in line to see *Ready to Rumble* just so I can mock it while it's playing. But what's even worse than that (Sorry, David) is that I get back in my car and go see it again the following week!

Hmmm?

But whatever; I'm not going to give you too much heat for it. I mean, I'm not going anywhere. Besides, if you don't have Vince Russo to hate, then who are you going to hate — Elisabeth Hasselbeck? Just remember, at the end of the day, I do it all for you, the fans — so chant to your heart's content.

And who are you kidding anyway — I know you all hate me because deep down inside, you truly *love* me!

Peace,
Vince

P.S. I truly hope they do "fire Russo!" (In order to save me the heartache of writing Book Three!)

How Did Things Go So Terribly Wrong?

It's four a.m. on Monday, October 26, and in approximately 32 hours the final chapter of my life in professional wrestling may be written.

I don't know how something so good could have turned so bad in a little more than three months . . . but that's how this business works. It seems like only yesterday we were meeting at Jeff's and writing the show, laughing, gossiping, taking lunch at Meat and 3, laughing some more and then calling it a day. But in a flash, life as we'd known it for the past three years didn't just change . . . it absolutely disappeared.

First it was Rudy, then it was Jeff, and soon after it was the Dutchman. Young Matt Conway and myself are the only two left standing — but that too seems destined to change.

How could things go so terribly, terribly wrong?

I returned to TNA a little over three years ago because I wanted to help my friend, whose wife was dying of cancer. Now she has passed, a friend may not even be a friend anymore and I'm about to be put in the worst possible situation.

It's easy for me to point the finger at Jeff Jarrett. The truth is, when you get down to it, it was his actions that triggered this entire encounter. It wasn't so much *what* he did — that's not for me to judge — but lying to Dixie's face was inexcusable. Jeff likes to dodge the word "lying." He prefers to say he just wasn't 100% honest with her.

No, Jeff, you lied. And because of that something that was both our lives, and our livelihoods, got taken away . . . from all of us.

Yeah, the human side of me wants to blame Jeff Jarrett for the nuclear bomb that fell on TNA, but that wouldn't be fair. I know in my heart that God has dealt me this card. Maybe this is His way of telling me that it's time to move on . . . again. It just seems that every time I leave this heart-breaking business, for some reason or other it just pulls me back in. Then the cycle starts all over again: it's great . . . it's good . . . it's ok . . . it's a living . . . get me the hell out of here.

It would be unfair for me to write about the issues between Jeff Jarrett and Dixie Carter that led to this; quite frankly, it's nobody's business but theirs. But, as you can read just a few chapters back, I'm almost embarrassed about how wrong I was in regard to their professional relationship. I really thought that in the end they would be on the same page and that TNA would prosper. Looking back, I don't know if that's what I really believed . . . or just really *wanted* to believe. I guess the latter is more appropriate.

Sitting here, I don't even know what Jeff and I *are* anymore. I haven't spoken to him in weeks. For 15 years various people have told me that Jeff was never *really* my friend. I never wanted to believe that . . . but now? I just don't know. To this day, I feel like I was always the one fighting for the friendship, always the one picking up the phone, the one apologizing. Even when I knew — I *knew* — that I wasn't in the wrong. But in this business, you get para-noid. Do they really care, or are they just playing you to their advantage? That's where it got to with Vince McMahon — and that's where it seems to be with Jeff. And even though the Hendersonville native would say, "Vince, that's a hard pill to swalla," it's a pill I've been choking on for the last 15 years.

But again, is it Jeff, or is it my own insecurity? This business will do that to you — every day, every minute, every second. You never know who has your back — *never*. It's a chess game that I hate with every single fiber of my being. I like to believe that people are "real," but in wrestling you never know. I've just been hurt so many times — so many freakin' times — by the Internet, by the fans, by the boys, by the bosses, by everyone that I have ever crossed paths with in wresting. McMahon recently went all out in a WWE DVD, telling their version of the demise of WCW. What an un-factual web of lies and BS. It was simply an exercise in vanity, to make Vince look mightier, while making others look imbecilic.

I was one of those imbeciles.

Chris Jericho? To call me one of the "three stooges" that brought down WCW when I never even worked there with you? Shame on you, Chris, shame on you. You must have confused your facts, being that I was the one who got you hired in WWF when I was still the head writer. I never worked a single day with you at WCW. Vince Russo brought down WCW when he brought KISS in? Lie: that was before my time. Vince Russo brought down WCW when he brought Megadeath in? Lie: I wasn't there.

But how can you blame Jericho? After all, he's just a puppet to the great puppet master himself, Vince McMahon.

Vince, through two books now, I have gone out of my way to take the high road. I get no joy out of attempting to build myself up by tearing you down. But here we are, ten years after the fact, and you continue to use every low blow you can. Why? Because I left your company at a time when it was the best thing for me and my family. For that reason I have suffered your wrath for ten years, and I'm sure that will not change. Unfortunately for you, Vince, the day will come when you will suffer a much greater wrath than the one bestowed upon me by an egotistical ex-boss.

And now, with another rant complete, I'm about 31 hours away from what may be my final chapter in professional wrestling.

I can't even release this chapter until sometime tomorrow afternoon, when *it* is out. I have known for weeks, but have had to kayfabe it from everyone to make sure it didn't find its way to the sheets. What a joke. I hate working people, I hate lying and I hate having to watch every word that I say in fear that *the truth* may come out. But again, that's the wrestling business.

Come tomorrow, October 27, 2009, Hulk Hogan and Eric Bischoff are joining TNA.

Wow.

How did it come to this?

As I type, I still can't believe it's going to happen. When Dixie called me almost a year ago and asked me which one person could make a difference in TNA, without hesitating I said, "The Hulkster." I even told Dixie if getting the Hulkster meant firing me then she should go ahead and fire me. I knew the move would be the best for TNA and everybody in it, and that's all that mattered. However, never once in my discussions with Dixie was it Hulk Hogan *and* Eric Bischoff; that was sprung on me at the last moment.

I don't know what it is between Eric and me; I just know that it's there. Eric has never disrespected me, and I don't think I have ever disrespected him, but we're just totally different. I guess what rubs me the wrong way about him is that at times I feel he's condescending towards me. I feel that every time we have a conversation he is talking down to me, rather than talking *to* me, and that bothers me. Could it be my own insecurity again? Of course it could, and I know that, but we have just never been able to get on the same page — never. I mean, even though Jim Cornette and I don't see eye to eye, we have worked together; I'm not sure that Eric and I can do that. More importantly, I'm not sure he *wants* to do that.

Sitting here, I have no idea where this thing is going — none — but I do know that like everything else in my life, this story is being penned by the Almighty Himself, and that gives me peace of mind . . . somewhat. Look, people change. I know I'm a different person than I was ten years ago, and look what Hulk has gone through. The trials and tribulations in his life of late make mine look like a pebble in the road. And who knows what Eric has endured over the last decade? I'm sure there were patches in his life when he had to take a long, hard look in the mirror. We have all grown, we have all endured . . . and we are all together again.

When this book hits the market in February, I can tell you without any hesitation that I have no idea where I'll be. I don't know what tomorrow brings, let alone four months from now. Do I hope this "experiment" works out? To be honest, I really hope it does. I hope that our working together — myself, Hulk and Eric — can really set an example for other people. It would be a good thing. But if it doesn't, it doesn't. Remember, this is God's plan, not mine — and no matter how much I try to control it, I can't. What He wants to happen . . . will happen.

Moving on.

In closing this second installment, there will be a third — you have to see it coming. I just want to thank a group of people that I had the privilege of putting together as my team in the last month at TNA. Guys who were comrades, friends, who helped me endure a very rough patch in my life. Pat Kenney, D-Lo Brown and Scott D'Amore are three of the finest agents you can have. No matter how negative things would get towards creative at times, these soldiers always had my back and that's all that you can ever ask. My two paisans, who I knew had my back no matter what the cost, Taz and Bubba. There is nothing like that Italian bond. If you're not a ginny, you will never understand. I love these two guys as if they were my own brothers. No matter what the situation, their red, green and white stripes were never going to change, not for anyone, anytime, anywhere. They are *real* people in a very phony world. I will be indebted to them no matter what happens. And what can I say about Terry Taylor? I love him — he will be a friend to the end no matter what happens.

A new paragraph is needed to address the last people I want to go out talking about: Matt Conway and Ed Ferrara. Not many people know the name Matt Conway, but in the future they will . . . unless the business kills him first. At the ripe old age of 26, Matt Conway is everything the wrestling business needs, but also everything that scares it to death. A wrestling fan since birth, Matt not only has a thorough knowledge of where the business has been, but a keen and youthful outlook at where it needs to go. Since this is my book, I'll say it right here: I have always been criticized for not having a "wrestling guy" on the creative team. You know what? If I still cursed, a gigantic *B@#$ S@#$* would go right here. You don't have to be a 20-year vet to understand the business. Believe me, it's not that complicated. Many people seem to forget that to this day, two non-wrestling guys drew the biggest ratings in the history of this business. Yeah, you remember: Vince Russo and Ed Ferrara. You can say Vince McMahon edited us all you want, but the truth is, he had to edit, because *he couldn't write it!*

Matt, don't ever give up. Don't ever listen to them, and don't ever give up. They will rip you and they will bury you because they want what you have and aren't intelligent enough to have it. If they were, they would be doing it. You have been an inspiration to me, and while my time winds down, the richest part of my labor was having the opportunity to teach you. Why? Because you were so grateful when a locker room full of wrestlers weren't. You understood what it was I was trying to pass along and you embraced it. That's rare in this business. When the time comes, I will miss you immensely and I want you to know that.

Ed Ferrara: it was the grace of God that I had the opportunity to work with Ed again — the grace of God. Ed's a guy who's more intelligent than I, but he's never used that to puff his chest out at my expense. We were a team, a true team. We were successful because we worked together. Every time Simon would leave Garfunkel . . . it was not. Throughout my career I needed Ed, and I needed him not just as a writing partner, but as a friend. Ed was always a friend, Ed will always be. There was magic between us; it was always so right. I can't thank him enough for being my co-pilot on the journey of a lifetime.

Jim, Fruitsy, what can I say? I love you both more than you'll ever know. It hurt me that for the majority of my career in wrestling I had to keep you in the dark about many things, but the truth is, I never wanted to let you know what I was going through. I never wanted you to know how tough it really was. I wanted you to think that your son was happy — as happy as he was when the Giants won the Western Division in 1971.

Amy, Will, vj and Annie: I cry when I think of all the sacrifices the family has made for a business that never gave a damn about any of us. A business that never knew any of you personally, but wanted to take you all down at my expense. I apologize for the time I took from each of you, while handing it to a locker room full of ungrateful wrestlers who only cared about themselves and their push (with the exception of a few). I can't get that time back and I now know that it was a mistake.

To those fans who supported me over the years: thank you. I'm just so grateful that at least some of you "got it."

To the critics: the negativity hurt . . . and it still does. If that was your intent, bravo. You win; I lose. I hope no other person has to endure the kind of criticism I've had to. What hurt most of all is that those taking the cheap shots never knew me, never knew what I was about. At the end of the day, I was a man just trying to do the best job he could in order to support his family. Nothing more, nothing less. Many of you took the fun out of it for me. I spent many, many years defending myself while still asking the question — why? What did I do so wrong that offended so many of you, and drove you to hate a person you didn't even know? But I guess in the big scheme of things, that's what this world is about: the more I tear you down, the better I look. My question: The better you look to who?

Peace.

Oh, and one last thing. For the record: I called Paul E. *personally* to ask him to join TNA . . . he declined.

***

November 5, 2009

Last update before we go to press.

To date, I have had one face-to-face with Eric Bischoff, and multiple phone conversations. And you know what? It's been cool. Thus far Eric and I have been working together, and I've enjoyed it. I have not yet met with the red and yellow icon, but I'm looking forward to doing so. If I can make all this work for the Hulkster, it will be my greatest accomplishment in this business. Not that it has anything to do with the story, or the angle, but rather it has to do with *life*. If two men who were just so far apart ten years ago can work in unity and for the betterment of the greater good, it will be the most significant achievement in which I can glorify my Maker.

I thank Him for this opportunity.